Citizenship and Welfare State Reform in Europe

This work examines the concept of citizenship in relation to social policy, in the context of the rapidly changing European welfare states. Leading academics analyse concrete changes in social rights and citizenship roles, and offer theoretical investigations of citizenship and the welfare state.

Issues discussed include:

- citizenship versus residence as a basis for social rights
- the relationship between rights and obligations
- workers' rights and non-workers' rights
- exclusion and inclusion in the labour market and community life
- the relationship between social and political citizenship
- poverty and social exclusion
- new roles for citizens as clients, consumers and participants in the welfare state

Discourses of citizenship in political debate are examined from an international comparative perspective and in single countries such as the UK, France, Spain, Sweden, Denmark and The Netherlands. Contributors demonstrate that welfare reform entails far more than cutbacks and retrenchment policies: it brings with it the need to critically re-examine the very concept of citizenship, leading to emancipatory and forward-looking social policy.

Citizenship and Welfare State Reform in Europe will be of value to scholars of citizenship, welfare states, social policy, comparative politics, sociology and political theory.

Jet Bussemaker is a Member of the Dutch Parliament for Labour. She is affiliated with the Department of Political Science and Public Administration at the Free University of Amsterdam, The Netherlands and has published extensively on welfare state issues, gender and social policy.

Routledge/ECPR Studies in European Political Science

Series editors
Hans Keman
Vrije University, The Netherlands

Jan W. van Deth
University of Mannheim, Germany, on behalf of the European Consortium for Political Research

The Routledge/ECPR Studies in European Political Science series is published in association with the European Consortium for Political Research – the leading organisation concerned with the growth and development of political science in Europe. The series presents high-quality edited volumes on topics at the leading edge of current interest in political science and related fields, with contributions from European scholars and others who have presented work at ECPR workshops or research groups.

1 **Regionalist parties in western Europe**
Edited by Lieven de Winter and Huri Türsan

2 **Comparing party system change**
Edited by Jan-Erik Lane and Paul Pennings

3 **Political theory and European union**
Edited by Albert Weale and Michael Nentwich

4 **Politics of sexuality**
Edited by Terrell Carver and Véronique Mottier

5 **Autonomous policy making by international organizations**
Edited by Bob Reinalda and Bertjan Verbeek

6 **Social capital and European democracy**
Edited by Jan van Deth, Marco Maraffi, Ken Newton and Paul Whiteley

7 **Party elites in divided societies**
Edited by Kurt Richard Luther and Kris Deschouwer

8 **Citizenship and welfare state reform in Europe**
Edited by Jet Bussemaker

9 **Democratic governance and new technology**
Edited by Ivan Horrocks, Jens Hoff and Pieter Tops

10 **Democracy without borders**
Transnationalization and conditionality in new democracies
Edited by Jean Grugel

11 **Cultural theory as political science**
Edited by Michael Thompson, Gunnar Grendstad and Per Selle

Also available from Routledge in association with the ECPR:

Sex equality policy in Western Europe, *edited by Frances Gardiner*; Democracy and green political thought, *edited by Brian Doherty and Marius de Geus*; The new politics of unemployment, *edited by Hugh Compston*; Citizenship, democracy and justice in the new Europe, *edited by Percy B. Lehning and Albert Weale*; Private groups and public life, *edited by Jan W. van Deth*; The political context of collective action, *edited by Ricca Edmondson*; Theories of secession, *edited by Percy Lehning*; Regionalism across the north/south divide, *edited by Jean Grugel and Wil Hout*

Citizenship and Welfare State Reform in Europe

Edited by Jet Bussemaker

London and New York

First published 1999 by Routledge
2 Park Square, Milton Park, Abingdon, Oxon, OX14 4RN

Simultaneously published in the USA and Canada
by Routledge
270 Madison Ave, New York NY 10016

Routledge is an imprint of the Taylor & Francis Group

Transferred to Digital Printing 2005

Editorial material and selection © 1999 Jet Bussemaker

Individual chapters © 1999 the contributors

Typeset in Garamond by
BOOK NOW Ltd

British Library Cataloguing in Publication Data
A catalogue record for this book is available
from the British Library

Library of Congress Cataloging-in-Publication Data
Citizenship and welfare state reform in Europe / edited by Jet
  Bussemaker.
       p.   cm.
   Includes bibliographical references and index.
   ISBN 0-415-18927-6 (hb)
   1. Citizenship – Europe. 2. Europe – Social policy.
3. Marginality, Social – Europe. 4. Public welfare – Europe.
5. Civil rights – Europe. I. Bussemaker, Jet.
JN40.C56 1999
323.6'094 – dc21   98–51214
                                                     CIP

ISBN 0-415-18927-6

Contents

Tables and Figures

Contributors

Berta Álvarez-Miranda is an assistant professor at the Department of Social Structure of the Complutense University Madrid and affiliated at the Analistas Sociopoliticos in Madrid.

Rob Atkinson is a Principal Lecturer in Urban Studies at the University of Portsmouth. He is co-author of *Urban policy in Britain* (Macmillan) and co-editor of *Public policy in Britain* (Macmillan). His current areas of research are on urban policy, social exclusion and the role of partnerships and community participation in urban regeneration.

Giuliano Bonoli is a Lecturer in social policy at the University of Bath. His publications include 'Classifying welfare states: a two-dimension approach', *Journal of Social Policy*, 1997; 'Pension policy in France: patterns of cooperation and conflict in two recent reforms', *West European Politics*, 1997; and 'Reclaiming welfare: the politics of social protection reform in France' (with Bruno Palier), *South European Politics and Society*, 1997. He is currently working on a project on welfare and culture in Western Europe.

Jet Bussemaker is a Lecturer at the Department of Political Science and Public Administration at the Free University Amsterdam. Since May 1998 she is also a Member of Dutch Parliament for Labour. In 1997 she was a visiting fellow at the Center for European Studies, Harvard University. Her recent publications include *Gender, Participation and Citizenship in the Netherlands* (Aldershot, 1998, co-editor) various contributions and co-editor of a special issue on Vocabularies on Gender and Citizenship in Northern-Europe from *Critical Social Policy* (August 1998).

Sandro Cattacin is a teacher and a researcher at the Universities of Geneva and Fribourg. He is the scientific coordinator of the Laboratoire de recherches sociales et politiques appliqués in Geneva. His main research areas are: social policy, governance and urban policies.

Elisa Chuliá is assistant professor at the Department of Political Science and Administration at the Spanish Open University and affiliated at the Analistas Sociopoliticos in Madrid.

Matteo Gianni is a research assistant of Political Science at the University of Geneva. His areas of interests include the normative theory of citizenship, multiculturalism and collective rights. He is currently working on two researches, one on racism and xenophobia in Switzerland and another on unemployment policies in Western Europe.

Randall A. Hansen is a Research Fellow at Christ Church, Oxford University. His research focuses on European politics, citizenship, nationality, migration and asylum, and social policy.

Markku Kiviniemi is Research Manager in the Department of Political Science, University of Helsinki, Finland. He is the author of *The improvement of the public services* (1988) and *Perspectives on structure, culture and action: studies in the public administration of the welfare state* (1994), in English, and also several books in Finnish.

Anna-Karina Kolb is a researcher at the Institute for Public Administration, University of Lausanne.

Marcus Mänz is an assistant lecturer and research assistant in the Department of Political Science at the University of Geneva. His general research interests are theories of justice and comparative social policy. He is currently working on a research which focuses on the normative basis of various income maintenance schemes of the welfare state.

Maurice Mullard is senior lecturer in social policy at the University of Hull. At present he is Visiting Professor and Adviser to the Malta Government. His most recent publications include *Public policy in Britain* (1995) *The politics of social policy in Europe* (with Simon Lee) (1997), and *Social policy in a changing society* (with Paul Spicker) (1998).

Bruno Palier is a political scientist from the Institut d'Etudes Politiques de Paris. His main area of research is comparative social policy. He is focusing his work on the recent reforms of the French Welfare State. From September 1998, he has been Jean Monnet fellow at the European University Institute in Fiesole, Italy.

Lawrence Rose is professor of political science at the University of Oslo. His research interests relate to political participation, local governments and politics, and comparative public policy. Recent books include *Local democracy and processes of transformation in east-central Europe* (Westview Press, 1996) and *Nordic local government* (with Erik Albaek *et al.*, Asociation of Finnish Local Authorities, 1996).

Birte Siim is an associate professor in the Department of Development and Planning, Aalborg University. She participates in a national Danish research programme 'GEP: The Research Program Gender, Empowerment and Politics'. Recent publications include: 'Engendering democracy – the interplay between citizenship and political participation', *Social Politics*, 1,3, 1994, and 'Citizenship and gender: the Danish case', *Critical Social Policy* 18,3, 1998.

Véronique Tattini is a research assistant of Political Science at the University of Geneva. Her areas of interests include unemployement policies and social theory. She is currently working on a research on unemployment policies in Western Europe.

Series Editor's Preface

Ever since Pericles' famous funeral oration the idea of an involved citizenry has been at the core of debates about democracy and individual rights. For the Athens statesman it was clear that citizens who do not take an interest in public affairs but are engaged in their own households only, are not to be seen as harmless, but as useless characters. Although he accepted a distinction between public and private affairs, Pericles stressed the need for citizens to be active in both public and private spheres as an essential characteristic of democratic societies. There is no democracy without engagement or – in other words – without citizenship.

The echo of Pericles' verdict still can be heard, but the focus has shifted from moral pleads with strong voluntarism overtones towards emphasis on structural and cultural preconditions for developing citizenship. The rise of welfare states in western Europe can be seen as an attempt to secure minimum living conditions for each and every citizen. Originally meant for the sick and disabled, coverage was rapidly expanded to the old, the young, and the unemployed. By the end of the 1970s, modern welfare states essentially provide an income guarantee for each citizen. In that way, these states attempt to secure the opportunities for people to act as a citizen even if conditions make it impossible for them to perform their roles as income earners. Without social policies of the welfare state poverty and inequality would imply even more social exclusion than can be observed already. And social exclusion is just another way to say that parts of the population are not able to materialize their citizenship rights.

Depicting welfare-state provisions as basically a guarantee for a lack of private income in order to support citizenship, however, is a view too biased and too limited for analyses of modern societies. First, citizenship is not restricted to the political arena only. Marshall's seminal account of the social, economic, and political aspects of citizenship already points to the fact that citizenship is relevant for virtually every aspect of social life. Politics is an important, but not the only, aspect of today's societies relevant for developing citizenship. Second, although welfare states indeed provide income guarantees, this does not imply that the relationship between welfare provisions and citizenship should be interpreted in a unidirectional way. An engaged citizenry is both a consequence and a precondition for the development of welfare states. Third, the conventional welfare-state provisions are strongly oriented on the professional labour market and the position of the (male) breadwinner. Yet, the life courses of increasing parts of the population are not – or no longer – defined in these terms and citizenship should not be conceptualized in relation to labour-market dependencies only. Finally, it is evident that in the last two decades the development of the welfare states is characterized by attempts to reform (that is, to reduce) the provision offered. If citizenship is to be understood in terms of both social and political engagement, and is seen as both a consequence and a precondition for welfare provisions which are not primarily defined in labour-market terms, then the reform of the welfare state provides a fundamental challenge for democratic decision-making processes in these societies.

It is this combination of discussions about citizenship and democracy on the one hand and about welfare-state reforms on the other, which define the unique character of the collection of essays presented in this volume. While there is certainly no lack of research on citizenship or on the development of welfare states, there are only very few publications aiming explicitly at the relationships between these two areas. The contributors to this volume approach this complex recursive connection by selecting various perspectives and objectives. Most chapters pay some attention to conceptual complications taking Marshall's well-known demarcation as a starting point. These problems are discussed in a more extended way in Jet Bussemaker's introduction and especially in Markku Kiviniemi's elaboration of a framework for empirical analyses. Maurice Mullard brings the problems to the point with his typology of citizens and especially with his objections against a static concept of citizenship as '... a set of clothing and as a matter of wearing the right clothing, identifying the individual who is not properly dressed'. Citizenship is a contested concept which actual meaning can only be understood properly in specific and specified contexts and discourses. Welfare-state reforms probably establish the most important stage for such dynamic and flexible conceptualizations in democratic societies.

The context dependency of changing definitions of citizenship is illustrated by the analyses of specific aspects of welfare-state reforms in a number of contributions to this volume. For instance, Randall Hansen shows the differences in justifying social provisions in terms of social solidarity in France and Britain, while Elisa Chuliá and Berta Álvarez-Miranda pay attention to the particular problems in Spain as a model of a society characterized by relatively low levels of state intervention. Taken together, the contributions to this volume cover several aspects of welfare-state reforms and discussions about the meaning of citizenship in Britain, France, Sweden, Denmark, The Netherlands, Finland, and Spain. In addition, in the final chapter Anna-Karina Kolb addresses the implication of the ongoing process of European unification for national welfare-state provisions and social rights. This selection of different objects, then, provides the variation in different contexts required for understanding the specific consequences and opportunities for new definitions of citizenship and citizens' rights.

Poverty, inequality, and social exclusion are too important for the chances of democracy and the well-being of people to be left to specialists in distinct areas. The extraordinary quality of the collection of essays presented here is the attempt to bridge the gap between the conventional approaches towards welfare-state reforms and the discussions about citizenship. The contributors show the need for a critical re-evaluation of our concepts and they underline the relevance of institutional differences within and between countries for this task. Whatever will happen to the social provisions originally developed by national states in an upcoming era of continuing globalisation and inter-dependency, it is evident that there can be no democracy without citizenship. As Benjamin Barber put it so nicely: 'A global democracy [. . .] cannot be borrowed from some particular nation's warehouse or copied from an abstract constitutional template. Citizenship, whether global or local, comes first'. Pericles certainly would agree.

Jan W. van Deth
Series Editor
Mannheim, October 1998

Introduction
The challenges of citizenship in late twentieth-century societies

Jet Bussemaker

The purpose of this volume is to analyse citizenship in relation to recent changes in European welfare states. Various developments, such as rising unemployment and poverty, welfare state retrenchment and reform, the transition from industrial to post-industrial economies, changing gender relations and family structures, and the increasing role of European legislation in national policy making, engender new questions about the meaning and status of citizenship in relation to social policy. Consequently, a renewed interest in the concept of citizenship has emerged in many countries. Debates have arisen about such themes as the relationship between rights and obligations, the relationship between workers' rights and non-workers' rights, exclusion and inclusion in the labour market and community life, the relationship between social and political citizenship, and the new roles of citizens as clients, consumers and participants concerning welfare provisions.

This volume reflects on the meaning of citizenship in the context of welfare state reform and transition. It includes examinations of concrete changes in social rights and citizenship roles, and theoretical and normative investigations concerning citizenship and the welfare state. Special attention is paid to discourses of citizenship in political debates both in single countries and from an international comparative perspective.

The relationship between citizenship and welfare is complex. Citizenship is both a condition and a result of welfare policy. Therefore, the volume focuses on the one hand on the assumptions of citizenship underlying various welfare state structures and welfare state reform, and on the other hand on changes in the status of citizenship which result from new policies. The focus is simultaneously on legitimation of welfare state policy and reform – arguments used to support welfare state reforms – and on empirical aspects of welfare state reform – changes in social arrangements. As many authors in this volume demonstrate, welfare state reform is not only a matter of cut-backs and retrenchment policies, but also engenders challenges for a (re-)definition of citizenship which is emancipatory and suited to meeting both contemporary and future expectations.

The concept of citizenship

When discussing citizenship and the welfare state it is impossible not to mention T. H. Marshall. Indeed, his famous analysis of citizenship and social class returns in most contributions in this volume. Therefore, it is worth paying attention here to the value and the shortcomings of his analysis.

The meaning of social citizenship, the last step in Marshall's famous sequence of civil, political and social citizenship, has been closely related to the growth and expansion of welfare facilities in Western countries in the twentieth century, particularly since 1945. According to Marshall, the social principle of citizenship embodies:

> the whole range from the right to a modicum of economic welfare and security to the right to share to the full in the social heritage and to live the life of a civilized being according to the standards prevailing in the society.
>
> (Marshall 1964: 72)

Social rights were historically developed in order to mitigate the most negative effects of early capitalism. The development of social rights was mainly understood as the consequence of attempts to make civil rights actually work by removing the barriers that blocked the full and equal exercise of civil and political rights. Capitalist market relations, poverty and inadequate education tended to reduce these latter rights to mere formalities, a contradiction that created the necessity for social policy. The development of the welfare state according to this account is the historical process by which members of a national community as citizens became inclusively entitled to the material promises of civil freedom and political equality.

There is no doubt that the expansion of social welfare has indeed contributed to the material promises of both civil and political equality. The more extensive post-war welfare states, whether they belong to the liberal, social-democratic or conservative regime (Esping-Andersen 1990), certainly meant an important step in the improvement of the quality of life for many citizens. In the time of welfare expansion and consolidation, from around 1945 to 1975, the meaning of citizenship was not much discussed; the importance of social citizenship was taken for granted and the reason for an extension of social rights seemed rather evident. When first published in 1950, for example, Marshall's *Citizenship and Social Class* received little attention, especially outside the United Kingdom (cf. Rees 1996).

In the era of welfare reform and welfare pessimism (cf. George 1996: 2–4), there has been much more discussion about, and contested interpretations of, citizenship. Simultaneously with the rise of the welfare state 'crisis' (a notion that should be used with great caution) citizenship arose as a central concept in many discussions, both scientific and political. It has been used by intellectuals trying to grasp and explain recent transformations in welfare states, by politicians reformulating the relations between citizens' rights and duties *vis-à-vis* the state, among social organizations and social movements questioning dis-integrating and new forms of social cohesion and community life and by international institutions such as the EU to name and frame the position of citizens *vis-à-vis* the nation-state and supranational levels of policy making. Within this context Marshall's text on citizenship has been rediscovered (cf. Bottomore 1992; Roche 1992).

With the reappraisal of his text new questions have arisen and new criticisms have been formulated. With respect to contemporary questions on citizenship and welfare states, the most important criticisms concern Marshall's sequential order of citizenship and his positive attitude towards progress; the role of political struggle in the development of citizenship; the relationship between citizenship and social class and other inequalities such as gender and ethnicity; and finally the question of the extent to which his description has general value for European welfare states and supranational institutions such as the EU. It is useful to look into some of these comments in more detail.

The historical sequence Marshall presented is doubtful. Marshall argued that citizenship consists of civil, political and social components that correspond to successive phases in the history of capitalist countries. Eighteenth-century civil rights established individual freedom, nineteenth-century political rights in-augurated political freedom, and twentieth-century social rights provided the foundation of social welfare. This sequence of citizenship rights suggests a rela-tively autonomous development in which every new step of citizenship results progressively from a previous step. Consequently, social rights are regarded as more advanced than political rights. However, on closer inspection the relationship between various rights seems to be less sequential. For example, as Himmelfarb suggests (1984: 268), a sense of social citizenship was already being generated in the eighteenth century through ideas about the moral economy, although it might have been threatened in the nineteenth century by industrialization and modern political ideologies, such as Utilitarianism.

The idea of sequence and progress is particularly relevant for current developments. What does welfare state retrenchment, for example, mean for the assumption of the continuous advancement of citizenship? Recent developments show that citizenship rights do not automatically develop in a more advanced form, but that drawbacks and backlashes may also occur. For example, access to social security entitlements and the level and terms of benefits has recently been limited in many European countries. Moreover, the quality of social services, such as education and health care, has decreased in various countries, while there are sometimes long queues. Such developments jeopardize the idea of universality, as the development of the National Health Service in the UK clearly illustrates. Thus, it is not self-evident that social citizenship in itself is the end of a sequence. Instead, it needs to be continuously re-evaluated and redefined.

The establishment and redefinition of citizenship does not take place in a vacuum. Citizenship is a contested concept, and the definition of citizenship is part of a political and social struggle. Various actors articulate various definitions of citizenship and they argue for different programmes and instruments to implement their notion of citizenship within social policy. For example, recent discussions about the balance between rights and obligations of citizens *vis-à-vis* the state reflect political struggles about the articulation and implementation of contemporary citizenship. In this volume citizenship is linked to the social and political struggles about the restructuring of the welfare state.

Marshall's analysis strongly focuses on the relationship between work and welfare and, as a result, on social class. He did not pay much, if any, attention to other social inequalities. His analysis is restricted to activities related to public spheres (state, labour market and so forth) and leaves the private sphere of the family – and therefore unpaid care work and women's dependency on men – out of the picture. However, more recently the assumptions about gender relations and breadwinner arrangements underlying the concept of citizenship have been extensively analysed. The successive development of citizenship, as Marshall sketched, certainly does not incorporate women in most European countries (see Pateman 1989; Orloff 1993; O'Connor 1996; Walby 1994). Attention to gender relations has brought about recognition of the role of unpaid care work – both in the private and public spheres – as a dimension of citizenship. This is not only of theoretical interest, but also of political interest, since many countries are being confronted with new challenges resulting from changing gender and family structures and demographical developments (ageing and fertility rates).

Furthermore, citizenship is also challenged by migration and by questions of race and ethnicity. The entitlements of citizenship rights to migrants resemble, to a certain extent, the development of women's rights, especially because they often receive social rights before they are entitled to political rights (Soysal 1994: 130). Questions of race and ethnicity particularly challenge political and civil rights and the role of the nation-state in granting rights (see Brubaker 1992; Soysal 1994; Cesarani and Fulbrook 1996).

The strong focus on work and welfare, and consequently on social class, also hinders an appropriate analysis of people who are not able to participate in the labour market. These include the mentally or physically handicapped, and 'marginalized' groups such as drug addicts, the homeless, rejected asylum-seekers or the long-term unemployed, who have lost faith in the political system to help them. In many cases, the right to work does not help them. There is a risk that 'marginalized' groups may become a permanent underclass of citizens excluded from meaningful social participation. Here it becomes clear that citizenship is not only about work and welfare, but also about inclusion in social communities outside the labour market, whether this is through voluntary work, self-help projects or social initiatives by civil society organizations. Although the focus of this book is on the state – ultimately the welfare provider – the role of civil society in fighting social exclusion returns in several contributions.

Another issue concerns the extent to which we may generalize Marshall's description of civil, political and social citizenship to cover all European welfare states. Marshall's analysis was based on developments in the UK. His analysis may be appropriate for the UK, but it is not so accurate for many other European countries. For France, for example, the meaning of republican citizenship, inherited from the French Revolution, should be taken into account in describing the development of social rights. The German development of citizenship was again rather different from the French case. In Germany, social citizenship developed before political citizenship, mainly as an effect of the Bismarckian introduction of social insurances in the nineteenth century. For these reasons, we should be careful when expanding Marshall's description to countries other than the United Kingdom. Although the notion of social citizenship – and the related notion of social justice – has influenced Scandinavian social policies, it seems less accurate for other countries. As many authors in this volume demonstrate, solidarity rather than citizenship has been the cornerstone of social policy in many continental countries. Solidarity has been influenced both by the French notion of republicanism and the catholic notion of organicism. Both refer to a national social and moral order in which citizens are integrated. While, to an extent, this notion of solidarity reflects – in an abstract sense – Marshall's notion of citizenship, the continental notion of occupational solidarity certainly does not, for this kind of solidarity is directed towards distribution of income within a professional group, emphasizes status and is certainly not universal.

Finally, Marshall's notion of citizenship is firmly rooted in the idea that citizenship and the nation state are closely linked. For a long time, the nation state has been viewed as the one and only provider of citizenship rights. However, increasing internationalization, particularly as an effect of European integration, has challenged the notion of national citizenship. The question is whether a European or supranational notion of citizenship will develop, and if so, how this will affect national citizenship rights. Recently, a fast growing list of publications have been published in this field (see, among others Meehan 1993: Rosas and Antola 1995). Whatever the answer may be on these questions, it is clear that the role of the national state is changing.

All in all, Marshall's analysis of citizenship no longer seems adequate. The development of the interrelation between civil, political and social rights is far more complex than we may conclude from Marshall's analysis. Marshall's idea of sequence and progress in the development of citizenship is certainly problematic. Moreover, it shows much more variation if one pays attention to other forms of inequality apart from class. Although his analytical distinction of civil, political and social rights is still frequently used, even this should be reformulated, as some of the authors in this volume argue. Furthermore, the configuration between the context and the content attached to various rights has in recent welfare reforms proved to be very complicated. Finally, the picture is further complicated if we look to countries other than the UK. Particularly in continental Europe the concept of citizenship in itself does not suffice; the concept of solidarity seems to be equally important. This also generates new questions concerning citizenship and the EU.

The contributions in this volume develop in more detail the problems and challenges in analysing citizenship and contemporary welfare states. All authors agree upon the shortcomings of Marshall's concept of citizenship, but they show that there are different options and alternatives for dealing with this.

In the first chapter, Maurice Mullard argues for the need to move beyond Marshall's concept of citizenship. Marshall represented a discourse which was emancipatory and had validity at a time when the welfare state was still being established. The challenge for the present is to construct a definition which is equally emancipatory but which has relevance to contemporary challenges and expectations. Mullard identifies various discourses that seek to define and redefine citizenship; he elaborates on the discourses of the 'public', the 'independent', the 'entitled', the 'communitarian' and the 'consumer' citizen. According to Mullard, none of these discourses in itself suffices to redefine citizenship, although they represent useful elements for a renewed notion of emancipatory citizenship. Such a renewed notion should be built on four components: universal human rights, the right to be different, the public dimension and the social dimension. Mullard gives a succinct overview and analysis of current discourses on citizenship which have distinctive implications for the future of welfare states. In the following chapters, some of these discourses will return in relation to more specific analysis of welfare and citizenship in various countries.

In Chapter 2, Randall Hansen compares discourses on citizenship, examining welfare state debates in the UK and France with attention for two notions that play a similar role: social citizenship in the UK, and *solidarité* in France. These concepts both refer to an individual's claim to welfare, but there are also key differences. In the UK, the concept of citizenship is linked to either communitarianism or liberalism to defend social provisions as a citizenship right. Hansen asserts that both are inadequate to give a secure defence of vigorous social provision which includes welfare for those on the social margins. In France, the historical and dominant role *solidarité* has played in the development and justification of social provision, as well as the related concept of risk, have been undermined by recent socio-economic changes. Hansen argues that it is necessary to undermine the distinction between civil, political and social rights to adopt a view of rights that includes an essential social component, and thus to establish a social democratic defiance of welfare provisions that does not presume a degree of commonality which no longer exists.

Giuliano Bonoli and Bruno Palier elaborate on the French case in more detail. Like Hansen, they deal with the difference between social security based on social citizenship and that based on occupational solidarity through contributory social insurance. The authors show that the social insurance model has become inadequate in the context of current changes in the labour market and rising unemployment. These concerns are reflected in political debates; since the early 1990s politicians have questioned the adequacy of the French occupational welfare system. As an alternative, policy makers argue for entitlements based on need or citizenship which would guarantee coverage of the entire population. (Although we should note that illegal immigrants are still excluded, and most third country nationals most likely also.) Bonoli and Palier illustrate how the contributory principle is being abandoned in a number of areas, particularly health care and family benefits, as a result of 1990's discourse and particularly the 1995 Juppé plan. Although these transformations may be regarded as a step towards the establishment of social citizenship in French welfare policy, this shift does not necessarily imply a reinforcement of welfare state institutions. Instead, it may make the French system more vulnerable for radical reform and cutbacks.

While Bonoli and Palier analyse the shift from contributory to more universal social programmes, in the fourth chapter Sandro Cattacin, Matteo Gianni, Markus Mänz and Véronique Tattini examine developments away from universal schemes, demonstrated particularly clearly in the introduction of workfare schemes. Such schemes have already been implemented in the United States, Canada and Switzerland and are a subject of debate in France, Italy, the United Kingdom and Germany. Workfare schemes can be understood as a reaction to the limits of the Marshallian model of social citizenship in the fight against social exclusion in a rapidly changing society. But the basic assumptions on social citizenship underlying the notion of workfare, particularly the obligation to work, are also problematic. The authors argue that the introduction of compulsory requirements in welfare programmes is an unsatisfactory response to the multifaceted problem of social exclusion. Moreover, the defenders of workfare share with Marshall the notion that a single set of solutions is capable of confronting the complexity of the problem of social exclusion. As an alternative, the authors argue for a pluralistic conception of social citizenship which pays attention to heterogeneous forms and paths of exclusion. In such a strategy, not only the state, but also civil society should play an important role.

My own chapter also examines the limits of the model of social citizenship in a rapidly changing society. Pluriformity is also a keyword in this contribution, but here in relation to life courses which are both changing and diversifying. I argue that the transition from Fordist to post-Fordist life-cycle is creating a challenge to reformulate the basic conditions of social citizenship in such a way that both security and respect of diversity can be guaranteed. It is argued that the basic conditions for emancipatory citizenship can be found in universality, flexibility and the integration of work, welfare and care in social policy. Various policies and welfare state initiatives, particularly in Sweden and the Netherlands, are examined from this perspective. Although they give some examples of 'good practices' more far-reaching initiatives may be needed. Ideas concerning a citizen's basic income and negative income tax, as well as the idea of vouchers and a sabbatical account are evaluated. Such ideas may provide perspectives to implement a concept of social citizenship in social policy that is both universal and flexible, and incorporate care as well as gender and family relations.

Although this volume focuses particularly on social citizenship and welfare, the issue of social citizenship is closely related to political citizenship. Citizenship not only refers to the character and quality of social rights, but also to the political participants involved in shaping the particular content and structure of welfare benefits, as well as to the political right to participate in the (political) arena in which decisions on welfare are taken. Although many articles refer to the relationship between social citizenship and democracy in general, some of the contributions in this volume give this relation a central role.

In Chapter 6, Birte Siim compares recent developments concerning social and political citizenship in Denmark, the UK and France from a gender perspective. Inspired by feminist analyses of breadwinner dimensions and women's political agency, she redefines Turner's framework of public and private dimensions of citizenship and active and passive dimensions of citizenship to make it useful for understanding gender relations. Next, she uses this framework to analyse the interplay between women's welfare and political agency in relation to recent shifts in discourses and practices of citizenship in the three countries. There is no clear pattern in the way social and political citizenship influence each other. For example in France, there is a contradiction between the ambitious programmes for gender equality in the labour market, and low female representation in political institutions. In the UK, women's social rights are not well protected, while women's political participation is increasing. In Denmark, on the other hand, social citizenship for women is advanced, and women's political representation is rather high. Here, welfare seems to have been the cause rather than the effect of political agency.

Elisa Chuliá and Berta Álvarez-Miranda also investigate the relationship between social and political citizenship. The debate in Spain started later than that in most other countries, due to the transition from an authoritarian regime to democracy. It was only from the late 1970s on that a more comprehensive system was developed in Spain. Here, similar to France (see the contributions by Hansen and Bonoli and Palier) concepts of redistribution and solidarity were much more important than social citizenship. The concept of citizenship was linked to democracy rather than to welfare state provisions. Chuliá and Álvarez-Miranda argue that the nature of the political regimes which laid the foundations for the construction of a public system of social protection was essentially incompatible with a discourse of rights. To the extent that social protection was developed, it was from the perspective of workers, rather than citizens. It addition to workers' social insurance programmes, the family has played a crucial role in Spain. Recent attempts at welfare state reform challenge these characteristics. There is a tendency among citizens to move to private insurance and services. The recourse to private services is, the authors argue, another source of distinction which adds to the fragmentation of the Spanish public system, and explains the existence of a rather heterogeneous Spanish social citizenship.

The relationship between social and political citizenship returns in the contribution of Markku Kiviniemi, Chapter 8. He aims to develop an analytical framework for empirical analyses of citizenship. Kiviniemi emphasizes the relationship between rights (and duties) of citizenship and the political ideology, and political culture, in which they are framed. The framework is then used to analyse the development of citizenship in Finland. The ideological background of the Finnish Constitution (1919) has been influenced by Swedish legislation, particularly concerning civil rights, and by European liberalism, particularly with respect to political rights. The construction of the welfare state has been accompanied by the rise of a consensual political culture in Finland. Welfare state reform in the 1980s and 1990s has not changed this political culture – the welfare state is still highly appreciated, both among citizens and among the political élite. However, the influence of various international factors, such as globalization, the development of the EU and transnational mobility, are a main challenge for the Finnish welfare state and the political culture in which the welfare state has been embedded.

Historically, the welfare state has been a national state and the basis for citizenship has been the nation state. So far, most authors in this volume examine citizenship and welfare policies on a national level, or compare various national policies concerning citizenship and welfare. However, at the end of the 1990s the national level seems to be losing power both to the local level (decentralization) and to the supranational level (internationalization), particularly as an effect of European union. The 'diffusion of politics' engenders new questions about the formation of citizenship at both the local and supranational levels. Both levels are subject to explicit analysis within this volume. In Chapter 9, Lawrence Rose examines the shift in attitudes of citizens towards municipal welfare politics. Various authors in this volume argue that individuals seem inclined to emphasize their roles as consumers rather than as active political citizens. Rose tests this hypothesis, presenting the results from a Norwegian survey about citizens' attitudes towards local government. In Norway, local governments are responsible for providing most public goods and services. Rose finds that there is a clear tendency among Norwegians to define themselves as consumers of public goods, while they place less emphasis on their role as taxpayers and active political citizens. In addition, Norwegians value the efficiency of local government more than democracy. The results of the survey also suggest that those residents who place high value on their consumer role are typically young, well-educated women working in the public sector, suggesting the emergence of a new public sector class. The shift in attitudes among citizens has consequences for the relationship between social and political citizenship; it seems that there is a risk that social rights may weaken the meaning of political rights, instead of reinforcing them.

From the local level we move to the supranational level of the EU. At stake is the extent to which economic integration engenders new challenges for European social and political rights, and the extent to which account is taken of the risks of marginalization and exclusion.

Rob Atkinson takes up the issue of social exclusion and citizenship within the European context in Chapter 10. He distinguishes two concepts of social exclusion: the first derives from the 'French tradition', while the second has its origins in European programmes and institutions. The first places great emphasis on the need to create social solidarity and to ensure that all citizens are integrated into and participate in a national social and moral order (here the notion of solidarity in the contributions from Hansen and Bonoli and Palier returns). The second, dominant in EU-publications, is much more embedded in a discourse of economic neo-liberalism and social-conservatism which emphasizes the market, competitiveness and individual responsibility. Social exclusion is primarily defined as a problem of marginalized individuals and their pathologies. From this perspective, Atkinson is rather sceptical about the development of a broad concept of social exclusion and citizenship on the European level. He concludes that the attention paid to social exclusion at a European level is more an element of policy symbolism than a signal that full citizenship rights are granted at that level.

The relationship between citizenship and social exclusion within the context of European integration also returns in the contribution of Anna-Karina Kolb. She examines the consequences of the EU's specific institutional framework for the development of social rights, and explores the differences with state-level experience of social rights. She presents those social rights which are firmly anchored in EC legislation and jurisprudence and related to the creation of the Common Market, and the rights promoted through different Structural Funds programmes. Kolb argues that the rights related to the Common Market are most developed and stable, whereas the rights related to Structural Funds are diffuse. Moreover, the notions of social cohesion and equality related to the Structural Funds show more dissension among national actors than in the case of workers' social rights. The development of social citizenship in Europe therefore depends largely on workers' rights. Although Kolb argues, similarly to Atkinson, that in the current context the use of the notion of 'European citizenship' may only have a symbolic function, she is more positive about the possibilities of European citizenship. Kolb concludes that the danger of policy symbolism may be averted through the social rights developed via the implementation of the Common Market.

This volume contributes to the analysis of citizenship and welfare both at a theoretical and at an empirical level. It emphasizes the need for a critical re-evaluation of the concept of citizenship, and presents some directions to develop a renewed understanding of the concept of citizenship. It underscores the interest of the analysis of political discourses on citizenship and the assumptions about the roles of citizens underlying these discourses. In addition, it not only examines differences in citizenship and welfare among various European countries, but also features the relevance of institutional differences, not only between countries, but also between the national and the local and supra-national levels. This volume suggests that the study of the interrelation between discourses, institutional settings and politics can contribute to a better understanding of contemporary challenges concerning citizenship and welfare states.

Acknowledgement

We would like to thank Joanne van Selm-Thorburn for her assistance in the final language correction of this text.

Bibliography

Brubaker, R. (1992) *Citizenship and Nationhood in France and Germany*, Cambridge: Harvard University Press.

Bottomore, T. (ed.) (1992) *Citizenship and Social Class*, London: Pluto Press.

Cesarani, D. and Fulbrook, M. (eds) (1996) *Citizenship, Nationality and Migration in Europe*. London: Routledge.

Esping-Andersen, G. (1990) *The Three Worlds of Welfare Capitalism*, Cambridge: Polity.

George, V. (1996), 'The future of the welfare state', in V. George and P. Taylor-Gooby (eds), *European Welfare Policy. Squaring the Welfare Circle*, Houndsmill: Macmillan.

Himmelfarb, G. (1984) *The Idea of Poverty: England and the Early Industrial Age*, New York: Alfred A. Knopf.

Marshall, T. H. (1964) *Class, Citizenship and Social Development*, Garden City/New York: Doubleday.

Meehan, E. (1993) *Citizenship and the European Community*, London: Sage.

O'Connor, J. (1996) 'From women in the welfare state to gendering welfare state regimes', Special issue of *Current Sociology* 44, 2, 1–130.

Orloff, A. (1993) 'Gender and the social rights of citizenship: the comparative analysis of gender relations and welfare states', *American Sociological Review*, 58, 3: 303–28.

Pateman C. (ed.) (1989) *The Disorder of Women*, Stanford: Stanford University Press.

Rosas, A. and E. Antola (eds) (1995) *A Citizen's Europe. In Search of a New Order*, London: Sage.

Rees, A. (1996) 'T. H. Marshall and the progress of citizenship', in M. Bulmer and A. M. Rees (eds), *Citizenship Today. The Contemporary Relevance of T. H. Marshall*, London: UCL Press.

Roche, M. (1992) *Rethinking Citizenship. Welfare, Ideology and Change in Modern Societies*, Oxford: Polity Press.

Soysal, Y. (1994) *Limits of Citizenship. Migrants and Postnational Membership in Europe*, Chicago: University of Chicago Press.

Walby, S. (1994) 'Is citizenship gendered?', *Sociology* 28, 2: 379–95.

1 Discourses on citizenship
The challenge to contemporary citizenship

Maurice Mullard

Introduction

The concern of this chapter is to outline a number of arguments which need to
be taken into consideration in making the concept of citizenship relevant to the
challenges of the millennium and their impacts on welfare states. The welfare
states established in the aftermath of World War II were founded on a series of
assumptions which need to be re-evaluated in the context of continuing change.
Demographic pressures, public expectations, the constraints on government
and the globalized economy are all major factors influencing new thinking
about welfare states. The concern of this chapter is the relationship between
citizenship and welfare states. It will argue for the need to move beyond
Marshall's concept of citizenship. Defining and redefining citizenship has to be
located within people's life experiences – it has to reflect people's expectations,
hopes and aspirations at a certain point in time. In this sense Marshall's attempt
at a definition of citizenship has to be contextualized. Instead of focusing on the
limits of that definition it would be better to argue that it represented a
discourse which was emancipatory and had validity in the aftermath of war and
at a time when the welfare state was still being established. The challenge for
the present is to construct a definition which is equally emancipatory, but
which has relevance to the expectations of the 1990s and beyond.

The concept of citizenship is a contestable site (Connolly 1994) occupied by a
number of competing discourses that seek to define and redefine citizenship.
This chapter identifies five discourses associated with the concept of citizenship:
the discourses of the 'public'; the 'independent'; the 'entitled'; the 'communitarian' and the 'consumer citizen'. They bring different emphases to the
constitution of the meaning of citizenship and have distinctive implications for
the future of welfare states. These discourses are shaped and influenced through
the process of political practice. Each discourse moves beyond Marshall in the
sense that there is increased awareness that welfare states have created their
own forms of discrimination and hidden oppression. Although none of these
discourses in themselves suffices to redefine citizenship, it shall be argued that
they represent forms of resistance within the spaces of democracy. The notion of
resistance, it will be argued, is very central to a redefinition of emancipatory

citizenship. Citizenship as resistance shifts the debate on citizenship from attempts at defining who is a citizen and who is excluded, to citizenship as a form of resistance against bureaucracy and uniformity. Instead, it argues for accountability, transparency and diversity. Such a renewed notion of citizenship should be built upon four components: universal human rights, the right to be different, the public dimension and the social dimension.

Citizenship as process

Like democracy citizenship has to be continuously recreated, re-evaluated and analysed. The difficult task is to agree on a series of components which are seen as essential to constituting the meaning of citizenship and therefore components which are valued in themselves. Within a liberal context, individual rights are described as being inalienable rights, preferably written within a constitution. These rights are of major importance for migrants, refugees, asylum seekers and ethnic groups who feel that their rights to residence are continuously threatened. The concept of citizenship has to confer a number of rights that are seen as essential human rights and which cannot be negotiated between generations or in between elections. However, citizenship is also about a sense of belonging, to share in the experiences of a community and not to be excluded from access to areas such as health care or education because of income, ethnicity or gender differences. Marshall, in his attempt at defining social citizenship, focused on issues of income and income acting as a barrier to access. Fifty years later the awareness of new problems of access and belonging point to issues that Marshall did not consider. Welfare states have not been benign institutions. They have created their own forms of discrimination and forms of suppression. Furthermore, the attempts to deal with child abuse, violence against women, racial harassment and the abuse of the elderly have created new agendas as to the meaning of citizenship.

The literature on citizenship since the 1980s has tended to focus on two major issues. These involved, via the rediscovery of the citizen of Marshall, making Marshall the cornerstone of the citizenship debate and asking whether Marshall's citizen as developed in the early 1950s could deal with the challenges of the 1990s (Mullard 1997). The second debate focused on the problems of citizenship and exclusion and emphasized the nature of political, social and economic exclusion. This debate has tended to concentrate on the nature of the exclusion of women, problems of racism and exclusion, social exclusion and social policy and economic exclusion and problems of unemployment and poverty. The common theme to emerge from these debates is that they all provide a definition which is static in both place and time. Citizenship is associated with the individual, the nation state, institutions and issues of inequality of access. It is approached as a set of clothing and as a matter of wearing the right clothing, identifying the individual who is not properly dressed. The concern with a static definition assumes that there is some agreed vision of what a citizen should look like yet the presence of competing discourses in itself confirms that citizenship is a contestable site. It is a space to be filled by discourses and narratives. There is no agreed yardstick to compare whether a person living in Germany or France is more citizen than a person living in Italy or in Britain. There is no agreement as to whether welfare states are aimed at creating citizenship. It is assumed that by constructing universal public services it is more likely that such a context will create citizenship, yet in Sweden and France citizenship has a different meaning. The welfare state in France does not feature in the debate on citizenship while in Sweden the problem of citizenship is equated with questions relating to migrants and minorities.

The concept of citizenship is a contestable concept in the real sense that it is a contestable terrain.

> To say that a particular network of concepts is contestable is to say that standards and criteria of judgement it expresses are open to contestation. To say that such a network is essentially contestable is to contend that the universal criteria of reason as we can now understand them do not suffice to settle these contests definitively.
>
> (Connolly 1983: 225)

At present, the terrain is occupied by a number of discourses which in themselves confirm the meaning of pluralism. We no longer live in a world of one truth but a world which is influenced by a number of truths. The building of consensus can no longer be achieved through the ascendance of one paradigm. Furthermore, the idea that there is a context where all discourses are given equal access and that one discourse can or will emerge as a new consensus suggests a lack of understanding of the nature of discourse. The recognition of discourses is the confirmation of pluralism, of having to live with uncertainty but also with hope. The excavation of discourses allows for issues of power and dominance previously hidden to be exposed and made transparent. It implies a need for transparency and the necessity of trust.

In the following section it will be argued that there are five discourses on citizenship each emphasizing a different definition and meaning of citizenship. However, there are elements within the various discourses which can be utilized to create a meaning of citizenship founded on sincere consensus.

Discourses on citizenship

The public citizen

The discourse of the public citizen combines the concepts of deliberative democracy, thick democracy as outlined by Barber and the democratic culture of Bowles and Gintis (Mullard 1997). The public citizen makes the public space central because it is essential in defining personal freedom. The commitment to public space is the commitment to listen to the other; to accept plurality and differences, to accept the priority of dialogue, compromise, honesty, sincerity and transparency.

At present, public spaces are perceived to be corrupted by policy processes which are not accountable and are remote and centralist. The present definition of the public space leaves the majority as the quiet audience sitting passively and silently in the darkness of the auditorium. The audience of liberal democracy is encouraged between acts and to judge the political actors when it comes round to the next election. By contrast, public citizenship is correlated with the widening of public space that includes the workplace, which creates a democratic culture and what Barber refers to as thick as opposed to thin democracy (Mullard 1997).

In developing the theme of public citizenship there are two issues which need to be taken into consideration. First, there is the issue raised by Hannah Arendt that the notion of the public citizen might be incompatible with the social question. Hannah Arendt (1951) argued that welfare policy, poverty and housing represented projects which could not be dealt with honestly within the public sphere. The social question represented particular interest and therefore hindered any attempt to create a public sphere. Second, there is the issue of whether the commitment is to democracy as an end itself or whether democracy becomes a means to an end to satisfy particular interests and creating increased expectations which result in overload and undermine governance. Bobbio (1987) has pointed to six broken promises of democracy to explain the disillusionment with public space. According to Bobbio the broken promises include the persistence of oligarchy, the limited spaces for democracy, the uneducated citizen and the stalemate of pluralism. All these factors have contributed to a functional rather than a citizens' democracy.

The independent citizen

The interpretation of the independent citizen is located within the discourse of classic market liberalism and the commitment to competition and the market economy. The rational individual continually makes decisions aimed at maximizing his or her well-being – decisions based on natural competence (individuals pursue happiness whilst avoiding pain) and technical competence or the ability to acquire and accumulate information. The individual makes decisions based on knowledge and information. The independent citizen prefers to live with the injustice of the market rather than the injustice of the political process. The injustice of the political process is founded on arbitrary decisions made by politicians. Politicians make decisions which seek to please majorities, decisions which favour specific interest groups, and which therefore tend to disadvantage the individual who does not belong to the pressure group which has muscle or has the ability of voice and exit.

According to the discourse of the independent citizen the injustice of the market is the result of the price mechanism. In the market people are not discriminated against because of colour or gender difference – the barrier to the market is price. The independent citizen is an end and not a means to an end. While politicians use people as means to an end – as instruments to create their vision of the good society, market Liberals have no vision of the good society – individuals decide for themselves their life projects. There is no attempt to moralize about what is the good society, each individual has a view and an interpretation.

While the discourse of the public citizen seeks to make central the importance of public space, the independent citizen seeks to squeeze and put limits on public space. The independent citizen discourse is about redefining the public–private divide. The independent citizen discourse is about less government – less intervention and more reliance on markets and competition.

The limits on government have to be outlined within a written constitution including written rules on the conduct of economic policy and rules on the financing of government. Money supply policy, setting limits on public sector deficits and declaring pathways for inflation represent examples of a constitutional approach to economic policy making.

The independent citizen is respected for making decisions as a rational individual – all individual decisions are therefore rational and of equal value – individual life projects have to be respected and people have to be given the autonomy and the choice to fulfil their projects.

The entitled citizen

The emphasis of the entitled citizen is a commitment to the social dimension of citizenship and the role of welfare states in the making of citizenship. Within a Marshallian approach to citizenship the meanings of belonging and membership indicate the sharing of life experiences. The life experience suggests that there has to be more to citizenship than the commitment to formal and procedural citizenship. Individuals may have a legal claim on citizenship but unless they have access to provisions of health care, education, social security, the courts and the justice system then that citizenship remains formal. Citizenship requires a series of policies which ensure that, irrespective of income, individuals have access to these provisions and can experience belonging.

Policy commitments to equal pay, equal opportunities, and non-discrimination all need processes of access to ensure that individuals who feel injured can have their case adjudicated with minimum costs and minimum delay. In addition, membership involves social membership which means access to a multiplicity of issues which influence daily life. Membership of community therefore involves sharing experiences in access to health and education services. If membership means a shared experience, it means shared environments which deliver health care and education services. This would imply expanding welfare services with a commitment to universal rather than selective public services.

Universal access to public health and education ensure that income is not a barrier to entry. Furthermore, with public services directed at meeting individual need, it makes it possible for individuals to be self actualized and fulfil their life projects. Commitment to life projects, choice and autonomy cannot be delivered in a context of income inequality and in a context of gender and race discrimination.

The discourse of the entitled citizen is at present being questioned by discourses which point to various crises of social citizenship. The entitled citizen is at present being undermined by the language of fiscal crisis which suggests that the entitled citizen has put too many claims on the state. The commitment to the entitled citizen has created a number of unintentional consequences including problems of moral hazard and dependency. The attempt to replace the network of families, friendships, communities and neighbourhood through state-financed services has created a vacuum where people feel that the duty starts and finishes with the taxes they pay and there is no obligation to care for others as this is the responsibility of the state professionals and bureaucracies. The problem is that despite major increases in expenditure, governments cannot replace the plurality of networks which deliver services.

The communitarian citizen

The communitarian citizen is firmly embedded in a community deriving identity from the story of the community. Rather than being unencumbered the individual identifies with responsibility, attachments, friendships and commitments. In the discourse of the communitarian citizen it is attachment which gives the individual identity. Issues of freedom, liberty and individualism are meaningless when discussed in abstract. It is only through context that such concepts gain meaning and are given value. We experience freedom and liberty in the context of community (Taylor 1979; McIntyre 1981).

> we all approach our own circumstances as bearers of a particular social identity. I am someone's son or daughter, someone else's cousin or uncle; I am a citizen of this or that city, a member of this or that guild or profession; I belong to this clan, that tribe, the nation. . . . I can only answer the question 'what am I to do?' if I can answer the prior question 'of what story or stories do I find myself a part?' The story of my life is always embedded in the story of those communities from which I derive my identity.
>
> (McIntyre 1981: 205)

Community is the anchor, it provides certainty, regularity and rhythm – in community people know their place, they know what is expected of them. Life is stable and predictable and it is the stability, the durability and continuity which give people a sense of belonging, identity and citizenship.

The communitarian discourse is a criticism of the independent citizen because the independent citizen seeks citizenship in the context of the market and has no attachment or responsibility. The market creates the ethic of competitive individualism, of personal striving without taking into consideration the impact this has on the wider context. In the context of the market there is no commitment to solidarity. The drive towards the market creates the emptiness of city centres and of public places which feel unsafe.

The communitarian citizen is located within the context of collective memories and of shared histories. Community is inclusive where the 'in group' is made up of those who share in the story or narrative. The community is exclusive with respect to those who do not traditionally belong to the 'in group' because it builds on tradition, institutions and authority.

The consumer citizen

Post-modernity points to fragmentation, disintegration, neotribalism and competing discourses. Within a post-modern discourse the consumer citizen is no longer attached to community, tradition, authority or institutions. The consumer citizen lives in a post-traditional, post-scarcity society where life politics replaces the emancipatory politics of modernity (Giddens 1991).

The consumer citizen lives in a world of continuing changes in wants and desires. There is no fixed essentialism; no fundamentals but continuing evaluation and self-reflection. The consumer citizen is the citizen of temporary and voluntary contract, of temporary attachment while searching for emotional democracy and the pure relationship. The consumer citizen seeks to deal with the problems of living in a society of strangers where there is no community but where the challenge is to live with uncertainty and fear (Bauman 1995). The consumer citizen perspective is implicitly critical of the assumptions that construct communitarian citizenship. Communitarianism is perceived as the attempt to re-occupy the vacuum of uncertainty and the emerging pluralism with pre-modern notions of community; with pre-modern anchors of family, neighbourhood and authority.

The consumer citizen replaces the politics of emancipation with life politics. There is no longer an emancipatory class category which is likely to deliver the promised land or the 'New Jerusalem'. Instead, the world is taken as it is; a series of contradictions of both optimism and pessimism; of wonder and tragedy; of hope and despair; of fear and security and of certainty and uncertainty. In the absence of an emancipatory category, politics becomes a politics of issues, of pressure group politics and of neotribalism with each tribe having its own language.

Life politics emerges as the politics of lifestyles. It emphasizes difference and the discovery of personal identity as opposed to the politics of life chances and opportunity. The consumer citizen retreats from the public sphere as presently constituted. Politics is increasingly perceived to be irrelevant. The strategy of retreat into increasingly privatized lives confirms the degree to which political discourse becomes a non-issue. Political parties elections and parliaments reflect the self serving interests of political élites.

The consumer citizen lives in a world of knowledge and information where knowledge increasingly leads to uncertainty and fear. Information provided by experts is inherently conflictual, research findings are temporary decisions and therefore become increasingly individualized. Unemployment is no longer a social issue but a personal experience – people are increasing learning to live with the market, a context which they cannot shape, so rather than shaping the market they come to accept to live with the market. Unemployment in this sense becomes a personalized experience of acquiring skills and knowledge, of human capital investment where investment is an individual decision.

In a consumer society we construct identity around the consumer products that we have and that we possess. The clothes we wear, the car we own, our leisure pursuits and the football team we support give us identity. Consumer society lives on the emotions of signs. This is the age of the superhighway of images in which we experience climbing Mount Everest without leaving the armchair. This is the age when we continually see images of starvation, of atrocity on TV screens and we continue to get on with the routines of our daily life. In this sense therefore we are becoming global citizens. We are sharing emotions with the rest of humanity and yet being the global citizen sometimes proves to be too much, we cannot take in all the emotions of the globe, while at the same time feeling powerless and hopeless.

The discourses identified in this section posit different challenges to Marshall's conception of citizenship. The public citizen discourse, for example, confirms that there is now a need to move beyond Marshall's political rights as being equated with the right to vote. The need to widen democracy, to create greater transparency and accountability of governments is rooted in the belief that welfare states have created an 'expertocracy' of bureaucrats of health and education professionals who need to be made accountable. Marshall's definition of citizenship assumed a certain homogeneity of people being treated in the same way: that is as members as of a community. After 50 years of experiencing the welfare state it is now very clear that homogeneity creates forms of oppression and defines the outsider and the stranger. The problem is that homogeneity creates irreconcilable tensions for those who are committed to citizenship and pluralism. If pluralism seeks to confirm the right to be different and to live in an environment which is heterogeneous, then it acknowledges diversity and celebrates difference, and thus pluralism does not sit comfortably with the citizen of Marshall.

The entitled citizen of Marshall is homogeneous as a claimant on the welfare state. Marshall made assumptions as to the definition of the family, of men claiming family allowance, encouraging women to contract out of pension contributions. Marshall's assumptions were utilized by governments in constructing social policies on income tax and the benefit system which contributed to the subordination of women and children. Marshall's welfare state assumed that there would not be long-term unemployment and was therefore unable to deal with the problems of recession and unemployment present since the early 1980s. Marshall's citizenship did not deal with the problems of institutional racism in public services.

The views on the independent citizen confirm that since the 1980s the boundaries between the public and private spheres have been challenged. Increasingly, governments are accepting that welfare states need to be reformed, that the private market can provide welfare services and that market disciplines can be introduced into areas of public provision by creating internal or quasi-markets for public services as the means of breaking with the monopoly of public provision.

Citizenship and resistance

Although the discourses mentioned above are in themselves not adequate to outline a definition of citizenship which is emancipatory and has relevance to current expectations, they represent elements of another approach to citizenship: citizenship as resistance.

Citizenship as resistance shifts the debate on citizenship from attempts at defining who is a citizen and who is excluded, to citizenship as a form of resistance which is awkward and which perpetually challenges the world as it is. This includes resistance against the expansion and influence of bureaucracy and rule by 'nobody'. It also includes resistance to the new knowledge estates of the so-called expertocracy including health professionals, military, environmental and economics experts and their language of exclusion and their disavowal of responsibility. Citizenship as resistance wants to give priority to processes of democratic politics, accountability and transparency (Beck 1992).

Citizenship has to be inclusive of the other, of plurality, diversity and the uniqueness of the individual. Citizenship as resistance configures the resistance of women and their attempt to make private issues into public concerns; of resistance to fundamentalist religious beliefs which seek to glue together new communities yet create new oppression and new forms of exclusion. Citizenship as resistance is confirmed in Northern Ireland when attempts are made to bridge the divide between Catholic and Protestant communities, in Bosnia, in Rwanda and in the new South Africa when resistance becomes the condition that replaces fear and suspicion with trust and hope. Resistance is confirmed when in the midst of fundamentalist surges there is a demand for pluralism and tolerance.

In the context of welfare states, citizenship as resistance challenges the debate on citizenship, which is passive, and which identifies who benefits and who loses from welfare provision. By contrast, citizenship as resistance questions the assumptions of welfare provision, questions, for example, images of households when governments outline taxation and benefit proposals. Citizenship as resistance seeks transparency in the delivery of health and education. Citizenship as resistance, therefore, seeks greater accountability of the professionals and also of government.

In arguing for citizenship as resistance the aim is to move towards an approach that makes citizenship fluid, permeable and a continuing agenda that does not come to a stop. Citizenship becomes a journey of resistances, of trying to create accountability, transparency and involvement in decisions which have an impact on the individual's life experiences. Citizenship as resistance is associated with awkwardness and discomfort. It provides the climate that seeks to deconstruct languages of power and oppression. It resists the closure of government so that what is perceived as being inevitable comes to be understood as choice and autonomy. Resistance is the ability to say 'No' to integration, assimilation and incorporation into a real or imagined community that denies reflection and criticism. Resistance is the ability to unmask veiled hypocrisy.

Citizenship as resistance is related to the process of personal biography. In the context of personhood, identity is very often defined by external factors which on reflection are contingent. The person attempts to resist those parts of identity which are increasingly experienced as suppressive including sexual orientation and gender oppression. The process of negotiating personal biographies reinforces the view that many dispositions of identity are contingent and could have been otherwise different in a different context. Concerning collective identity, resistance is the attempt to create a context that questions assumptions and points to the world as we know it as being contingent rather than inevitable and that it is also a world which is susceptible to change.

> The one who construes her identity to be laced with contingency, including branded contingencies, is in a better position to question and resist the drive to convert difference into otherness to be defeated, converted, or marginalized.
>
> (Connolly 1994: 180)

Components of citizenship

The number of discourses on the meaning of citizenship re-affirms the lack of agreement as to what constitutes citizenship. Citizenship incessantly reflects changes in expectations and hopes. Citizenship has to be continuously recreated and redefined. The concern of this chapter is to outline an argument which suggests that the concept has to be firmly located in people's daily lives and that there has to be a continuous engagement with the term to give it meaning and make it relevant to the here and now. Citizenship as resistance may provide a useful notion of citizen which fulfils these demands. Such a notion of citizenship should be built upon four central components.

Universal human rights

The first major concern of citizenship must revolve around the issue of human rights. The preservation of individual human rights constitutes safety, freedom from fear and the arbitrary loss of civil liberties. The problem with human rights is that such rights are now very often abused within the boundaries of nation states. The democratic process is no longer a guarantor of human rights for minority groups. Human rights therefore need to be protected at the global level through international agreements and a universal human rights discourse.

Freedom from fear is an essential component of human rights. Campaigns by women to recapture the right to walk inner city streets free from fear is an important component of citizenship. Freedom from racial harassment is equally important to the daily life experience of ethnic minorities.

The right to be different

The commitment to universal human rights is compatible with the commitment to the right to be different. The right to be gay or lesbian, the right to worship as a Muslim are connected with a commitment to the recognition of difference of living within a plurality of paradigms. The commitment to human rights guarantees the rights of the individual. The person with physical disability or learning difficulty has to be treated differently only in the context of difference as a commitment to the rights of the individual.

The recognition of communities, of the need to recognize difference between communities and to give communities autonomy tends to confirm separatism and segregation. The attempt to create ethnic enclaves in former Yugoslavia might be a short-term answer to bring about peace and stability but in the longer term the commitment must be to recreate the state of Bosnia Herzegovina committed to ethnic pluralism and human rights.

The emphasis on difference, on collective memories and collective histories are important because they enable minorities to live in dignity in the context of majority cultures. People seek enclaves and safe areas and to be with those of common views as a strategy, and an avenue to safety. It is suppression for an Afro-Caribbean, Asian or Chinese to be asked to make a commitment to Britain and to surrender ethnic identity in an oath of allegiance to British citizenship. To have a plurality of identities does not constitute a threat. Identity with collective memory or history only becomes a threat if it creates a climate of intolerance and the negation of the right to be different.

The right to be different within the context of the modern state is only of limited relevance since the modern state is a territorial state and individuals, groups and communities are located within the territory of the modern state. According to Parekh

> . . . the modern state privileges the territorial identity. Its members do, of course, have multiple identities, affiliations and allegiances, but the territorial identity is overarching and dominant. . . . Unlike its earlier counterparts, it territorialises and totalizes human relations and activities, and gives them a wholly new dimension.
>
> (Parekh 1995: 28)

Policies of integration and multiculturalism have to be understood in the context of the modern state. Most modern states are constituted of pluralities of identities, of communities and ethnic minorities. The nature of legislation has often been constructed within the framework of sustaining a majority paradigm that does not question the nature of dominance and oppression and does not seek to be reflexive and critical. Modern European states have tended to be nationalistic, emphasising homogeneity and commonality, where the individual is deeply situated within the imagined community as constituted by the state. The nationalistic nation state of Europe creates a policy framework which hides and disavows oppression of those who do not belong to the imagined community. Collective memories and living with the past imprisons individuals in the past and creates an obstacle to optimism and the ability to be different.

> The dangers of nationalism are all too well known to need elaboration. It is exclusive and chauvinistic . . . it is suspicious of differences between individuals and groups, and postulates a non existent national soul or spirit. Privileges national identity, denies the role of mediating agencies, has a collectivist thrust, fears outsiders, and rules out intercultural borrowing.
>
> (Parekh 1995: 48)

Public dimension

Despite the post-modernist criticism of the notion of the public citizen there are still a number of elements of the discourse of the public citizen which need to be safeguarded and reclaimed. The commitment to human rights needs an environment of transparency. The confirmation of human rights in a written constitution is not sufficient since human rights need to be protected in an environment of political accountability, a democratic culture and public participation. This commitment requires governance which is decentralized and governance which encourages a 'thick' democracy. The post-modern scepticism needs to be attracted from the retreat of private life to the public space. The problem is that public space needs to be made safe, the discourses of difference and of neotribalism have to be replaced with commitments to compassion, tolerance, forgiveness and negotiation.

Social dimension

Aspects of Marshall's social argument are still relevant to the challenges of consumer capitalism. Denial of access to health care, education and social security are still major barriers to citizenship. Civil liberties and human rights need to be combined with social rights.

Since the mid 1970s, Keynesian conventional wisdom has been abandoned as a macro economic framework. The conduct of economic policy during the past 20 years has been about control of inflation, money supply and reducing the public sector deficit. Most European countries have now experienced long-term unemployment in the 1990s. Unemployment is likely to remain at about 25 million people out of work or 12 per cent of the total European workforce.

Whilst a Keynesian economic strategy might still be viable in the 1990s, the question is whether governments are likely means to demand management policies. The evidence suggests that most countries over the next 5 years at least will remain committed to a monetarist framework. The criteria for European Monetary Union (EMU) are set within a monetarist framework. The consequence of this policy approach is that governments have accepted that unemployment is here to stay. Furthermore, reducing unemployment seems to be tied to governments reducing their deficits, reducing interest rates, reducing non-wage labour costs and providing employers with a context of falling labour costs. The present logic is that Europe has to compete with the Asian 'tigers' and European workers need to reduce their costs if they are to remain competitive.

The abandonment of the Beveridge/Keynesian paradigm has major implications for the social citizen of Marshall. Monetarism has resulted in widening income differentials and inequality. The welfare state no longer creates citizenship but dependency targeted at specific income groups. The welfare state looks more and more like a place of deterrence and a place to stay away from. Reducing taxes have meant that the tax base for funding the welfare state has been eroded which in turn means that future governments will have to depend on growth to fund additional expenditures whilst at the same time they will be under equal pressure to deliver tax reductions so that people can feel they are sharing in prosperity.

> If we can, we buy ourselves individually out of the underprovided, shabby schools, the overcrowded, undernourished hospitals, the miserly state old-age pension. The more we do so, the more reasons we have for doing it, as the schools grow shabbier, the hospital queues longer, and old-age provisions more miserly still.
>
> (Bauman 1995: 272)

Conclusion

According to Beck (1992) the globalized economy and the age of risk society require a commitment to widening political accountability where people feel that they are part of the universe, involved in decisions which affect their lives, their environment and the world to be left to future generations. It is within this context that civil society, civic virtue and citizenship have to be redefined.

In the making of contemporary citizenship there is a need to combine the lessons of modernity with the criticisms of post-modernity. Citizenship has to be developed in a post-enlightenment context or in a post-modern civic culture which still needs to be coined:

> The new vocabulary of citizenship will be shaped by concepts of moral liberal ideals that emphasize their cultural particularism and their partial nature. . . . This requires a re-thinking of virtually every aspect of liberal democratic citizenship
>
> (Bridges 1994: 114)

The new citizenship has to combine a commitment to universal human rights with the right to be different. The citizenship of modernity was founded on a civic culture which emphasized the rights of the individual. By contrast the citizenship of post-modernity needs to be underpinned by a civic culture which recognizes that the construction of the individual of post-modernity has to be accompanied by an explicit commitment to 'the other' in a language which seeks to build sincere consensus.

The civic culture of post-modernity represents a commitment to transparency, to accountability and decentralized government. Rorty (1989) has tended to provide a pragmatic defence of liberal democracy arguing that liberal democracy continues to be our best hope despite its limitations. By contrast Lyotard (Pangle 1992) has tended to argue that liberal democracy is a form of government which replaces monarchy but that the form of power in liberal democracy continues to be despotic. There is therefore a need to reclaim public space for a democratic culture. Public space still offers the best hope for dialogue and compromise.

The argument for the post-modern citizen is also an argument which accepts that we are living in a different age and that we are witnessing the emergence of a new society qualitatively different to that of modernity. There are no longer emancipatory categories of class, or women or black tribunes but there is the potential for the emancipated citizen.

The emancipated citizen has to be continuously recreated and re-invented. The nature of power, domination and oppression needs to be replaced by the language of human rights, justice and tolerance. The citizen is the individual who has autonomy and choice, who can identify with a plurality of identities, recognizing the right to be treated as different and unique, and willing to treat the other with the same respect and dignity.

Bibliography

Arendt, H. (1951) *The Origins of Totalitarianism*, New York: Harcourt.

Bauman, Z. (1992) *Imitations of Postmodernity*, London: Routledge.

Bauman, Z. (1995) *Life in Fragments: Essays in Postmodern Morality*, Oxford: Basil Blackwell.

Berstein, R. (1991) *The New Constellation. The Ethical–Political Horizons of Modernity/Postmodernity*, Oxford: Polity Press.

Beck, U. (1992) *Risk Society: Towards a New Modernity*, London: Sage.

Bobbio, R. (1987) *The Future of Democracy*, Oxford: Polity Press.

Bridges, T. (1994) *The Culture of Citizenship: Inventing Postmodern Civic Culture*, New York: State University of New York Press.

The Commission on Global Governance (1995) *Our Global Neighbourhood*, Oxford: Oxford University Press.

Clifford, J. (1997) *Routes: Travel and Translation in the late 20th Century*, Cambridge MA: Harvard University Press.

Connolly, W. E. (1983) *The Terms of Political Discourse*, Oxford: Martin Robertson.

Connolly, W. E. (1994) *Identity/Difference: Democratic Negotiations of Political Paradox*, Ithaca/London: Cornell University Press.

Eistenstein, Z. (1989) *The Female Body and the Law*. Berkeley: University of California Press.

Foucault, M. (1975) *Discipline and Punish: the Birth of the Person*, Harmondsworth: Penguin.

Giddens, A. (1991) *Modernity and Self Identity: Self and Society in the Late Modern Age*, Oxford: Polity Press.

Gilroy, P. (1987) *There Ain't No Black in the Union Jack. The Cultural Politics of Race and Nation*, London: Hutchinson.

Gilroy, P. (1993) *The Black Atlantic Double Consciousness and Modernity*. Cambridge MA: Harvard University Press.

Hobsbawm, E. (1995) *The Age of Extremes: the Short Twentieth Century*, London: Abacus.

Kymlicka, W. (1989) *Liberalism, Community and Culture*, Oxford: Clarendon Press.

Lyon, D. (1994) *Postmodernity*, Oxford: Oxford University Press.

Lyotard, J. F. (1984) *The Postmodern Condition: a Report on Knowledge*, Manchester: Manchester University Press.

McIntyre, A. (1981) *After Virtue, A Study in Moral Theory*, Notre Dame: University of Notre Dame Press.

Mullard, M. (1997) 'Discourses on citizenship', in M. Mullard and S. Lee (eds) *The Politics of Social Policy in Europe*, Aldershot: Edward Elgar.

Norris C. (1993) *The Truth about Postmodernism*, Oxford: Basil Blackwell.

Nozick, R. (1984) 'Moral constraints and distributive justice', in M. Sandel (ed.) *Liberalism and its Critics*, Oxford: Blackwell.

Pangle, T. (1992) *The Ennobling of Democracy: the Challenge of the Postmodern Age*, London: Johns Hopkins University Press.

Parekh, B. (1995) 'Ethnocentricity of the nationalist discourse', *Nations and Nationalism*, 1: 25–52.

Rorty, R. (1989) *Contingency, Irony and Solidarity*. Cambridge: Cambridge University Press.

Sartori, G. (1987) *The Theory of Democracy Revisited*, Parts 1 and 2, New Jersey: Chatham House Publishers.

Selbourne, D. (1997) *The Principle of Duty*, London: Abacus.

Soysal, Y. (1994) *Limits of Citizenship: Migrants and Postnational Membership in Europe*, Chicago: University of Chicago Press.

Steenbergen, B. van (ed.) (1994) *The Condition of Citizenship*, London: Sage Publications.

Taylor, C. (1979) *Hegel and Modern Society*, Cambridge: Cambridge University Press.

Turner, B. (1990) 'Outline of a theory on citizenship', *Sociology* 24, 2: 189–218.

Vogel, U. (1991) 'Is citizenship gender-specific?'. In: U. Vogel and M. Moran (eds) *The Frontiers of Citizenship*. Houndsmills: Macmillan.

Walby, S. (1994) 'Is citizenship gendered?', *Sociology* 28, 2: 379–95.

2 Against social solidarity and citizenship

Justifying social provision in Britain and France

Randall A. Hansen

Introduction

In both France and the United Kingdom, public and academic debate about the role and character of social provision has implicated questions of citizenship.[1] In France, this debate reflects a long tradition of post-revolutionary public discussion about citizenship, and the language of citizenship is employed in a wide range of contexts.[2] In the United Kingdom, public discussion of citizenship has been traditionally less pronounced, and it has only been in the last two decades that an active public debate about citizenship has developed.[3] Recent British interest in citizenship partly reflects efforts, led by 'Charter 88', to lobby for an entrenched bill of rights (Stewart 1995), but also a desire by intellectuals and journalists on the political Left, marginalized in the 1980s, to find a bulwark with which they could resist the neoliberal reforming zeal of Margaret Thatcher's governments. 'Citizenship' seemed to promise a means of defending the modern British welfare state against neoliberal threats to dismantle it. This chapter examines citizenship discourse, as it relates to social provision, through a focus on two notions that play a similar role: social citizenship, in the United Kingdom, and *solidarité*, in France. It highlights the concepts' shortcomings, and sketches the outlines of an alternative foundation for defending social provision.

Social citizenship and *solidarité* fulfil the same role of justifying, at the level of theory, an individual's claim to welfare.[4] In the discussion that follows, the manner in which these two concepts exercise this legitimizing function will be examined. In the UK, such an examination involves paying close attention to two representative scholarly efforts at defending social provision as a right of citizenship, one communitarian, the other liberal. In France, it involves consideration of how *solidarité* justifies, through the related concept of risk, the maintenance of welfare programmes.

Although the manner in which the two concepts justify social provision contains important differences, they both suffer from an identical shortcoming. Neither is able to justify welfare provision in the most pressing instance: when a shared citizenship does not generate the common attachment that they presume. In addition, the concepts suffer from particular flaws. In the United

Kingdom, scholarly efforts to defend social citizenship founder either on their inability to link social provision to citizenship without reference to (not obviously related) principles, such as fairness, or on their inability to provide a persuasive account of why social citizenship would impel economically secure citizens to transfer their resources to the socially marginalized. In France, despite the historic role that *solidarité* appears to have played in the development of French social provision, the assumptions on which it is founded, above all the random distribution of risk, have been undermined by socio-economic changes in the last 20 years.

The foundation of a surer defence of welfare provisions, this chapter suggests, depends on our ability to undermine that which is at once the foundation and the central weakness of the neo-liberal critique of social provision: the distinction between kinds of rights. Such a defence bases claims not on common membership, but on an approach which links welfare to a definition of rights that does not recognize the distinction, elucidated by T. H. Marshall, between social, political and civil rights. Although the contours of such an approach remain open for debate, its outlines are found in recent liberal rights theory.

Citizenship and social citizenship in the United Kingdom

During the last 15 years, there has been an increased interest in citizenship as the basis for a justification and defence of a redistributive welfare state. The strands of the argument are various, but they are united by the claim that full membership in a political community, that is, citizenship, creates an entitlement to welfare.

Those making this argument draw on the work of the Cambridge Sociologist, T. H. Marshall, beginning with his claim that there has been, in this century, an extension of the rights of citizenship to include social rights – a right to education, unemployment benefits, pensions and so forth (Marshall 1992: Introduction, this volume). Although Marshall's thesis had always been read in intellectual circles, the ideological and political attack on the welfare state, associated with the Thatcher governments, led to a renewed interest in his views on citizenship (Harris 1987; Plant 1988; Vogel and Moran 1991). Casting about for the means to defend welfare provisions against Thatcher's ideological and political attack, British theorists seized on the concept of citizenship. If welfare could be defined as a right pertaining to citizenship, then the neoliberal assault could be rejected as not only objectionable but illegitimate. Such a move, however, required more than simply invoking Marshall's thesis. Marshall's work concerned itself with describing a historical evolution rather than normatively *defending* a link between welfare and citizenship; for Marshall, the link was self-evident. Consequently, scholars have sought to articulate a normative defence linking citizenship with a right to welfare.[5] The next section considers two of these approaches, one rights- and the other communitarian-based, which are representative of broader arguments about citizenship and welfare.

Grounding the right to welfare

Adopting a rights-based approach, Jeremy Waldron has recently articulated a sophisticated set of arguments defending a Marshallian conception of social citizenship rights (Waldron 1993).[6] There is a sense in which he is not definitively committed to any of these. Following a common practice in political theory, employed by such figures as Ronald Dworkin and John Rawls, Waldron is using theory to justify what he believes to be our basic intuitions.

Waldron's first argument rests on 'legitimate expectations'. On this view, the welfare state as it has developed since 1945 has encouraged certain beliefs about what Britons could legitimately expect in terms of child benefits, funding for education, retirement pensions and so forth. It was in the knowledge of these guarantees that people entered particular professions, decided to go to university rather than take school-leavers' jobs, opted for larger families and so forth. To withdraw these provisions now, the argument goes, is to alter illegitimately the terms of long-term choices halfway through citizens' lives. It is an affront to British citizenship:

> To violate these expectations is not merely to disappoint people. It is also to radically disrupt their personal planning. Social security expectations crucially affect the risks people think they can run in making their decisions. I have in mind here things like forming and breaking marital or quasi-marital relationships, conceiving children, moving away from close-knit communities, making employment decisions, taking certain attitudes to one's employer, starting a small business, opting for higher education, and so on. . . . My sense of what it is to be a member of this community is going to be centrally linked to my awareness of the conditions under which I am to think about making a life for myself in this community and about taking the various risks that that involves. . . . So we can see immediately the force of the argument that would say it is unfair to change the terms of the gamble – by abolishing the welfare safety net – halfway through.
>
> (Waldron 1993: 295–96)

Although the 'legitimate expectations' argument is intuitively appealing, it is undermined by its own conservatism. The argument, taken to its logical conclusion, freezes a given welfare distribution at any moment. Consider the example of a young doctor making life-plans five years before the implementation of a publicly-funded medical system. He makes a reasonable estimate of the fees he can charge in the medical market, opts for a large family, commits to costly college funds for all his children, and assumes a large mortgage based on what he believes will be substantial earnings. Assuming that the subsequent implementation of medical care reduces his earning potential (a reasonable assumption if one considers, for example, doctors' salaries in the USA and Canada), he could then use a variant of Waldron's point to provide moral back-up for the claim that the imposition of state health care conflicts with his legitimate expectations about the 'conditions under which (he is) to think about making a life for (himself)'. He could argue that his plans were 'radically disrupted' by a change in the rules halfway through the game. As any fundamental change in distribution will 'radically disrupt' life-plans of some members of the citizenry, the 'legitimate expectations' argument can equally justify the wholesale rejection of welfare reform in the 1940s and its retention in the 1990s. Such indeterminate outcomes cast serious doubt on the argument's usefulness as a normative defence of social citizenship.

Waldron recognizes that, were his argument taken seriously in 1945, there would have been no modern British welfare state. He retreats to the following arguments: first, that what he wishes to preserve is a good, as opposed to (for example) slavery, and thus the argument still carries weight; second, that his argument demonstrates that, if we are going to change social arrangements, we must do so slowly, over decades or generations; and, third, that his argument highlights in any event the importance of expectations (Waldron 1993: 297–98). These points remain open to objection. In the first instance, many will dispute that social rights are a good; otherwise, the welfare state would not have to be defended at all. In the second, the modified suggestion suffers from the same conservatism – a 'legitimate expectations' argument could have delayed for generations the creation of the modern British welfare state. Finally, it would still be possible in the third instance for those who wish to block the development of the welfare state to appeal to the importance of their expectations.

The argument, moreover, is further weakened by the fact that it has strayed from the language of citizenship. The argument appears to be based not on citizenship, as such, but on *fairness*. That is, altering people's life-plans is not morally wrong because it denies their social citizenship rights; rather, it is wrong because it is unfair. It is unfair to allow people to make plans based on a certain set of expectations and to 'radically disrupt' them. The adoption of such a claim, whatever its merits, involves surrendering the defence of welfare to the language of fairness.

Recognizing that the 'legitimate expectations' argument is a defence of particular arrangements rather than a defence of social provision *per se*, Waldron makes the suggestion that provisions of welfare are constitutive of the very concepts of community, membership and citizenship. He opts for two versions of the argument used by John Rawls in his discussion of the original position, which holds that the legitimization of our institutions requires that we consent to them in advance under fair conditions (Rawls 1971). The first of these draws on Rawls' controversial 'veil of ignorance', in which institutional and social arrangements are considered from the perspective of those ignorant of their wealth and status in society. As such, it raises difficult issues concerning contract theory, and Waldron views it as peripheral to his argument.[7] He develops a second defence based on contractarian principles: a system of distribution is only just when all individuals consent to it. Each 'original chooser' enters the pre-social negotiations, which are subject to a unanimity requirement, with a veto:

{I]t is worth noting that the argument [for the welfare state] can be made out even without Rawls's controversial 'veil of ignorance'. All one needs is a veto and the requirement of unanimous agreement. Those who happen to be poor or untalented may be expected to veto the adoption of any social system that does not attempt to ameliorate their plight. . . . If an argument like this can be made, then there is a reason for having welfare rights in a society whether it has a tradition of such institutions or not. Social rights of citizenship are a necessary condition for genuine and meaningful consent to social and political arrangements.

(Waldron 1993: 306–7)

The difficulty with this approach, however, is that it defends not Marshallian social distribution, which alleviates the more extreme economic inequality and strives for equality of status, but a rigid equality requiring a massive transfer of property and income. If the participants knew they were poor, *and* possessed a veto power over the final distribution, then they would be irrational if they accepted anything but a rigidly equal distribution of wealth.[8] This use of Rawls thus has redistributive consequences well beyond that which Waldron seems to intend, and certainly beyond what Marshall would have wanted (Marshall 1992: 31). Even if their original position sustains a concept of social citizenship, it does so at the price of 'decoupling' the concept from the welfare rights that it was supposed to justify.

Welfare provision as familial care

An alternative defence of welfare provision, founded on principles that might broadly be called communitarian, is suggested by David Harris' work. In the same vein as Marshall and Waldron, Harris holds that access to welfare provision should be guaranteed by membership in the national community:

The core of my theory of social justice is not that social justice amounts to the satisfaction of needs *per se*, but that it consists in protecting the status of individuals as full members of the community. The notion of full membership in the community I treat under the rubric of 'citizenship'. . . . Citizenship rights, as their name suggests, are held by individuals in virtue of their membership of the society in question. They are ascribed to persons *qua* citizens rather than directly or exclusively *qua* human beings.

(Harris 1987: 3, 147)

As full membership depends on the ability to participate effectively in a society's forms, members of the community may claim from the community those goods necessary to participation (Harris 1987: 148–49).[9] Yet, what is it about membership that generates this claim?

According to Harris, the claim on welfare results from the nature of membership in a political community: the national community is analogous to the family.[10] Children with particular needs, such as extra tuition in the case of learning difficulties or special equipment in the case of physical handicaps, are able to claim resources from their parents, and a disproportionate share of the family's resources relative to other children. In the same manner, citizens with particular needs, because of unemployment or other disadvantage, may claim special assistance from the state. Such citizens may also claim a disproportionately large amount of society's public resources relative to other citizens. Once the national community is recognized as the political equivalent of the family, the claim to welfare provisions follows.

Although Harris' familial understanding is among the most sophisticated defences of social citizenship around, it fails in its ultimate aim because a defence of welfare must justify distribution not between family members but between strangers.[11] It requires a theoretical justification of and political support for the transfer of resources towards those whom we do not know and for whom we have no sentimental attachment. It is precisely because the national community is not a family that such a conception of the welfare state is deficient.

Citizenship and solidarity in France

Before considering how *solidarité* ties citizenship to welfare in France, it is necessary to distinguish two types of solidarity: national solidarity (*solidarité nationale*) and occupational solidarity (*solidarité professionnelle*) (Ashford 1982: 253–55; Bonoli and Palier 1996: 242–43). National solidarity involves something akin to the Beveridgian ideal – solidarity across all social and professional groupings – and recommends a tax-financed, non-means-tested system of social protection offering flat-rate benefits. Occupational solidarity, by contrast, concerns solidarity within a given professional grouping, and it recommends a system of social protection funded through insurance contributions and offering earnings-related benefits. National solidarity promotes distribution across classes and aims at the prevention of poverty; occupational solidarity distributes income within a professional group and aims at the maintenance of income (Hantrais 1994). When discussing *solidarité* and social protection in France, one is largely discussing professional solidarity (Béland and Hansen, in press).

Solidarité, in so far as it concerns the welfare state, has two main intellectual influences in France. The first is Emile Durkheim, who distinguished between mechanical and organic solidarity. Mechanical solidarity is essentially tribal, resulting from the homogeneity of an isolated community (Durkheim 1947: 74–80), whereas organic solidarity is the consequence of social pluralism. Society is divided by technology and labour, and individuals are demarcated into a series of groups performing different tasks; it is from this division of labour that organic solidarity arises. As professional lives intermesh, we become increasingly dependent on one another: the car manufacturer relies on the production of motor parts, and both rely on the commercial industry, all three rely on the maintenance of the city's infrastructure and so forth. The second influence was exercised by Léon Bourgeois (Hayward 1961; Hazareesingh 1994: 88–9). An advocate of *solidarisme*, Bourgeois emphasized the individual's social interdependence (Bourgeois 1912: 46). In the same vein as Durkheim, he argued that the fulfilment of this debt necessitated a system of social protection, founded on the principle of insurance, which would neutralize the risks associated with industrial life: accidents, illness, the poverty of the aged.

Central to *Solidarité* in both these traditions is the notion of social inter-dependence, a collective recognition that each individual is dependent upon others (Milhau 1993: 77). This interdependence originates not from citizenship directly, but rather from *risk*. The fact that we all encounter a series of risks, notably illness and unemployment, which could interrupt our earnings, makes us all interdependent, and it renders social solidarity imperative (Chevallier 1992).

After 1945, a series of programmes was established with the specific aim of counter-acting socio-economic risk (Dupreyoux and Prétot 1995: 1; Ashford 1991: 25), and the choice of the insurance principle as the dominant policy instrument reflected a pursuit of professional solidarity as the dominant policy aim. The insurance principle, the institutional core of the post-war French welfare state, has three components: (1) the system is designed to insure workers; (2) benefits are earnings-related; and (3) they are paid to workers and their families on the basis of their contributions (Bonoli and Palier 1996: 242). Finally, the overall system was an institutional reflection of interdependence: French social insurance is based on the idea of *mutualité*, the notion that each individual should do as much as possible for his or her needs in co-operation with similar efforts by others (Ashford 1991: 34). Social protection was thus to be achieved through a system of mutual aid (*entraide*), in which all contributed, and in which those periodically without employment were supported by the con-tributions of those within it (Ashford 1991: 34; Ferrand-Bechmann 1993: 243).

The limits of solidarité

If the problems of citizenship as the foundation of a theoretical defence of welfare are primarily theoretical,[12] those of *solidarité* are empirical. The funda-mental assumption on which *solidarité* is premised – that risks are unpredictable – no longer applies. In Durkheim, this belief stems from the fact of functional interdependence; in the modern justification of the French welfare state, it stems from the belief that risks are randomly distributed. Along with retire-ment, which we all share, all citizens are at risk of illness and unemployment, both of which were assumed during the first three decades of the post-war period to be largely unpredictable. This assumption is no longer defensible. The emergence since the first oil shock in the 1970s of mass, structural unemploy-ment (*la crise*) means that a large portion of unemployment insurance funds support individuals who contribute only a portion, if anything at all, to that which they claim as benefits (Rosanvallon 1995: 92). In 1996, at least 1,650,000 individuals in France were without insurance.[13]

Mass unemployment has led to the emergence of *les exclus*: identifiable groups of individuals, of which a disproportionate number are immigrants and the poorly educated, who find themselves excluded from the labour market and society itself (Madec and Murard 1995; Bouvier 1996; Donzelot 1991). Those who are born into these disadvantaged ranks are unlikely to leave them, and the cycle of educational failure, poverty and unemployment repeats itself (Donzelot 1996: 59). In both these instances, the French educated middle and upper classes can be confident that their chances of finding themselves permanently unemployed, and/or a victim of exclusion, are markedly lower than those of poorly educated children of immigrants or the working class (Mongin 1992). The very word *la banlieue*, which creates an image of crime and indigence, graffiti and burned-out cars cut off from central Paris and other French cities, highlights the extent to which the extreme deprivation of segments of French society is marginal to the majority's daily existence and life chances. As there is little commonality between the two groups, there can be little interdependence and little solidarity.

Under such conditions, solidarity cannot be an effective foundation on which to defend welfare provisions. There is, moreover, a perspective from which *solidarité*, like social citizenship in the British debate, is theoretically as well as empirically flawed. The essential difficulty with *solidarité* as the foundation for the welfare state is that it justifies only those programmes that are least in need of theoretical justification. If there is full solidarity, such that the interests of all citizens are inseparable from those of all others, then mutual assistance naturally and logically follows. As this does not occur, what is most required, in France and throughout the Organization for Economic Cooperation and Development (OECD), is an argument for welfare provisions in which those contributing and those receiving have nothing in common beyond their shared citizenship. Like Harris' familial model of citizenship, *solidarité* cannot justify social provision when it is most needed. The phenomenon of *l'exclusion* in France is a telling example of this inadequacy.

Alternatives to citizenship and social solidarity

To summarize, I have argued that both 'citizenship' and *solidarité* are unsure foundations on which to construct a defence of robust social provision. Social citizenship, in the British case, is inadequate because the most promising efforts to use citizenship as a 'ground' of a right to welfare succeed only by reducing citizenship to a derivative status; citizenship defends welfare only by subordinating itself to independent principles, namely fairness. *Solidarité* is inadequate in so far as its core notion of interdependence presumes socio-economic conditions – most importantly the random distribution of risks – that no longer obtain. Finally, both approaches fail in that they cannot justify welfare provisions for the most compelling cases on the social periphery. To the degree that 'citizenship' and *solidarité* depend on a basic underlying common attachment, they hold little promise in those instances when a case for welfare is most needed: when a shared citizenship creates neither solicitude nor solidarity.

In considering an alternative to these approaches, it is instructive to reflect on the character of social citizenship's critique. The appeal of citizenship theory, in the UK, lies in its scepticism about the neoliberal effort to construct a rigid distinction between political rights (rights to free speech, freedom from arbitrary arrest), which are unassailable, and social rights, which are subordinate to considerations of cost or efficiency. The most effective way to give persuasive force to that scepticism, however, is to engage the distinction between kinds of rights *directly*, to highlight its fragility, and to demonstrate that if the state wishes to respect political rights, it is logically committed to respect social ones as well.

There are two steps involved in such an alternate defence: first, to offer a view of rights which undermines the traditional distinction; second, to show why those hostile to social rights – neoliberal theorists in the UK, for example – hold to a view of rights precluding reliance on the distinction. The first task offers an alternative view of rights; the second establishes that the choice between the two views of rights is not arbitrary.

Although the argument can be developed from several angles, it is possible to illustrate its outlines by drawing on liberal rights theory and, in particular, on the work of Joseph Raz (Raz 1988).[14] In *The Morality of Freedom*, Raz argues that a right is established when an individual possesses an interest vital to well-being. The core of this formula is the duty, for rights are grounds of duties (Raz 1988: 170–71). For Raz, a right exists when an interest is tied to an aspect of a person's well-being, an aspect that will create the duty. Quoting Raz:

> To assert that an individual has a right is to indicate a ground for a requirement for action of a certain kind, i.e. that an aspect of his well-being is a ground for a duty on another person. The specific role of rights in practical thinking is, therefore, the grounding of duties in the interests of other beings.
>
> (Raz 1988: 180)

In the same way that 'interest' is subject to a particularity requirement (not any interest will do, only those linked to well-being), rights are not applicable to any being or object which has an interest in well-being. Only those whose well-being is *intrinsically* valuable can possess rights. This must be so because it is only when someone's well-being is of intrinsic value that the rights they enjoy will be non-derivative, that is, explicable only with reference to their interest.

Thus, once an interest is vital to well-being, a right exists. The indeterminacy and expansiveness of Raz's formulation is intentional,[15] varying among agents and across social contexts. This indeterminacy provides an understanding of rights that cuts across our traditional distinctions among rights. Rights exist because there is an interest of sufficient importance (linked to well-being), and whether that right falls into a category of political, social or civil is entirely irrelevant. Although the precise implications of this approach are debatable, the form of the defence is clear: if particular welfare programmes are interests essential to individuals' well-being, then they are, on such an understanding, *rights*.

The question that remains is why we should abandon the traditional view of rights in favour of this new understanding. To answer this, it is necessary to consider the neoliberal argument in favour of keeping political and civil rights distinct from social.

The neoliberal argument invokes the philosophical distinction between negative freedom (absence from coercion in pursuing one's ends) and positive freedom (possessing the resources to pursue one's ends). Such a distinction between freedom and ability exists for two reasons: first, if freedom is defined as the ability to fulfil one's desires, then the agent is enslaved unless he or she is omnipotent, which is absurd; and, second, if we accept the liberal ideal of equal freedom for all citizens, then it cannot be achieved because we would equalize ability at time $T(1)$ only to see this distribution changed at $T(2)$, when a new inequality would reassert itself (Nozick 1974: chapter 7). Only if freedom is distinct from ability, and defined as the absence of intentional coercion, can it be secured through general legal provisions.

The negative/positive distinction, which ultimately sustains the traditional threefold view of rights, relies on the capacity of neoliberals to keep freedom and ability analytically distinct. Conversely, the success of an attempt to see social rights as indistinguishable from political rights depends on our capacity to undermine this distinction. Two possibilities present themselves. First, the coherence of the negative/positive distinction can be questioned. In an influential essay, Gerald MacCallum argues that *all* statements about freedom are triadic; they all involve elements of both negative and positive freedom. Whenever the freedom of persons is in question, it is always the freedom of agent X from constraint Y to do, not do, be, not be Z. To seek freedom from imprisonment is to seek freedom from chains to walk unimpeded. To seek freedom from scarcity is to do so in order to live a full life, or to purchase expensive art, or to travel the world. Freedom, *pace* the neo-liberals, is inherently concerned with ability (MacCallum 1991).

More concretely, the most common empirical argument used by neoliberals relies on scarcity. Negative rights, they argue, are free of cost; positive rights, given their open-ended character, are insatiable. There is no enforceable right to scarce resources and, without enforceability, a right becomes only rhetorical. Raymond Plant suggests a riposte to this argument: scarcity is a problem that affects *kinds* of rights rather than *categories* of rights. He cites the classic negative freedom: security of person and property. Enforcing non-interference requires resources, including police, courts and prisons. These costs are substantial in themselves and subject to unexpected increases as new threats (aircraft hijacking, urban riots) emerge. Finally, although absolute security can never be realized, neither the conceptual coherence of such a right nor the value of its pursuit is ever questioned (Plant 1988: 25). If the fact of scarcity is to undermine social rights, its indictment will extend to political and civil rights as well.

If these two arguments undermine the distinction between freedom and ability, then there is a *prima facie* case for shifting towards a conception of rights that rejects the Marshallian tripartite distinction. On Raz's conception, once the interest criterion is achieved, the right grounds a duty to provide for that interest regardless of category. Social welfare provisions can be defended not because they are part of citizenship, but because they are necessary for individual well-being. As such, they are rights that ground a duty on the part of the state to do everything within its capacity to ensure their realization. This does not mean that present resource constraints will be irrelevant. It does, however, mean that welfare provisions are not privileges to be extended or withdrawn at the whim of the ruling party; rather, their grounding is fundamental. If the state wishes to take seriously political and civil rights, then it must recognize and respect social rights.

Conclusion: citizenship, solidarity and social provision

In summary, this chapter has analysed citizenship discourse, as it concerns social provision, through an examination of the British concept of social citizenship and the French concept of *solidarité*. There is a little-noticed similarity in the role fulfilled by the two concepts in justifying the individual citizen's claim to social provision, though this role is exercized in importantly different ways. 'Citizenship' in the United Kingdom has been explicitly seized upon by intellectuals on the political left as a means of rebutting the neoliberal critique of the welfare state, while *solidarité* has long been viewed as the political motivation and theoretical justification for French social provision.

In analysing these concepts, the chapter has highlighted their shortcomings as justifications of social provision. Both concepts are flawed as theoretical foundations for such provision in a period of limited economic growth and, at least in France, mass structural unemployment. In the French case, *solidarité* has largely been discredited because the socio-economic conditions that supported the concept have altered. In the British, efforts to defend a link between citizenship and welfare rights succeed only by relegating citizenship to an analytically derivative status. In both cases, the two concepts cannot justify welfare for those on the social margins, those with whom there is no underlying attachment, no belief that their predicament is comparable to ours.

Finally, the inadequacy of these approaches does not suggest impotence in the face of pressure for welfare retrenchment. The strength of attacks on social provision depends on their ability to distinguish clearly between political/civil rights and social rights. If such a distinction is undermined, as recent political theory suggests it should be, then it is possible to adopt a view of rights that includes an essential, through indeterminate, social component. This conclusion naturally does not explore the argument that establishes a link between welfare entitlements and human well-being. This link is intuitive, though not uncontroversial. If the argument presented coheres, it none the less establishes the shape of a social democratic defiance of welfare provisions that does not presume the degree of commonality that no longer exists, if it ever did, in modern, industrialized and atomized societies.

Notes

1 Although this volume is devoted to analysing the 'welfare state' in Europe, the term is inappropriate in the French case, as many of the main components of French social provision (namely the insurance programmes) rest outside the state. I will thus use the term 'social provision', which can be taken as the equivalent of the 'welfare state' in the British case. The point on France was emphasized by Bruno Palier at the workshop leading to this volume (European Consortium for Political Research workshop on citizenship and the welfare state, Bern, 27 February– 4 March 1997). In using the terms 'social provision' and 'welfare state', I refer to the complex of programmes designed to ameliorate the condition of those who find themselves unable to participate in the labour market, because of sickness, unemployment or age.

2 In France, it is common, among journalists and scholars, to speak of *citoyenneté d'enterprise, citoyenneté culturelle* and so forth.

3 This is not to claim that there is no citizenship tradition in the United Kingdom. The work of the Fabians, the British idealists and William Beveridge, founding father of the modern British welfare state, was informed by their views on the rights and obligations of citizenship. It is rather that the language of citizenship has implicated fewer aspects of social life in the UK than it has in France, and that discussion of the concept outside the universities and élite intellectual circles has been, until recently, rare. On British conceptions of citizenship, see Rodman (1964) on T. H. Green, Harris (1995) and McBriar (1987). A conversation with José Harris clarified this point.

4 *Solidarité* has arguably exercised a greater practical influence in the development of the post-war French welfare state than the (relatively recent) notion of 'social citizenship' has in the UK. Although my concern is largely theoretical, I return to this point later in the chapter.

5 It is generally assumed that Marshall was a partisan of a redistributive welfare state. A recent article has challenged this assumption, arguing that attention to Marshall's other writings suggests that he adopted the liberal view that citizenship should be restricted to the political sphere. See Rees (1995).

6 This article was originally published as King and Waldron (1988). Waldron actually pursues both historical and normative arguments. My concern is with the latter. In the former, he discusses the belief among thinkers in the Western tradition, from Aristotle to Arendt, that a degree of economic security is a precondition to political participation. Such a belief, Waldron argues, suggests that citizenship has been historically understood to have a social component (283–94).

7 For critiques of the original position, see Dworkin (1977) and Kymlicka (1990: 66–8).

8 In making this argument, I borrow from G. A. Cohen, who presented this argument against Rawls' difference principle at All Souls College, Oxford, March 1993.

9 Harris relies on the assumption that there are a range of 'activities, patterns of consumption and types of relationships in the community' that are 'highly valued' and a prerequisite to full membership in it. These, which will vary according to community, may be claimed as rights of citizenship.

10 Harris argues that two characteristics of the family generate familial claims: first, it is a scheme of mutual support – parents support children, and children may be called on to support their parents and each other – and, second, certain claims exist

solely by virtue of membership, and not by virtue of contribution. In the latter, which is important for Harris' thesis, a handicapped child will have a claim against all other family members, while a father who deserted his children will none the less have some claim to their support in his old age. See Harris (1987: 152–3).

11 I owe this point to a conversation with Lesley Jacobs. Professor Jacobs also develops the argument in his *Rights and Deprivations* (1993: 43–6).

12 I say primarily because the language of citizenship has done little to prevent successive restrictions of social support in the United Kingdom since 1979.

13 Statistics on those without insurance are extremely difficult to find. I arrived at the above by adding those receiving the French minimum income (*le Revenu Minimum d'Insertion*), and labour market programmes designed for those without insurance: *les contrats emploi-solidarité, les contrats emplois consolidés* and *les contrats emplois ville* (*L'Annuaire* 1997: 310, *Contrats*, 1997: 2). These statistics do not take into account those who drop out of the labour market altogether. They should be construed as conservative estimates.

14 In discussing Raz's work, I intend only to give one example that rejects the civil–political–social distinction, rather than to endorse his position as the ideal. Recent work by Amartya Sen also suggests itself. Sen argues that the aim of social policy should not be to promote equality, as such, but to ensure that individuals possess the range of goods necessary to function in a given society. Relating the argument to the debate over relative and absolute poverty, Sen argues that the 'capability function' is absolute – all individuals may claim it – but that the range of goods associated with it, the range of goods needed to function, is relative to region, financial means, physical health and so forth. See Sen (1992). For earlier discussions of the capability function, Sen (1983) and (1985).

15 This point was stressed by John Gray in a 1992 seminar. In this respect, Raz shares common ground with Sen, who views the particular range of goods associated with the 'capability function' to be a question of context.

Bibliography

Ambler, J. S. (1991) *The French Welfare State: Surviving Social and Ideological Change*, New York: New York University Press.

Annuaire des Statistiques Sanitaires et Sociales (ASSS) (1997), Paris: Service des Statistiques des Etudes et des Systèmes d'Information.

Ashford, D. E. (1982) *Policy and Politics in France: Living with Uncertainty*, Philadelphia: Temple University Press.

—— (1991) 'Advantages of Complexity: Social Insurance in France', in J. S. Ambler (ed.) *The French Welfare State: Surviving Social and Ideological Change*, New York: New York University Press.

Béland, D. and Hansen, R. (in press) 'Solidarity, Social Exclusion and the Three Crises of Citizenship in France', *Western European Politics*.

Bonoli, G. and Palier, B. (1996) 'Reclaiming Welfare. The Politics of French Social Protection Reform', *Journal of South European Politics and Society*, 1, 3: 240–59.

—— (1999), 'From Work to Citizenship? Current Transformations in the French Welfare State', Chapter 3 this volume.

Bourgeois, L. (1912) *Solidarité*, Paris: Arman.

Bouvier, P. (1996) 'Citoyenneté et exclusion', *Ethnologie Française*, 26, 2: 248–54.

Chevallier, J. (1992) 'La résurgence du thème de la solidarité', in J. Chevallier and D. Chocart (eds) *La Solidarité: un Sentiment Républicain?* Paris: Presses Universitaires de France.

Les contrats emploi-solidarité (CES), les contrats emplois consolidés (CEC), et les contrats emplois ville (CEV) en 1996 (1997), Paris: Direction de l'animation de la recherche des études et des statistiques, August.

Démier, F. (1996) *Histoire des Politiques Sociales: Europe, XIXᵉ – XXᵉ Siècle*, Paris: Seuil.

Donzelot, J. (1996) 'L'avenir du social', *Esprit* 219: 58–81.

——— (1991) 'Le social du troisième type', in J. Donzelot (ed.) *Face à L'Exclusion*, Paris: Éditions Esprit.

Dupreyoux, J. J. and Prétot, X. (1995) *Droit de la Sécurité Sociale*, Paris: Dalloz.

Durkheim, E. (1947) *The Division of Labor in Society*, Illinois: The Free Press.

Dworkin, R. (1977) 'Justice and Rights', in R. Dworkin *Taking Rights Seriously*, Cambridge MA: Harvard University Press.

Euzéby, C. (1996) (ed.) *Les solidarités: fondements et défis*, Paris: Economica.

Ferrand-Bechmann, D. (1993) 'Le Bénévolat comme modèle d'identité', in M. Thierry (ed.) *Exclusion et solidarité: Comment Repenser Le lien Social?* Paris, La Fondation l'Arche de la Fraternité.

Gewirth, A. (1982) *Human Rights: Essays on Justification and Applications*, Chicago: University of Chicago Press.

Hansen R. A. (1998) 'The Politics of Citizenship in 1940s Britain', *20th Century British History*, 10, 1: 67–95.

Hantrais, L. (1994) 'Comparing Family Policy in Britain, France and Germany', *Journal of Social Policy* 23, 2: 135–60.

Harris, D. (1987) *Justifying State Welfare*, Oxford: Basil Blackwell.

Harris, J. (1995) 'Le Compromis de Beveridge. Contrat et Citoyenneté dans la Protection Sociale, 1934–1948', *Revue Française de Science Politique* 45, 4: 596–606.

Hayward, J. (1961) 'The official social philosophy of the French Third Republic: Léon Bourgeois and Solidarism', *International Review of Social History* 6: 19–48.

Hazareesingh, S. (1994) *Political Traditions in Modern France*, Oxford: Oxford University Press.

Jacobs, L. A. (1993) *Rights and Deprivations*, Oxford: Clarendon, 1993.

King, D. S. and Waldron, J. (1988) 'Citizenship, Social Citizenship and the Defence of Welfare Provision', *British Journal of Political Science* 18: 414–43.

Kymlicka, W. (1990) *Contemporary Political Philosophy: An Introduction*, Oxford: Clarendon.

MacCallum, G. (1991) 'Negative and Positive Liberty', in D. Miller (ed.) *Liberty*, Oxford: Oxford University Press.

Madec, A. and Murard, N. (1995) *Citoyenneté et Politiques Sociales*, Paris: Flammarion.

Marshall, T. M. (1992), *Citizenship and Social Class*, London: Pluto (with an introduction by T. Bottomore).

McBriar, A. M. (1987) *An Edwardian Mixed Doubles: the Bosanquets versus the Webbs*, Oxford: Clarendon.

Milhau, J. (1993) *Solidarité: L'Avenir d'un Héritage*, Paris: Essai/Editions Sociales.

Mishra, R. (1977) *Society and Social Policy*, London: Macmillan.

Mongin, O. (1992) 'Le contrat social menacé?', *Esprit* 15:182: 5–11.

Nozick, R. (1974) *Anarchy, State and Utopia*, New York: Basic Books.

Parry, G. (1991) 'Conclusion: Paths to Citizenship', in: U. Vogel and M. Moran, *The Frontiers of Citizenship*, London: Macmillan.

Paugam, S. (1996) 'Le revenu minimum d'insertion en France après six ans d'expérience, un bilan contrasté', *Interventions Economiques* 27: 21–45.

Plant, R. (1988) *Citizenship, Rights and Socialism*, London: Fabian Society, No. 531.

Rawls, J. (1971) *A Theory of Justice*, Cambridge: Harvard University Press.

Raz, J. (1988) *The Morality of Freedom*, Oxford: Clarendon.

Rees, A. M. (1995) 'The Other T. H. Marshall', *Journal of Social Policy* 24, 3: 341–62.

Rodman, J. R. (ed.) (1964) *The Political Theory of T. H. Green*, New York: Appleton-Century-Crofts.

Rorty, R. (1989) *Contingency, Irony and Solidarity*, Cambridge: Cambridge University Press.

Rosanvallon, P. (1995) *La Nouvelle Question Sociale: Repenser l'État-Providence*, Paris: Seuil.

Sayah, J. (1996) 'Le droit à l'assistance ou la solidarité reconnue par le droit', in: A. and Ch. Euzéby (eds) *Les Solidarités: Fondements et Défis*, Paris: Economica.

Sen, A. (1983) 'Poor, Relatively Speaking' *Oxford Economic Papers* 35, 2: 153–69.

—— (1985) 'A Sociological Approach to the Measurement of Poverty: A Reply to Professor Peter Townsend', *Oxford Economic Papers* 37, 4: 669–76.

—— (1992) *Inequality Reexamined*, Oxford: Clarendon.

Stewart, A. (1995) 'Two Conceptions of Citizenship' *British Journal of Sociology* 46, 1: 63–78.

Thierry, M. (1993) 'RMI et lutte contre l'exclusion', in: *Exclusion et Solidarité: Comment Repenser le Lien Social?* Paris: Fondation l'Arche de la Fraternité.

Vogel, U. and Moran, M. (eds) (1991) *The Frontiers of Citizenship*, London: Macmillan.

Waldron, J. (1993) 'Social citizenship and the defense of welfare provision', in J. Waldron *Liberal Rights: Collected Papers 1981–1991*, Cambridge: Cambridge University Press.

3 From work to citizenship?

Current transformations in the French welfare state

Giuliano Bonoli and Bruno Palier

Introduction

The conservative–corporatist model of social protection found in most continental European countries is, of all such models, the one facing the biggest difficulties in adapting to current socio-economic change (Esping-Andersen 1996). Critics of this model have pointed to two key problems. First, systems falling into this category tend to use employment as a basis for social rights, as opposed to either need or universal social citizenship. In the current context of high and persistent unemployment, the appropriateness of such a system is being increasingly challenged (Rosanvallon 1995). In particular, it is argued that employment-based benefits are of little use in the fight against social exclusion. Since entitlement to benefits must be earned, those who are most in need are often unable to gain access to provisions. Yet, in most industrial countries, unemployment and social exclusion together are widely regarded as the most pressing social problems.

The conservative–corporatist model has also been criticized for its inability to create new jobs, since high levels of entitlement for workers and high levels of contributions have created a ring-fenced labour market to which 'the excluded' have little or no access (Esping-Andersen 1990, 1996). This model is seen as being at an impasse; because of its emphasis on contribution financing, contributory social insurance and high benefits for workers, it is vigorously defended by those who are in employment. These latter are generally unwilling to trade some of their privileges in order to create more jobs for those excluded from the labour market (Esping-Andersen 1996). In general, the fact that trade unions are powerful, or at least have a significant mobilizing capacity, is seen as an additional explanation for the 'frozen' status quo. The overall impression is that social insurance-based welfare states are finding it difficult to adapt to current socio-economic change (see Clasen 1996).

These concerns are reflected in national political debates. In the case of France, entitlement to benefits is gained through the payment of employment-related contributions in various social programmes. In the context of persistent unemployment in the late 1990s, policy makers are increasingly questioning the adequacy of a welfare system in which access to benefits is based on work.

The alternative would be to base entitlements on need or citizenship, which would, or at least should, guarantee coverage to the entire legally resident population.

Policy makers have responded to these concerns in two ways. The initial approach, predominant throughout the 1980s, saw the introduction of a number of new non-contributory social programmes, such as a guaranteed minimum income (social assistance). This process found widespread support and did not generate controversy. It included measures aimed at improving the financial situation of those excluded from the social insurance system, as well as active labour market policies, seeking to ease their entry into employment. The subsequent approach has seen increased momentum in the discussion on moving from the current employment-based arrangement to one which makes reference to residence or need criteria, and in fact some steps in that direction have already been taken (Palier and Bonoli 1995).

Until recently, however, this second approach to welfare restructuring has emerged mainly in intellectual and political debates, but has not been followed by actual changes in policy, arguably because of resistance from some actors (Bonoli and Palier 1996). Politically, it has proved easier to introduce new schemes than to rethink existing ones. Since 1995, however, structural change in the French welfare state has begun to look more likely (Taylor-Gooby 1996: 121). The government plan for reform of social security put forward in November 1995 (known as the Juppé plan) involves a clear intention to move away from contributory social insurance in a number of social policy areas. In spite of the impressive protest movement generated by the announcement of this reform, having made some concessions to the trade unions, the government appears to be in a position to make substantial progress towards this goal.

While the movement away from social insurance in certain areas of policy became increasingly evident in 1996–98, the direction the French welfare system is taking is still not clear. The contributory principle is being abandoned in a number of schemes, particularly health care and family benefits. However, it remains to be seen whether it will be replaced by need or citizenship. The emphasis on universality which is often found in government discourse, is met with scepticism by the trade unions, who fear that by weakening the contributory principle the government is actually paving the way for more radical reforms such as increased targeting.

In this chapter, we look at recent and current changes in the entitlement basis of French social programmes. In particular, universal entitlement is understood here as a key indicator of social citizenship. On this basis, we argue that while it may be true that some recent reforms are bringing France closer to the establishment of full social citizenship, with universal entitlement to social rights, this does not necessarily mean a reinforcement of welfare state institutions.

There are two main dimensions to this argument. First, in France the political forces which instigated the development of a welfare state did not fight for the recognition of social citizenship. Instead these groups traditionally argued for employment-related rights (Baldwin 1990; Ferrera 1993). To some extent, T. H. Marshall's vision of citizenship-based social rights as the climax of a three-century long emancipation process, is not fully reflected in the developments that have taken place in France. Second, with regard to ongoing change, the abandonment of the social insurance principle might in fact make the French welfare state more vulnerable to radical reform, such as targeting.

After a brief overview of the developments that lead to today's structure of the French welfare state, we will look at current debates and recent policy changes. Finally, we conclude that while the current transformation is a step towards the establishment of social citizenship in welfare policy, this shift is simultaneously making the French welfare state more vulnerable to cutbacks and targeting.

From social assistance to social insurance

As in other European countries, social policies in France originated in charities, administered by the church or local authorities. Assistance was available only to individuals who were unable to work or were in particularly difficult situations (sickness, invalidity, single motherhood, etc.) (Castel 1995). Towards the end of the nineteenth century, in the context of the ideological and political struggle opposing the state and the church, attempts were made to regulate and improve this form of social intervention, by adopting a number of laws on public assistance: on free medical treatment for the poor in 1893; on assistance for the elderly, disabled and chronically ill in 1904–05; and on assistance to large families in 1913 (Pollet and Renard 1995).

Social assistance, provided either by the state or the church, was seen as a moral duty towards the most disadvantaged in society as well as a means of social control. A significant amount of stigma was attached to recipients of social assistance, causing assistance to be increasingly regarded as an inadequate means of social intervention. From the end of the nineteenth century social insurance schemes were gradually introduced to the benefit of workers, through the establishment of friendly societies or on the initiative of socially-aware employers (Ewald 1986; Saint-Jours 1982). Social insurance was considered to be an instrument that gave individuals responsibility for themselves, since entitlement must be earned through work. To some extent, social insurance was seen as a morally superior form of social intervention in comparison to the previous assistance-based approach.

The replacement of social assistance by insurance was a long incremental process, from the nineteenth century until the end of World War II. The establishment of a social security system in 1945 can be seen as the climax of this movement. At that time, social assistance was seen as residual, and it was assumed that the expansion of social insurance would eventually make it redundant, as the whole population would be integrated in the social insurance system. Social rights were understood to a large extent as employment-related rights, and social insurance was seen as the best instrument to guarantee these rights.

During much of the post-war period, the gap between employment-related and social rights was not seen as a major problem. Access to benefits was guaranteed to workers and their families (see also note 1 on page 55). Although the French welfare state never managed to get rid of its assistance component, the context of full-employment and dominance of traditional patterns of family life made a relatively satisfactory approximation of universal coverage possible, though this was not achieved through the granting of citizenship rights. In addition, groups that were not covered by the initial (1945) arrangement, for example the self-employed, were gradually integrated into the system. As a result, during the *trente glorieuses* (1945–75) the employment-based French welfare state came close to the establishment of de facto citizenship rights for the whole population. Since the mid-1970s, however, the gap between the basis of the welfare state (i.e. workers) and the population affected by new social problems, has become increasingly evident.

The French model: a workers' welfare state

As seen above, the social insurance system (*Sécurité sociale*), established in 1945, is often presented as the final stage of an evolutionary process from social assistance to social insurance. The main component of the French social protection system remains its social insurance system. That is why France is generally recognized as belonging to the Bismarckian family of welfare states (Merrien 1995).

At the time of its introduction, the social insurance system was centred on male workers (*les travailleurs*) and their families. In this respect it clearly reflected a vision of society characterized by traditional gender roles, based on the male breadwinner model.[1] It is divided into a number of different schemes covering different risks[2] (health care, old age, family allowances) and different occupational groups. The system is highly fragmented along occupational lines. Besides the main scheme (*régime général*), which caters for employees in industry and trade, there are 122 separate schemes (*régimes spéciaux et particuliers*) covering occupational groups that were already covered by insurance arrangements before the introduction of *sécurité sociale* in 1945, and that declined the offer to join the *régime général*. For instance, separate schemes exist for civil servants and for employees of nationalized industries (electricity; SNCF, the national railway company; RATP, the Paris Metro; etc.). Nearly 20 per cent of the population is covered by separate schemes. There are also nineteen autonomous schemes for self-employed (*travailleurs indépendants*) non-agricultural workers: shopkeepers, employers, artisans and independent professionals (*professions libérales*) willing to decide for themselves the importance and the level of financial participation they want to assign to social security. Nearly 10 per cent of the population insured by the social security system is covered by one of these autonomous schemes. Finally, the agricultural scheme covers people working in the agricultural sector (employers and employees) and their families. Its institutional framework, the *Mutualité Sociale Agricole* (MSA), is supervised by the Ministry of Agriculture.

The *régime général* can be viewed as the most important and complete scheme, as it covers two-thirds of the working population, and provides insurance against the major social risks. It accounts for approximately 60 per cent of the benefits delivered by all the compulsory schemes. The other schemes cover only some social risks, with different level of contributions and benefits. Autonomous and agricultural schemes are less generous for some benefits (sickness being one exception), but also require a lower level of contributions. The *régimes spéciaux et particuliers* (for public sector employees) are significantly more generous in the areas of health care and pensions.

The French social insurance system is managed by representatives of employers and employees. Each scheme is divided into different funds (*caisses*), headed by one of the trade unions involved in the management of the system. The initial intention was to set up a system with relative independence from the state. The rationale behind this was that the insurance system should be managed by those who paid for it and had an interest in it (Kerschen 1995; Pollet and Renard 1995). Social insurance schemes, however, are subject to governmental supervision, and responsibility for setting the levels of benefits and contributions lies with the government. This considerably reduces the effectiveness of the social partners' control over the system. The fact that social insurance is managed by the social partners serves to strengthen the link between social policy and employment: in France the social insurance system is not seen as a government policy but as belonging to the realm of employment.

The emphasis on work as the basis for entitlement to social benefits has been somewhat mitigated during the postwar years. It was particularly strong before the unemployment compensation reforms carried out in the 1980s. In contrast, there is a minimum guaranteed pension, granted on the basis of a means test, and access to health care is virtually universal (about 99 per cent of the population is covered), although this is due to the combination of various schemes (with different levels of provision) rather than the existence of a universal scheme.

Pressures for change

Besides the financial problems common to virtually all Western welfare states, recent and current French debates on social protection have identified two additional pressure points resulting from the particular structure of social policy in France. First, a welfare state financed to a very large extent through employment-related contributions inflates labour costs and is thus an obstacle to job creation. Second, a worker-orientated welfare state seems increasingly inadequate in the context of mass and long-term unemployment. In France, unemployment stood at 12.5 per cent of the active population at the end of

1997, i.e. over 3.1 million. More than one million people had been unemployed for more than one year (20 per cent for more than two years) (Table 3.1).

Contribution financing and employment

As mentioned above, schemes geared towards employees are financed solely through employers' and employees' contributions, without government subsidies. This is by virtue of a strong normative perception whereby the collectivity that receives benefits (workers) must coincide with the one which pays for welfare (also workers).[3] In short, it is not seen as acceptable that money collected through taxation be used to finance social insurance schemes, as it is not accepted that people who did not contribute might receive contribution-financed benefits. This perception underlies the strong relationship between the debate on financing and that on entitlement. A change in the financing method from contribution to taxation would entail a shift in the basis of entitlement away from work.

Contribution financing plays a bigger role in France than in any other EU country (see Table 3.2). This issue is central to the French debate, since the high level of contributions is perceived as having an overall negative impact on the country's economic competitiveness and as being responsible for the high rate of unemployment. This claim is supported by international comparisons, which highlight the poor job-creating performance of the French economy. Between 1983 and 1991 total employment increased on average by 0.5 per cent in France, whereas it grew by 1.7 per cent in the EU as a whole, by 1.3 per cent in Japan and by 1.9 per cent in the US (OECD 1994: 5).

Overall labour costs are not significantly higher in France than in other similar countries (Euzéby 1994). However, it is argued that the negative impact of insurance contributions on employment is strongest in the case of low wages. The proportion of gross salary paid in contributions is in fact higher in the low wage range than for higher wages due to an upper limit on contributions to the old age pension scheme. For instance, total contributions paid on the minimum wage amount to 48 per cent, while the proportion for a salary three times as high is only 41.6 per cent (Join-Lambert 1994: 334). This,

Table 3.1 Unemployment rate in France as percentage of active population, 1993–97

Date	%
March 1993	11.1
March 1994	12.4
March 1995	11.6
March 1996	12.1
March 1997	12.3

Source: INSEE, *Chômage et Emploi en Mars*, 1997, No 530.

Table 3.2 Contribution financing as a percentage of total social expenditure (EU-12
 countries, 1992)

Country	%	Country	%
Belgium	68.5	Ireland	34.5
Denmark	10.8	Italy	61.9
Germany	69.9	Luxembourg	52.3
Greece	8.3	Netherlands	61.5
Spain	65.1	Portugal	62.6
France	79.9	United Kingdom	41.9

Source: Eurostat, *Basic Statistics of the European Communities 1994*, Brussels, 1995, table 3.35: 164.

together with the existence of a minimum wage, results in an artificial inflation of the cost of low-wage labour being artificially inflated.

The minimum wage, currently set at around 6,000 FF (920 euro) per month, is strongly supported by French public opinion (Rosanvallon 1995: 80), and it would be suicidal for any government to try to reduce it substantially.[4] Indeed, it was raised by 4 per cent in 1995 (well above the rate of inflation). This reflects French scepticism towards the Anglo-American approach to job-creation (Esping-Andersen 1996: 13–15), which, though perhaps more successful in numerical terms, creates other problems such as poverty traps and the 'working-poor' (Albert 1991). The only viable option left to policy makers dealing with the high cost of low-wage labour, is a reduction in contributions. This view is shared by a majority of French commentators (see for instance Hirsch 1993: 43; Join-Lambert 1994: 331).

Some steps in this direction have already been taken, the most notable of which is the creation of an ear-marked tax, the *contribution sociale généralisée* (CSG). This new tax has played an increasing role in the overall financing of social protection. It was first introduced in 1990 at a rate of 1.1 per cent. The rate on 1 January 1998 was 7.5 per cent. The CSG is levied on a variety of incomes including wages, capital revenues and welfare benefits. Since financing does not only come from the working population, the CSG breaks the link between employment and entitlement. Access to CSG-financed benefits cannot be limited to any particular section of society. The ongoing shift in protection financing from employment-related contributions to the CSG is thus creating the conditions for the establishment of citizenship-based social rights.

The link between contributions and entitlements has also been weakened in the context of fiscal incentives for job creation. Since the late 1970s, governments of different political orientations have adopted contribution exemptions in order to encourage firms to take on new employees. These measures usually target socially disadvantaged groups, such as the long-term and young unemployed, or small companies, which are considered to be the most affected by the relatively high cost of unskilled labour. Employees hired under these programmes, though not contributing fully to the system, are granted full access to benefits (see Join-Lambert 1994).

It has been argued that this series of measures, aimed either at reducing the impact of contributions or at replacing them (CSG), *de facto* amounts to a partial shift away from social insurance (Pellet 1995). The Jospin Government's (elected in 1997) plan to replace health insurance contribution by CSG is evidence of acceleration in the trend towards shifting social protection financing from contributions to taxation.

Protecting the 'socially excluded'

With its emphasis on contributory social insurance, the French system is increasingly open to question for its inability to deal with those who do not have access to it, such as the long-term unemployed or the young unemployed, who have never been involved in the labour market. The size of these groups has grown constantly in recent years, and they represent the most pressing social issue in the country. For them, the social insurance system, which is the main provider of social welfare, is of little use. The result is the emergence of a two-tiered system which exacerbates social divisions and inequality between employees with full entitlement to generous social insurance protection and those with little or no connection to the labour market, who rely on minimum income or social assistance programmes (Hantrais 1996). In this context, the weakness of the French system in terms of recognition of social rights regardless of employment status, constitutes a major issue.

Problems of this nature have developed significantly since the late 1970s, as a result of economic recession. In France, such problems were seen as radically new. The scale of the social problems (the numbers of unemployed people and of long-term unemployed and the seriousness of the recession; see Table 3.3) and the economic changes at their root (e.g. economic globalization, more flexibility in the labour market and job insecurity) were also unprecedented. In this context, the inadequacy of a welfare state based on contributory social insurance became increasingly evident. Pressure to develop new policies was the inevitable consequence.

Table 3.3 Long-term unemployment in France (as a percentage of total unemployment)

	1975	1985	1995
Unemployed for:			
less than 1 year	82.8%	54.5%	60.5%
Between 1 and 2 years	—	21.7%	19.9%
More than 2 years	—	23.8%	19.9%

Source: INSEE, *Enquêtes emploi*, 1975, 1985, 1995)

Policy changes

The policy makers' response to these pressures can be divided into two periods. First, in the period up to the early 1990s, the non-contributory component of the French system was expanded. New programmes were introduced to supplement existing schemes without aiming to replace them. Possibly for this reason, they were established without major political problems. In a way, this was an extension of the dominant approach of the post-war years, which based the establishment of *de facto* citizenship rights not on the granting of universal access to benefits, but through the juxtaposition of numerous schemes designed to cover various social groups.

In contrast, since the early 1990s, but particularly after the 1995 plan for the reform of social security (Juppé plan), changes have been affecting and transforming the very structure of existing schemes. The contributory principle is being abandoned in a number of areas, particularly health care and family benefits.

The new policies in the 1980s

The family benefits scheme is increasingly considered as part of the non-contributory component, though this has not always been the case (Borgetto and Lafore 1996). Family benefits were first introduced purely as a social insurance scheme, financed by employers' contributions, covering only employees, and managed jointly by representatives of employers and employees. However, the coverage of some family benefits was gradually extended to the whole population, with the scheme becoming universal in 1978 (Dupeyroux and Prétot 1993: 71). Any legally resident family with one or more dependent children is entitled to family allowance. The benefits are delivered to households (as opposed to the mother or the father). The universal benefits (*allocations familiales*) are granted, without means-testing, for the second child and all subsequent children. Their amount varies according to the number and the age of the children. In addition, the scheme now grants a number of means-tested benefits, which are not seen as consistent with the principles of social insurance. Finally, as a result of the introduction of the CSG, family benefits are now financed partly through taxation. The family benefits scheme represents a hybrid, blending elements of both the social insurance and non-contributory tax-financed provisions systems. A universal right to family allowances has been granted, in France, not through the combination of a variety of categorical schemes, but through a transformation of the existing programme which initially covered only employees. However, family benefits have long been cited as an exception in the French social protection system.

A number of new programmes designed to cover those who did not have access to the labour market have been introduced since the early 1980s in response to growing social problems. These policies contrast starkly with the traditional features of social insurance, emphasizing the inadequacy of the former system. While the social insurance system is centred on employees, the new policies target the most disadvantaged, or socially excluded. Instead of treating all sorts of situations with the same instruments, social re-insertion policies are geared towards specific groups and are designed according to local needs. That is why re-insertion policies are characterized by a high degree of devolution to local authorities. In addition, unlike the social insurance system which treats social risks separately (old age, sickness, unemployment), re-insertion policies address a whole range of relevant social problems in an integrated manner, so that housing and vocational training are now included in the realm of social policy.

These features are typical of the policies, developed since the mid-1980s, aimed at vocational training and at integrating the young or long-term unemployed. In this context, the creation of the RMI (*revenu minimum d'insertion*) is certainly the most significant achievement. As it became evident that the social insurance system did not cover the whole population and that a new safety net was needed, former president Mitterrand, during the presidential campaign of 1988, proposed the creation of a guaranteed minimum income to cover those who '. . . have nothing, can do nothing, are nothing. It is the pre-condition to their social re-insertion' (Mitterrand 1988). A local authority-run social assistance system existed already, but was regarded as highly stigmatizing and inadequate for dealing with the problems of mass and long-term unemployment.

The law establishing the RMI was accepted by a unanimous vote of the French parliament at the end of 1988. Its main feature is the guarantee of a minimum level of resources for each individual, which takes the form of a means-tested differential benefit, and a re-insertion element, in the form of a contract between the recipient and 'society'. People resident in France and over 25 years old are eligible for the RMI (subject to a means test). The recipient must commit him or herself to taking part in re-insertion programmes, as stated in the contract, which is signed by the recipient and a social worker. Such programmes include job-seeking, vocational training or activities designed to enhance the recipient's social autonomy. It should be noted that both the aims and the implementation of RMI are very different from American workfare programmes. While the latter are generally geared towards making dependency on benefits a less comfortable situation than employment (often regardless of pay and working conditions), the French variant is much more about avoiding the social and psychological consequences of long-term unemployment, by keeping recipients involved in other social networks.

The RMI must be seen in the context of an ongoing adaptation process of the French welfare state, consequent to the recognition of the inadequacy of a system predominantly based on social insurance. The RMI, being tax-financed, belongs to the realm of government provision (as opposed to social insurance) and is an example of the recent orientation of the French welfare state. The new benefit responded to a real social need. In December 1997, over one million citizens were receiving RMI (including spouses and children of recipients, over 2.5 million people were covered by this scheme).

A new system?

Since the early 1990s, but particularly from 1995 onwards with the Juppé plan, reforms have not been concerned with creating new schemes but with replacing or transforming existing structures.

Some of the elements included in the 1995 Juppé plan can be seen as part of this trend. The plan is supposed to provide a framework for the reform of the welfare system over the coming years. Juppé's intentions were disclosed to Parliament in November 1995. The plan was generally regarded as highly ambitious, as it tried to achieve substantial savings and structural change in the social protection system.

First, with regard to financing, a new tax has been created to pay off the accumulated debt of the social insurance system, estimated at FF 250 billion. This tax, called RDS (*remboursement de la dette sociale*) will be levied on all incomes at a rate of 0.5 per cent for the next 13 years. The creation of this new tax reinforces the shift from contribution to taxation discussed above. Revenues have been further boosted by an increase from 1.4 per cent to 3.4 per cent in the rates of health insurance contributions payable by pensioners and unemployed people. A ceiling of 2.1 per cent on the rate of growth in health expenditure has also been imposed, although it is difficult to see how this measure can be implemented in practice. Finally, family benefits were not upgraded in 1996, and in 1998 they have been made income-tested (but have been upgraded).

Additional savings and equity improvements were expected to come from a reform of the separate pension schemes (*régimes spéciaux*) that exist for particular occupational groups. The government's intention was to erode some 'peaks of generosity' in harmonizing benefit formulas and entitlement conditions between private sector employees covered by the *régime général* and separate schemes, mainly in the public sector. It was this measure that triggered the massive wave of strikes of November 1995. One week after the announcement of the Juppé plan, strikes began on the SNCF (national railways) and RATP (Paris Metro), and spread across the public sector. The intensity of the movement, peaking on 12 December 1995, when some two million people were reported to have taken to the streets in various French cities, forced Juppé to make some concessions. As a result, pension reform was dropped from the package. While reductions in public sector pension rights were certainly what triggered the reaction of the strikers, it seems clear that some trade union federations, CGT (*Confédération Générale des Travailleurs*) and FO (*Force Ouvrière*), were deeply concerned with other elements of the package, specifically elements relating to the control of the social insurance system.

The Juppé plan also included structural change in the areas of health care and family allowances. With regard to health insurance financing, a shift from contribution to taxation (CSG) is planned. This is supposed to make the system more compatible with economic requirements and more equitable, as it expands the financing basis of the scheme from only wages to all sorts of revenues. Changes in health care financing are to be complemented by changes in the coverage of health insurance. The government intends to introduce a universal health insurance scheme, under which everyone would receive the same benefits in kind, and where contributions would be harmonized. This project is still being debated, but a first series of measures was adopted in Autumn 1996. With regard to the universal family allowance (*allocation familiale*), the plan's stated intention is first to make them taxable, and subsequently to make them means-tested, which would finally do away with the social insurance principle, thereby completing the transformation of a scheme which was initially introduced as a pure insurance-based programme.

From work to citizenship?

Access to benefit is not the only dimension of the current crisis and transformation of the French welfare state. As seen above, financial concerns, the impact on employment and the issue of who controls the system (whether it is the state or the social partners) are all central to the current debate and reform movement. In this final section, however, we will try to assess whether the current crisis in French welfare constitutes an opportunity to bring about what social reformers failed to achieve in 1945 – a social security system in which entitlement is based on a notion of citizenship.

What the founders of the social security system had in mind in 1945, in fact, was to achieve universal and uniform coverage for the whole population. Nevertheless, given the strong resistance coming from those groups who already had access to some form of social protection, they chose to remain within an employment-related social insurance framework. The hope was that, in the context of full employment, the difference between a universalist and employment-based system would be negligible. To some extent, French social reformers tried to achieve Beveridge's aims with Bismarck's instruments. Subsequent developments showed this challenge to be too ambitious. Universality, uniformity and unity were never achieved. Furthermore, with the economic recession and its consequences, the inadequacy of an employment-based system has become increasingly evident.

Until recently, this problem was tackled through the introduction of additional programmes, targeted at those who did not have access to the social insurance system. However, with the 1995 Juppé plan the aim of transforming the basis of entitlement has become clear, at least with regard to health insurance. Does that mean that the French welfare state is moving towards the recognition of a notion of social citizenship ?

The following quote, taken from Juppé's introduction to his plan, would suggest that this is the case:

In the name of justice, we want social security to be for everyone. Today, this is not exactly the case. French people are not yet equal in front of social protection. . . . We will introduce a universal health insurance scheme . . . which will offer the same sort of benefits to everyone. . . . It will guarantee that the whole population is in fact covered by health insurance, or in short that every French person is well treated.

(Juppé 1996: 221)

This argument has some strength. Disparities between employees in different sectors and problems involved in covering the non-working population, are difficult to justify in the current context. As argued elsewhere, however (Bonoli and Palier 1996), these changes can also be interpreted as a move to increase the state's control over social protection. The plan, in fact, takes these trends even further, proposing a new 'architecture' for the entire system, a new 'chain of responsibilities'. Changes reflecting this new direction were implemented in 1996 when the French constitution was amended to allow Parliament to decide on the general orientations and political objectives of the social security system, particularly with reference to expenditure. Each social insurance fund will be given a spending target fixed by Parliament. On the basis of these spending targets, the government will then negotiate a series of 'agreements on objectives and management' (*conventions d'objectifs et de gestion*) with the different funds. In other words, the social partners remain responsible for the management of the social insurance funds, but within a framework which has to be negotiated with the government.

The organization of the management structure of the system is also being transformed. The composition of the governing boards of the insurance funds is being changed. Employers and employees will be represented in equal numbers (previously employees were in a majority). More importantly, there will be four new members appointed by the government, and one or two additional representatives from mutual and family associations. The director of each fund, even the regional and local ones, will be appointed by the government. These changes are intended to increase state penetration within the social insurance system. During the summer of 1996, the presidency of the main health insurance fund changed: FO (*Force Ouvrière*) was replaced by CFDT (*Confédération Française Démocratique des Travailleurs*), a trade union which supports the trend of structural transformation of the French social protection system.

Increased state control over the social insurance system is likely to make it more vulnerable to reform. Radical changes, in the context of a health insurance scheme managed by the social partners, are relatively difficult to implement. Their acquiescence, if not their agreement, is needed in order to apply new rules in the day-to-day management of health insurance. In addition, the social insurance principle, which links the amount paid into the system to the right to benefits, is an obstacle to radical reforms such as targeting. These could be more easily implemented in the context of a tax-financed scheme. Contrary to social insurance contributions, taxes are payments that do not give the right to benefits. Finally, the introduction of spending limits decided by Parliament might provide a powerful institutional support for reform.

In this respect, it is instructive to draw a parallel between current developments in French health insurance and past changes in the family benefits scheme. As seen above, family benefits were introduced in the 1930s as an insurance-based scheme and only employees were entitled to receive them. In the late 1970s, however, the scheme was made universal, and financed by employment-related contributions and general taxation (Dupeyroux and Prétot 1993: 71). In the following years the balance between contribution and tax-financing has progressively shifted towards taxation. As a result, in the 1995 Juppé plan, it was announced that family benefits will become means-tested from 1998 onwards. This sort of reform would have been unthinkable if previous changes had not done away with the contributory principle. More recently, this measure has been picked up by the new socialist government, and it is actually the latter which will implement targeting in the area of family benefits.

These changes have been opposed by the trade unions. According to the leader of the *Force Ouvrière* union, increased state control over health insurance is a preliminary move towards a residualization of public provision (through targeting) and an expansion of the private sector in the area of health care (Blondel 1996: 241).

As of now, it is rather difficult to assess the validity of these two competing explanations. What is clear, however, is that the shift away from social insurance removes some of those mechanisms that Pierson has termed 'lock in effects', a notion that refers to policy choices '. . . that greatly increase the cost of adopting once-possible alternatives and inhibit exit from a current policy path' (Pierson 1994: 42). This is typically the case with contributory social insurance, which creates strong expectations with regard to benefits that are generally recognised as legitimate. From this point of view, the French government could to be trying to remove one of these 'lock in effects'.

If this element is taken into account, then the scepticism of the labour movement with regard to reforms that extend the scope of existing arrangements is understandable. To some extent, social rights based on citizenship are not part of the French tradition in social policy, which is characterized by a constant tension between the state (regardless of the political orientation of the government) and the labour movement. The reluctance of the trade unions to go along with the government's desire to introduce a universal right to medical care, must also be seen in this light. From their point of view, social insurance has the advantage of being less vulnerable to radical reform. A step towards the establishment of full social citizenship, in the French context, does not necessarily imply a reinforcement of social rights.

Notes

1   As the first article of the law establishing the social security system says: 'Il est institué une organisation de la Sécurité social destinée à garantir les travailleurs et

leurs familles contre les risques de toute nature susceptibles de réduire leur capacité de gain, à couvrir les charges de maternité et les charges de famille qu'ils supportent' (ordonnance du 4 octobre 1945). For a complete presentation of the French social protection system, see for example Join-Lambert 1994; Dupeyroux 1993.

2   Unemployment benefits are also insurance-based in France, but they are not delivered through the *sécurité sociale* system.

3   This is not entirely true. There are some indirect taxes on alcoholic drinks, tobacco and car insurance premiums that are earmarked for health insurance. However, in order to comply with the normative perception described below, these taxes are justified in so far as they come from activities (drinking, smoking and driving) which are likely to increase health expenditure.

4   In 1994, the Balladur government attempted to introduce a scheme involving exemptions to the minimum wage, allowing companies to employ first-time young employees at 80 per cent of the minimum wage. The government, however, had to renounce this measure following a massive protest movement led by the trade unions.

Bibliography

Albert, M. (1991) *Capitalisme Contre Capitalisme*, Paris: Seuil.

Baldwin, P. (1990) *The politics of Social Solidarity. Class Bases of the European Welfare State 1875–1975*, Cambridge: Cambridge University Press.

Blondel, M. (1996) 'L'Etatization, Antichambre de la Privatization', *Droit Social* 3: 241–45.

Bonoli, G. and Palier B. (1996) 'Reclaiming Welfare. The Politics of Reform of the French Social Protection System', *Journal of South European Politics and Society* 1,3: 240–59.

Borgetto, M. and Lafore, R. (1996) *Droit de l'Aide et de l'Action Sociales*, Paris: Montchrestien.

Castel, R. (1995) *Les Métamorphoses de la Question Sociale*, Paris: Fayard.

Clasen, J. (1996) (ed.) *Social Insurance in Europe*, Bristol: The Policy Press.

Dupeyroux, J. (1993) *Droit Social*, Paris: Dalloz.

Dupeyroux, J. and Prétot, X. (1993) *Droit de la Sécurité Sociale*, Paris: Dalloz.

Droit Social (1996), special issues on the *Plan Juppé*, No.3, and Nos. 9–10.

Esping-Andersen, G. (1990) *The Three Worlds of Welfare Capitalism*, Cambridge: Polity.

—— (1996) 'Welfare States Without Work: the Impasse of Labour Shedding and Familialism in Continental European Social Policy', in G. Esping-Andersen (ed) *Welfare States in Transition*, London: Sage.

Eurostat (1995) *Basic Statistics of the European Communities 1994*, Brussels.

Euzéby, A. (1994) 'Cheres Charges Sociales', *Le Monde* 1/2/94, p.VII.

Ewald, F. (1986) *L'Etat-Providence*, Paris: Grasset.

Ferrera, M. (1993) *Modelli di solidarietà*, Bologna: Il Mulino.

Hantrais, L. (1996) 'France: Squaring the Welfare Triangle', in V. George and P. Taylor-Gooby (eds) *European Welfare Policy. Squaring the Welfare Circle*, London: Macmillan.

Hirsch, M. (1993) *Les Enjeux de la Protection Sociale*, Paris: Montchrestien.

INSEE (1997) *Chômage et Emploi en Mars*, No. 530.

Jobert, B. (1991) 'Democracy and Social Policies: The Example of France', in J. Ambler (ed.) *The French Welfare State*, New York: University Press.

Join-Lambert, M.-T. (1994) *Politiques Sociales*, Paris: Dalloz.

Juppé, A. (1996) 'Plan pour la reforme de la sécurité sociale', reproduced in *Droit Social*, No. 3.

Kerschen, N. (1995) 'The influence of the Beveridge report on the French social security plan of 1945' in MIRE (Mission Interministerielle Recherche et Experimentation) (ed.) *Comparing Social Welfare System in Europe* Vol.1, Paris: MIRE.

Merrien, F.-X. (1995) 'The French Welfare-State and its Crisis', paper presented at the conference, *La Fin du Modèle Suèdois?*, Paris, January.

Mitterrand, F. (1988) *Lettre à tous les français*, Paris.

OECD (1994) *Employment Outlook*, Paris: OECD.

Palier, B. and Bonoli, G. (1995) 'Entre Bismarck et Beveridge, "Crises" de la Sécurité Sociale et Politique(s)', in *Revue Française de Science Politique* 45, 4: 668–98.

Pellet, R. (1995) Etatization, fiscalization et budgetization de la Sécurité sociale, *Droit Social* 3: 296–305.

Pierson, P. (1994) *Dismantling the Welfare State? Reagan, Thatcher and the Politics of Welfare Retrenchment*, Cambridge: Cambridge University Press.

Pollet, G. and Renard, D. (1995) 'Genèses et Usages de l'Idée Paritaire dans le Système de Protection Sociale Français', *Revue Française de Science Politique*, 45, 4.

Rosanvallon, P. (1995) *La Nouvelle Question Sociale. Repenser l'Etat-providence*, Paris: Seuil.

Saint-Jours, Y. (1982) 'France', in P. Koehler and H. Zacher (eds) *The Evolution of Social Insurance, 1881–1981*, London: Frances Pinter.

Taylor-Gooby, P. (1996) 'Eurosclerosis in European Welfare States. Regime Theory and the Dynamics of Change', *Policy and Politics* 24, 2: 109–23.

4 Workfare, citizenship and social exclusion

Sandro Cattacin, Matteo Gianni, Markus Mänz and Véronique Tattini

Introduction[1]

Current debates on the reorganization of the welfare state as well as new divisions of tasks between public and private actors within welfare societies are frequently associated with issues of citizenship. These debates are often put forward by left-wing critics who emphasize the dangerous consequences of increased restrictions on individual agency within a free society. Particular concerns arise from the tendency which Ralf Dahrendorf describes as the 'Two-Third Society', where the excluded will systematically be placed in the minority within the political process by a majority that controls welfare and enjoys a stable social status.[2] At the same time, conservative critics (Murray 1984; Mead 1986) worry about the effects of social entitlements for the 'privileged class' of welfare recipients who are not interested in leaving a situation in which their material needs are provided for.[3] This view criticizes welfare programmes for creating social dependency on the care of the welfare state, and for breeding 'demotivation'. Recent developments in unemployment regulation policies indicate that the universal approach to the treatment of social welfare recipients is increasingly being replaced with selective programmes characterized, first, by lower subsidies compared to those of the 1970s and 1980s and, second, by the introduction of workfare schemes in social welfare.[4] These schemes require people who benefit from social welfare to perform some kind of work in return. In this chapter, we criticize these demands as constraints that contradict understandings of modern citizenship. In particular they do not respect individual choice in seeking employment and confuse a right to assistance with duties pertaining to membership of a concrete nation-based society.

More precisely, we argue here that the current tendency to introduce compulsory requirements in welfare programmes is an unsatisfactory response to the multifaceted problem of social exclusion. Indeed, workfare schemes risk introducing unjust treatment of already disadvantaged groups of citizens. They create a sharp division between employees with stable jobs and their associated advantages, such as purchasing power and social status, and those people in a multiplicity of precarious situations oscillating between unemployment and forms of flexible and unstable 'under-employment'. As a result, workfare schemes appear to be not only a useless mechanism for ensuring full social citizenship, but also to contribute to the reproduction of social exclusion.

Our argument will follow three steps. First, we consider Thomas H. Marshall's theory of social citizenship as a justification for social integration through the institution, during the twentieth century, of social rights. According to Marshall (1965), social rights are the condition for giving the formal status of citizenship a material foundation, thus ensuring the full integration of all citizens in the national community. Indeed, social rights have constituted a powerful mechanism against major aspects of social exclusion in the course of the development of the welfare state. Nevertheless, this model has been shown to have its limits, which have nourished the criticism already mentioned, and enabled the promotion of workfare. The second step of the argument thus assesses the implications of workfare with regard to social exclusion. To accomplish this task, we will clarify the basic assumptions underlying workfare by calling into question the conception of social citizenship as expressed by the theory of workfare, focusing especially on the work of Lawrence M. Mead (1986). We will maintain that workfare justified in Mead's terms is ill-suited for adequately dealing with the complex problem of social exclusion. Indeed, it seems to make things worse. As a result, Mead's theory of social citizenship, like Marshall's, appears to imply the questionable idea that a single set of solutions (rights on the one side, workfare on the other) is able to confront the complexity of the problem of social exclusion. We will argue for a pluralistic conception of social citizenship, justifying differentiated measures of social policy which take into account the heterogeneous forms and paths of exclusion.

Social rights and integration

In this section, we will discuss some of the theoretical links between citizenship and social rights. We start from the classic treatise of Marshall (1965), which can be considered the first formal systematization of citizenship that takes account of the notion of social citizenship. According to Marshall, citizenship rights are divided into civic, political and social components.

Marshall argued that social entitlements contribute to the construction of a comprehensive political citizenship. He analysed the process of the political integration of the working class in Britain and concluded that the profound class distinctions which existed risked not only producing significant in-equalities – with respect to opportunities to consume common cultural goods – but also, in the long term, would undermine the ability of many to participate in the destiny of England as a whole. The class factor explained the inequality of access to important political and social positions, thereby reinforcing the power of the powerful, and the powerlessness of the working class. In Marshall's view, limited resources and limited access to education for the working class were responsible for this situation. As a remedy, he proposed the extension of the system of social entitlements through reinforcement of the welfare state, and in particular the provision of material benefits to the working class, including increased access to education, health care, and social security programmes. In other words, the extension of social entitlements on a universalistic basis would create the conditions of political and social citizenship which would allow for the full integration of the working class in England (Kymlicka 1995: 180).

Marshall argues that the progressive implementation of forms of universal citizenship has led to the reduction of class inequalities. More precisely, class inequalities still exist in a welfare system, but, according to Marshall, because of the equality expressed by citizenship, individuals consider the inequalities to be more acceptable. In other words, social citizenship rights are a necessary condition for legitimizing the inequalities that are inherent to capitalism. Thus, citizenship rights constitute the recognition of the equal social value of all members of society, as well as the means by which this is supposedly achieved (see Moon 1988: 43). In this sense, the social and political integration of the least advantaged strictly depends on the existence of social rights. At the *symbolic* level, formal universal rights express the moral equality of each citizen, and at the *material* level, they allow citizens to live a decent life. Thus, social rights can be seen as an extension of civil and political rights (see King and Waldron 1988).

The spread of social problems is closely associated with the development of complex organizational structures, which has consequently led – especially in Europe – to various formulations of state solidarity. The formation of the welfare state may be described in terms of a substitution of civil society by the state in the production of responses to social problems. Solutions to various problems have been provided in the form of old-age pensions, medical care, and unemployment benefits. Such problems mainly concern users who are integrated in the economic production process for most of their lives and who thus contribute to social security funding. Nevertheless, since the beginning of the 1970s, the welfare state has had to cope with a double crisis: a crisis of its instruments and a crisis in the general social and economic context. The instruments of the welfare state pose problems of increasing inefficiency, raising questions of legitimacy. There are difficulties in adapting instruments to a changing environment and in creating appropriate new instruments. The changing environment is specifically characterized by an increase in those social problems which are ostensibly about to be solved: in particular unemployment but also all phenomena embodied in the term 'new poverty'. In other words, the welfare state is expected to act within an unpredictable and rapidly changing context, which can no longer be managed with traditional means and uniform solutions. Furthermore, the globalization of economies challenges the financing of welfare states. The middle class is coming under attack: the poorest and richest groups are growing at the expense of the middle class – which is destabilizing the project of a social policy benefiting the majority. Both national solidarity and the legitimacy of the redistribution project of the welfare state are now negatively affected and the current evolution of the state is increasingly criticized (Dufourcq 1994; Cattacin 1996: 73). This leads some scholars to claim that the rights of social citizenship are affected by the restructuring of the market (Birnbaum 1996: 61). In this vein, Dahrendorf (1988) warns against the 'collapse' of the welfare state by describing a division between the majority and those who are excluded from the status of citizenship.

Marshall's interpretation therefore seems to be too optimistic because he suggests that access to citizenship can prevent growing inequality. Several scholars have emphasized the excessive optimism of Marshall's conception of citizenship (see Giddens 1985; Zolo 1994). Barbalet argues that

> . . . those disadvantaged by the class system are unable to practically participate in the community of citizenship in which they have legal membership. The disability is a double one because in these circumstances citizenship rights which are only formal cannot influence the conditions which render the possession of citizenship ineffective, if not worthless.
>
> (Barbalet 1988: 2)

According to this perspective, social rights are not the expression of social and political integration, but represent a *conditional opportunity* necessary to reach such integration. In other words, to achieve social citizenship requires more than the exercising of social rights; it requires greater involvement of public agencies and social actors in order to achieve better social integration.

Social duties and exclusion

Workfare programmes are being heavily promoted as a response to growing social exclusion. Such programmes have already been implemented in countries such as the United States, Canada, and Switzerland. In others, particularly the Scandinavian nations, workfare programmes have recently been introduced. Other countries, for example, France (discussing the reform of the *revenu minimum d'insertion*), Italy (with initiatives of the Prodi government), Britain under Blair's leadership, but also Germany, are currently debating the introduction of workfare schemes. So far, however, these latter nations have only implemented some experimental workfare schemes and mainly at the subnational level. One of the main points in political debates about workfare schemes concerns the underlying notion of social citizenship.

Lawrence M. Mead (1986) is one of the leading authors aiming to justify workfare measures to achieve social citizenship in the particular context of American social policy. He emphasizes certain social duties that correspond to existing social rights. Yet his emphasis on obligations implies a reversal of priorities, compared to those of Marshall, which has important consequences for the analysis of social exclusion.[5] He holds that social exclusion has precisely been engendered by the narrow concern with social entitlements in the course of the development of the American welfare state. In this perspective, social protection builds up a kind of shield which is internalized by welfare recipients as a barrier, rather than an opportunity to become full citizens in the sense of morally equal agents. Welfare recipients are in some sense protected, but also detached from the constraints of the economic and social sphere which affects all other citizens. They are 'trapped' in a condition which does not stimulate them to work because work's limited advantages do not outweigh the advantages derived from welfare benefits (see Van Parijs 1996). Moreover, the longer a person lives on liberally granted welfare benefits, the greater the difficulty in successfully emerging from this welfare dependence that Van Parijs calls a 'trap'. Skills become obsolete and motivation dwindles. As a result, according to Mead, welfare recipients remain in a state of exemption which is incompatible with full social citizenship. Indeed they cannot be recognized as full citizens as long as they do not perform what are regarded as obligatory social activities, such as work.[6]

According to Mead, social citizenship implies not only the exercise of social rights but also the accomplishment of corresponding social duties, specifically the obligation to work. In his view, the commitment to work is a key factor in social integration. Therefore, he suggests measures which connect the granting of benefits to some effort in return in place of the existing income maintenance programmes. Work performed by the welfare recipients would thus express their contribution to the well-being of the community as a whole. The accomplishment of their duties towards the community represents the legitimate basis of their social entitlements:

> Today, the poor . . . must demand equal obligations from government the way they once demanded equal rights. Equality demands that they take back the [duty] to work. . . . For, given the evenhanded nature of citizenship, only those who bear obligations can truly appropriate their rights.
>
> (Mead 1986: 257)

Measures of workfare thus force people into reinsertion, and are supposed to enhance the possibility of pursuing a normal working life. Skills are preserved or new skills are learned, and Mead believes that, within a short period, the unemployed will find their way out of the sphere of exclusion through work.

A conceptual shift in the way welfare is provided can be noted in this proposal. The constraint of work as a condition for welfare had practically disappeared in the course of the development of modern welfare states. Indeed, the least advantaged members of advanced industrial societies have progressively acquired social rights that they can assert in the national community. This implies that duties rest mainly with the community which, through the state, has the obligation to provide a minimum of resources to the poor. The relationship between the state and the welfare recipient is thus largely one-sided, characteristic of an assistance relationship. By contrast, workfare aims at introducing modalities of exchange in this relationship, which is literally expressed by the term itself: *workfare* is *work* in exchange for *welfare*. As Dahrendorf puts it, through workfare 'rights are dissolved into marketable commodities; they are offered for sale' (1994: 13). By doing this, workfare radically transforms the relationship between the state and the welfare recipients, which is no longer one-sided, but reciprocal. The principle underlying this social policy is no longer a *compensation* for the recognized disadvantages suffered by the poor, but a *reciprocity* of actions requiring that the claimant works for the welfare benefits provided by the state. The argument is that through reciprocity, welfare recipients should not be understood as dependent persons – excluded from the 'normal' process of social integration (i.e. paid work) – but as persons who can be recognized as the moral equals of any other citizen who accomplishes his duty to work (Mead 1986: 12–13; Moon 1988).

We believe that this argument fails in various ways. First, if the welfare recipient is required to work, then this implies that the state provides employment. Indeed, to propose that 'they ought to work if they can work' means, among other things, that work is actually available. If the labour market does not offer them a job through which they could satisfy this requirement, then work has to be provided by other means. Who other than the state could be considered as liable to organize some kind of work? The first problems facing the organization of workfare thus consist in providing enough work to be performed and the kind of work that can be provided. In particular, there are difficulties in organizing workfare that is neither a hidden measure to subsidize or compete with private enterprises (which is contested by entrepreneurial organizations), nor a system to produce public goods on behalf of the public administration (which labour unions oppose). Objections are also raised against the organization of workfare in areas which are traditionally handled through voluntary work, because the obligation to work has different implications to those of voluntarism.

Thus, the basic problem is how to provide work for which there is sufficient demand. Otherwise, workfare appears less a measure of social integration and more a mere symbolic social act. The performance of the work is not perceived as important by society because it is not needed. Therefore, it cannot effectively contribute to social integration by the recognition, through a scheme of reciprocity, of welfare recipients as the moral equals of other citizens (see Elster 1988). Moreover, the work accomplished in this context is often devalued because those who, in the course of implementation of workfare, are charged with checking that recipients actually perform the required tasks are not themselves interested in the transaction. These social policy controllers are not really reciprocative to the welfare recipients; their actions are dictated by bureaucratic rules and they are only accountable to their immediate supervisors within the state agency. As a result, workfare merely constitutes a symbolic act which is constructed within a systemic environment of social control and cannot really be interpreted by the social actors of workfare programmes as an exchange based on solidarity principles (Offe and Heinze 1986: 486).

Second, reciprocal schemes such as workfare fail to take into account the reasons for which welfare provision is justified. Welfare is provided precisely because of the handicaps suffered by the least advantaged. Assistance serves those who cannot find employment which would enable them to earn a decent living. In this context, it is plausible to assert that with workfare, the recipients are punished twice. As Fullinwider suggests, 'tying welfare to work requirements adds insult to poverty. The poor are already powerless; making them perform for their hand-outs further confirms their powerlessness' (1988: 271). In this sense, what is controversial in workfare is that citizens are being denied social benefits on the basis of factors for which they are not responsible.[7] In particular, disadvantaged citizens are not responsible for the structural lack of availability of jobs or for such processes as decentralization of production on a global scale. Therefore, to compel them to work implies that welfare recipients are considered to be the only ones responsible for their situation. The obligation to work thus entails double punishment of the unemployed. They are first punished by exclusion due to their condition, and a second punishment is meted out in the obligation to work, which, in a paternalistic manner, adds to the burden of that for which they are not necessarily responsible (i.e. the difficulty to find a job).[8] Because of its social connotation as a form of punishment, workfare calls into question the possibility for welfare recipients to be socially respected by their fellow citizens. In as much as mutual respect is a basic condition for full citizenship in a democracy (Moon 1988), we are led to the conclusion that workfare could potentially undermine the basis of social integration.

As a result, the introduction of reciprocity schemes such as workfare further undermines the already shaky opportunities for social integration offered by the exercise of social rights, not to mention civil and political rights. Welfare recipients remain in a situation of dependency which is incompatible with the recognition of oneself as a full member of society, both from a personal and a societal point of view. Therefore, workfare, as it is advocated by Mead, appears to be an inadequate social policy for the social integration of the least advantaged members in our democratic societies.

Integration without work coercion

We have now determined that neither Marshall's approach nor Mead's are wholly satisfactory for dealing effectively with social exclusion. More precisely, social rights are not a sufficient condition for ensuring full social integration. However, it seems that the enforcement of a social duty to work undermines the possibility to achieve social integration even further. But both authors concur in a conception of social citizenship which implies monistic solutions in order to deal with social exclusion. We believe that they both fail in this respect, because the phenomenon of social exclusion is too heterogeneous to be solved by this type of measure (Paugam 1996). More specifically, if marginality and social exclusion can be somewhat alleviated by access to a minimum of resources, the lack of material means are not the only factor involved in social exclusion. Other factors concern physical and psychological disabilities, ethnic, cultural and sexual discrimination, non-traditional family structures, age, unconventional lifestyles, drug-addiction, and so forth. Even if work is an important aspect of social integration, to compel people to work in such cases is not an adequate solution leading to improvement in their social condition. The pertinent questions, therefore, are: is it possible to conceive of a set of measures which would allow for better social integration? And what would be the conception of social citizenship underlying this set of social policies?

We consider that a way out can be found through a combination of measures. First, we think that at least minimal social resources should be granted as a universal social right and that they ought not be conditional on a duty to work. Different proposals have been put forward in this direction: negative income tax, unconditional insertion subsidies or forms of universal basic income. These different instruments are necessary but not sufficient as a response to social exclusion. Social workers are well aware that the lack of material means is not the only reason for social exclusion. These different instruments are necessary but not sufficient as a response to social exclusion. Social exclusion demands much more complex and individualized intervention (see Ferroni 1991). These situations call also for more responsibility on the part of civil society to support people in distress. While distributive strategies toward a basic income will certainly protect some risk groups from social exclusion, notably single-parent families, long-term unemployed workers, or divorced people with contribution charges (i.e. visible and reachable categories) there are other segments of the population – the most marginalized – which remain untouched by a redistributive system and will thus be excluded from benefits.

This is why we think that, assuming that liberal democracies are marked by different paths of social exclusion, social integration requires differentiated measures of social policy. Not everyone is capable of developing autonomous initiatives. Hence, it is important that state agencies and civil society provide integration possibilities. They should operate on a voluntary basis, however, because only this can guarantee the motivation to integrate. If motivation is missing, all integration efforts are in vain; and motivation is only sincere when people can choose between an integration programme and other activities, secure in the knowledge that their basic needs will be met. When asking the question of what kind of intervention could strengthen social integration, we enter the territory of all the reformist strategies aimed at a revaluation and revitalization of activities stemming from the self-organization of society, such as mutual support between neighbours, volunteering, and so forth. These strategies refer to renewed forms of subsidiarity adapted to societies characterized by the research of modern forms of governance and by respect for plurality in life-worlds (see Heinze 1986). In fact, the new practice of subsidiarity implies that it is the state which asks civil society to organize solidarity. Compared to traditional subsidiarity where civil society, once it had failed to solve a problem, turned to the state, it is now state intervention that determines the shaping of the welfare system (Bütschi and Cattacin 1993; Cattacin and Kissling-Näf 1997). We do not want to enter here more deeply in this discussion but we will nevertheless give some indications on the directions such strategies could take:

- Regarding the quality of life: these measures have to ameliorate general living conditions, especially in places suffering from high levels of housing degradation, such as some urban peripheries. This can be done through urban planning with more respect for human beings. There should also be improvements in extended social services and leisure opportunities in general (see Höpflinger and Wyss 1994).
- The value of non-professional and volunteer work for the production of the collective welfare should be recognized. Most of these services are time consuming – therefore potentially expensive – and cannot (and should not) be guaranteed by the state any longer. Volunteer activities should come into play or at least contribute when such social interventions are time consuming but not specialized (e.g. elements of home-care, accompaniment of sick or old people). Various instruments exist, such as indirect subsidies (in the form of vouchers) for volunteers, which can then be exchanged to top-up other social benefits (e.g. old-age pension; see Heinze *et al.* 1988: 221ff).
- It is essential to introduce a clear strategy of reinforcement of all intermediary organizations – organizations between the state and the civil society – which are active in the production of welfare. This can be done through contracts of co-operation between the public actor and the private ones and by subsidizing activities realized by private actors (see Evers 1990). Still on the organizational level, it would be essential to re-think certain models of co-operation in the contemporary welfare system in order to rationalize their functioning and to harmonize their activities between various social domains.

In this perspective, we can conceive of a multifaceted social citizenship. The guarantee of universal social rights expresses respect for the equal moral value of citizens who have multiple interests and social identities in life. Nevertheless, it is plausible to think that phenomena of marginalization and exclusion entail the need to conceive of forms of differentiated treatments which are able to promote equality and social integration. This idea relies on the Aristotelian concept of justice, which consists of treating equal things equally, in turn implying treating different things differently (see Young 1990). From this perspective, with a differentiated treatment of people living on the edges of the society, we can imagine the creation of a pluralistic social citizenship which recognizes all forms of marginalization in order to socially integrate all persons according to their own biographies. In this sense, we can say that such a conception of citizenship entails some modifications regarding the universalistic conception of the *status* of citizenship, according to which all people must be treated in a similar way.

This conception of differentiated citizenship is based on the idea that social integration is an essential precondition for the achievement of full citizenship. Nevertheless, it must also be clear that social policy alone does not provide all the solutions to the problems of exclusion. In order to confront exclusion, political citizenship must also be considered. As Young asserts, 'a democratic public should provide mechanisms for the effective recognition and representations of the distinct voices and perspectives of those of its constituent groups that are oppressed or disadvantaged' (1990: 184). The argument centres around the idea that to oppose exclusion also means providing the excluded or disadvantaged groups with the political opportunities necessary for participation in the redefinition of the values and procedures that contribute to their oppression. In other words, one way to promote social integration is to conceive public policies not *for* the disadvantaged, but *with* the participation of the disadvantaged (see Phillips 1995; Gutmann and Thompson 1996). Only in this way will the conditions of the excluded be politically recognized. According to this point of view, such forms of empowerment (Phillips 1995) are a fundamental element in asserting the equal moral value of each citizen, linked to the liberal idea that freedom is based on self-determination. Moreover, such recognition can lead to important changes in the *practice* of citizenship, because group rights will improve the political resources for social actors in order to be more involved in the public space.

Conclusion

In conclusion, to achieve full citizenship requires different kinds of political and social measures. A well conceived policy mix of measures (affecting both the social and the political conditions of least advantaged citizens) appears to be the most suitable way to confront social exclusion. Workfare, being a one-sided approach to social exclusion, does not provide an adequate movement in the direction of social integration. In this sense, workfare is not an ameliorating feature toward social citizenship and, hence, toward the ideal of full citizenship.

Notes

1 We would like to thank Max Bergman, Jet Bussemaker, Antonella Ferrari and François Grin for their comments.
2 As Wehner explains: 'If the legitimization money goes beyond a certain level, it is effectively possible that a two-thirds-society will be created, characterized as a society of the strongest, in which only the upper one-third receive 'comfortable' salaries. Such a society would give not more than the existential minimum that the labour market offers to the lower third' (1992: 233, our translation).
3 A description which is essentially political and often expressed with little regard for its moral implications by, for instance, the Italian neoliberal right.
4 Tursi gives us a concrete definition of workfare: 'The expression work for welfare (= workfare) contains an implicit critique of inefficient and unproductive income-sustaining measures for unemployed people, and the poor in general. In this sense, workfare could be construed as a policy against "unemployment caused by welfare". In addition, as a labour market policy instrument, workfare can be used with different objectives and with different intentions. The most common is to encourage "social work" practices which aims at socializing marginalized people through their employment in totally or partially subsidized work which is useful to the community' (1996: 10, our translation).

5   It is important to point out that Marshall was also aware of the need of a balance
     between rights and duties concerning citizenship. In fact, according to him, 'if
     citizenship is invoked in the defense of rights, the corresponding duties of
     citizenship cannot be ignored. These do not require a man to sacrifice his individual
     liberty or to submit without question to every demand made by government. But
     they do require that his acts should be inspired by a lively sense of reponsibility
     towards the welfare of the community' (1965: 112). Elsewhere, Marshall
     emphasizes: 'of paramount importance is the duty to work,' but he also specifies
     that 'it is no easy matter to revive the sense of the personal obligation to work in a
     new form in which it is attached to the status of citizenship' (1965: 117–18).
     Despite the acknowledgement of the importance of social duties related to social
     rights, Marshall gives priority to the analysis of social rights. Notably, he never
     analyses the implications of the 'paramount' social duty to work as a means to
     improve social integration.
6   Concerning the relation between citizenship and work in the context of the United
     States, see also Shklar (1991).
7   This argument is inspired by Gutmann and Thompson (1996: 273).
8   In this respect, workfare programmes recall the ancient institution of the work-
     houses, which were indeed conceived as repressive measures of social control.

Bibliography

Barbalet, J. (1988) *Citizenship*, Milton Keynes: Open University Press.
Birnbaum, P. (1996) 'Sur la Citoyenneté', *L'Année Sociologique* 46, 1: 57–85.
Bütschi, D. and Cattacin, S. (1993) 'The Third Sector in Switzerland: the Trans-
    formation of the Subsidiarity Principle', *West European Politics* 16, 3: 362–79.
Cattacin, S. (1996) 'L'action politique face à l'exclusion. Quelques réflexions au secours
    de l'Etat-Providence et sur la situation Suisse', in D. Bütschi (ed.) *Inutiles au Monde?*
    Réflexions sur l'Exclusion à Genève, Genève: Parti Socialiste Genevois.
Cattacin, S. and Kissling-Näf, I. (ed.) (1997) Subsidiäres Staatshandeln. L'Agir
    Étatique Subsidiaire, Special Issue, *Swiss Political Science Review* 3, 3.
Dahrendorf, R. (1988) *The Modern Social Conflict: an Essay on the Politics of Liberty*,
    London: Weidenfeld and Nicolson.
—— (1994) 'The changing quality of citizenship', in B. Van Steenbergen (ed.) *The
    Condition of Citizenship*, London: Sage.
Dufourcq, N. (1994) 'Vers un Etat-providence sélectif', *Esprit* 207: 55–75.
Elster, J. (1988) 'Is there (or should there be) a right to work?', in A. Gutmann (ed.)
    Democracy and the Welfare State, Princeton: Princeton University Press.
Evers, A. (1990) 'Shifts in the welfare mix. Introducing a new approach for the study of
    transformations in welfare and social policy', in A. Evers and H. Wintersberger (eds)
    Shifts in the Welfare Mix, Frankfurt am Main/Boulder Co.: Campus/Westview.
Ferroni, A. (1991) 'Individualisieren. Gedanken zu einem strapazierten Begriff. Zur
    Rolle der öffentlichen Fürsorge im System der sozialen Sicherheit', *Zeitschrift für
    öffentliche Fürsorge* no 9: 132–37.
Fullinwider, R. (1988) 'Citizenship and welfare', in A. Gutmann (ed.) *Democracy and the
    Welfare State*, Princeton: Princeton University Press.
Giddens, A. (1985) *The Nation State and Violence*, Cambridge: Polity Press.
Gutmann, A. and Thompson, D. (1996) *Democracy and Disagreement*, Cambridge: The
    Belknap Press of Harvard University Press.
Heinze, R. G. (ed.) (1986) *Neue Subsidiarität: Leitidee für eine zukünftige Sozialpolitik?*,
    Opladen: Westdeutscher Verlag.

Heinze, R. G., Thomas, O. and Hilbert, J. (1988) *Der neue Sozialstaat. Analysen und Reformperspektiven*, Freiburg i.B.: Lambertus.

Höpflinger, F. and Wyss, K. (1994) *Am Rande des Sozialstaates. Formen und Funktionen öffentlicher Sozialhilfe im Vergleich*, Berne: Haupt.

King, D. S. and Waldron, J. (1988) 'Citizenship, social citizenship and the defence of welfare provisions', *British Journal of Political Science* 18, 4: 415–43.

Kymlicka, W. (1995) *Multicultural Citizenship. A Liberal Theory of Minority Rights*, Oxford: Clarendon Press.

Marshall, T. H. (1965) *Class, Citizenship and Social Development*, New York: Anchor.

Mead, L. M. (1986) *Beyond Entitlement. The Social Obligations of Citizenship*, New York: Free Press.

Moon, D. (1988) 'The moral basis of democratic welfare state', in A. Gutmann (ed.) *Democracy and the Welfare State*, Princeton: Princeton University Press.

Murray, C. (1984) *Losing Ground*, New York: Basic Books.

Offe, C. and Heinze, R. G. (1986) 'Am Arbeitsmarkt vorbei. Überlegungen zur Neubestimmung "haushaltlicher" Wohlfahrtsproducktion in ihrem Verhältnis zu Markt und Staat', *Leviathan* 14, 4: 471–95.

Paugam, S. (ed.) (1996) *L'exclusion l'État des Savoirs*, Paris: La Découverte.

Phillips, A. (1995) *The Politics of Presence*, Oxford: Clarendon Press.

Shklar, J. N. (1991) *American Citizenship: the Quest for Inclusion*, Cambridge MA: Harvard University Press.

Tursi, A. (1996) *Disoccupazione e lavori socialmente utili. Les esperienze di Stati Uniti, Germania e Italia*, Milano: Angeli.

Van Parijs, P. (1996) 'De la trappe au socle: l'allocation universelle contre le chômage', *Revue Suisse de Science Politique* 2, 1: 103–17.

Wehner, B. (1992) *Der Neue Sozialstaat. Vollbeschäftigung, Einkommensgerechtigkeit und Staatsentschuldung*, Opladen: Westdeutscher Verlag.

Young, I. M. (1990) *Justice and The Politics of Difference*, Princeton NJ: Princeton University Press.

Zolo, D. (1994) (ed.) *La Cittadinanza*, Bari: Laterza.

5 Citizenship and changes in life-courses in post-industrial welfare states

Jet Bussemaker

Introduction

The post-war welfare state was built upon the assumption of stable and standardized life-courses. Since the 1970s welfare states have been confronted by structural shifts which are fundamental in nature and undercut some basic assumptions on which they were built. Among these latter are assumptions about 'full-employment', family, gender relations, the 'standard worker' and the inclusiveness of social and political communities. In the last two to three decades there has been a shift towards what is called a more post-industrial life-cycle; life-courses are both changing and diversifying. These changes call for a rethinking of social citizenship, the relationship between various social rights and the welfare provisions to which they are related. The meaning of education, employment, care, and leisure-time has changed for the majority of citizens, both in their combination at any given moment in life, and in their relevance during the whole life-course. Consequently, the relations between different social rights, and the institutions that provide the facilities to implement these rights, are challenged.

This chapter focuses on the consequences of changing life-courses for the concept of social citizenship and related welfare policies. It starts with a brief overview of the challenges of changing life-cycles for the welfare state. Next, attention shifts to the consequences of these challenges for the definition of social citizenship. It will be argued that the basic conditions of social citizenship need to be reformulated in such a way that both security and respect of diversity are guaranteed. In the next section, various policy initiatives, particularly in Sweden and The Netherlands, will be examined from this perspective. Proposals which are not yet implemented in policies, such as ideas about a basic-income and vouchers systems, will also be explored. The main argument of this chapter is that – on a normative level – the basic conditions for emancipatory citizenship can be found in universality, flexibility and time autonomy, together with the integration of work, welfare and care in social policy. Fundamental changes are necessary to translate these notions into concrete policies.

Welfare and the life-cycle

The shift in life-courses and resulting changes for welfare states have not been extensively analysed by welfare state scholars. However, recently, concern for the issue of shifting life-courses has increased. For example, Myles (1990) examines the transition from a Fordist to a post-Fordist life-cycle. He starts from the construction of the Fordist life-cycle that emerged out of the Depression and World War II. He associates the Fordist life-cycle with a system of wage stabilization at historically high standards of living and the 'embourgeoisement' of the working class (Myles 1990: 274). Social policies were assumed to provide income security for all workers, not only for the poor. The Fordist life-cycle was considered to be a life-cycle for adult males; women were assumed to be dependent on the wages of their men and to take care of the family at home. Moreover, the Fordist life-cycle assumed stable life-courses; citizen's careers were assumed to be orderly, standardized and predictable. It could be summarized for men in 'once a worker, always a worker' (Esping-Andersen 1994: 167). In addition, marriage was assumed to last a lifetime, while moving to other places did not happen that often (and was mainly dependent on a breadwinner's career), which reinforced kinship and family care as well as the cohesion of small communities.

The post-Fordist, or post-industrial life-cycle, can partly be seen as the reverse of the Fordist life-cycle. It has been related to the rise of services and knowledge, more than industrial production. Particularly the rise of services opened the way for new jobs, especially among women, which, in turn, increased the possibilities for women to live independently of men. In addition, the labour market has asked for more flexible working schemes which has consequences for the division of work and care within families. Concurrently the public sector, particularly the service sector, has expanded, family forms have changed, flexibility in working schemes has increased, and welfare state policies have required adjustment. As a result, Myles argues that

> it seems, we are moving naturally, almost inevitably, towards a new kind of labour market, a new kind of welfare state and, as a result, a new kind of modal life-cycle for many and perhaps the majority. Instead of the predictable, orderly pattern that life-course implied, it is now claimed that the life-course is becoming increasing disorderly and fragmented.
> (Myles 1990: 278)

Esping-Andersen (1994) also points to such factors as industrial decline and revolutions in technology and the organization of work, the increase of service occupations, the changing economic status of women, and the revolutions in family life to sketch the transition from a Fordist welfare state towards a post-industrial society. As a result, the standard job trajectory is becoming atypical, while non-standard employment is becoming quite mainstream (Esping-Andersen 1994: 168). These developments create similar problems for welfare states. However, the way they respond to them, shows significant differences. Esping-Andersen (1996) distinguishes three routes of governmental response to current changes. Not surprisingly, these routes follow his famous former welfare state typology (Esping-Andersen 1990). He makes a distinction between a Scandinavian or social democratic route, which concentrated – until recently – on a strategy of welfare state-induced employment expansion in the public sector; an Anglo-American or neoliberal route, following a strategy of deregulating wages and the labour market, combined with a certain degree of welfare state erosion; and – third – a Continental or labour reduction route, favouring a strategy of induced labour supply reduction in combination with the assumption of family income maintenance systems. As Esping-Andersen argues, these three routes are, due to their distinct policies, confronted with different problems. The Scandinavian countries, and Sweden more particularly, are confronted with very high absenteeism, declining fiscal capacity combined with rising pressures on public job creation and income maintenance. Liberal welfare states, among them the UK, are confronted with the problem of poverty, and share a deepening inequality. The problems among the continental countries seem to be most fundamental. Esping-Andersen signals a real insider–outsider problem in the labour market: there is a predominantly male insider workforce enjoying high wages, expensive social rights and strong job security on the one hand, and a swelling population of outsiders (women, migrants, the elderly) on the other hand, depending either on the male bread-winner's pay or on welfare state transfers. The labour reduction strategy, is not working any more and must be drastically reversed, while families' dependence on the single, male earner should be diminished (Esping-Andersen 1996).

Challenges for citizenship

This kind of analysis is very useful for understanding recent changes in life-cycles and welfare policies, as well as changing work-patterns. However, it focuses strongly on the relationship between labour market participation and social protection through the state. To a certain extent, this kind of analysis still reflects some basic assumptions about social citizenship which can be traced back to Marshall.

Economic processes are regarded as the main driving forces in the face of which governments respond. Much is written about flexibility of the labour market, the structure of the service economy, the future of employment (Myles 1990) or about welfare state responses to economic change, the service economy, jobs and wages, employment dilemmas and social security (Esping-Andersen 1994). Although the notion of stable life-courses underlying Marshall's concept of citizenship is being challenged, the emphasis is still, as in Marshall's work, on the public sphere of work and welfare. This leaves the private sphere of the family – and consequently the role of unpaid care and dependent relations resulting from it – largely unnoticed, or only involved to the extent that they directly affect the public sphere of work and welfare.

The crucial interest of the family, dependent relations and care for welfare state and life-course issues, has been particularly emphasized by feminist scholars (see, among many others, Pateman 1989; Lewis 1992, 1993; Orloff 1993; Lewis and Ostner 1994; Fraser 1994; O'Connor 1996; Sainsbury 1994, 1996). This kind of research has engendered critical questions about the relationship between publicly organized, and usually paid care work on the one hand, and informal and unpaid care on the other, and about the relationship between care and citizenship. Care may be an important part of the welfare state, as laid down in the state's obligations towards its citizens, but the carrying out of the caring tasks themselves is not usually regarded as a basis for citizenship. It is only recently that scholars have started to redefine social citizenship to include care. For example, Taylor-Gooby (1991) argues that the central relationship between citizenship and welfare states is not just between paid work and welfare, but between paid work, welfare and unpaid (care) work. Also authors who examine the relation between care, gender and citizenship have raised the critical question of whether and to what extent care respon- sibilities, especially in the private sphere, tend to exclude people (women) from social citizenship or affect a distinctive identity of citizenship. Most of these authors seem to agree with the idea that care should become a dimension of citizenship (see for example Leira 1989: 208), although they do not agree about the way in which it should be integrated (Bussemaker 1997a). One way to integrate care is by paying attention to services which facilitate female labour market participation, such as public child-care and parental leave-entitlement to citizenship rights which have especially been developed in the Scandinavian countries (Siim 1993; Sainsbury 1996). Another way is through payment for informal care work (Ungerson 1995, 1997). Payment for care has been developed in various countries. For example, people who care for the disabled in the UK receive payment. However, the level of payment is low and the recipients are seen as not having a paid job. Yet another approach is to focus not only on the financial aspects of care work or accessibility to care provisions, but also on the right to have time to care. This can be implemented by part-time work strategies or generous leave schemes. The first strategy is well developed in The Netherlands, the second in Sweden and Denmark. None of these strategies are in themselves sufficient to integrate care in terms of citizenship. A perspective that includes both the right to care and the right to be cared for might be more attractive. This is what Knijn and Kremer (1997) call 'inclusive citizenship'.

However, such attempts to include the caring dimension within the concept of social citizenship, also have potential disadvantages, precisely because they tend to redefine care as matters of social rights. The question is which aspects of care can be formalized in terms of rights. As Sevenhuijsen (1998) argues, care is not only a matter of rights, but also of responsibilities, involvement, and personal and moral dimensions. In other words, interpreting care in terms of rights implies subjecting care to public intervention and control, which, at least in part, could be at odds with the moral and personal dimensions of care. Care, after all, has its own forms of logic, which restrict the degree to which it can be seen in economic, legal or even professional terms. Instead of a social rights discourse, these authors prefer to define care in terms of ethics or virtues. For example, Tronto defines care as a virtue and argues that the virtue of care lies in finding a middle path between 'excessive reliance upon others for our maintenance, and excessive self-reliance' (Tronto 1995: 14; see also Bussemaker and Voet 1998 and Sevenhuijsen 1998). Although these authors rightly warn us not to translate the caring dimension in terms of social rights only, the recognition of care as a matter of social rights is necessary to create the conditions for a more balanced relationship between work, welfare and care throughout the life-course.

Apart from care, the role of education and training is also becoming increasingly important, particularly in a service and knowledge economy. The traditional division between learning first and then working in one job until retirement age without any further training is diminishing. Instead, people undertake additional training, in or outside the job, and are more inclined to change from one job to another. In addition, firms and some governments have introduced sabbaticals, and work and learning or training are becoming more interrelated (Bussemaker 1997b). The concept of 'life-long learning', and the notion of 'employability' – one of the buzz-words in labour market debates at the end of the 1990s – both refer to the need to combine work and education, and to create career-breaks for learning. All these dimensions of social citizenship are closely interrelated and place the meaning of work in a new perspective, particularly in complex, post-industrial societies where no clear distinctions between different social spheres exist.

A preliminary conclusion is that social citizenship rights have been challenged by developments in labour market patterns, by changing and diversifying life-courses and by more equal gender relations. All together, there is increasing heterogeneity among workers and individual life-courses. In addition, there is increasing need for flexibility, among both employers and employees, in working standards and working times. Furthermore, care for children and other dependents is slowly becoming recognized as an issue closely related to work and welfare policies. Nowadays, social citizenship concerns the complicated relation of diverse needs between work, welfare and care.

Policy consequences

The discussion about a renewed notion of social citizenship is certainly not only an academic matter. It is a matter of politics as well. To uphold the welfare state in the future, it will be necessary to adjust social policies to changing life-courses. This can be done through various policy instruments. In this section, some advantages and disadvantages of existing policies in western Europe will be investigated. The emphasis will be on two countries which have been in the spot-light on these issues in the last decade, Sweden and The Netherlands. The emphasis will be on strategies of part-time work, leave schemes and social provisions such as child-care. Thereafter, more visionary solutions will be examined, such as ideas about negative income tax, sabbatical accounts and vouchers.

It is common to assume that Scandinavian countries do far better than others from the perspective of changing life-courses, especially because of their universal and generous citizenship rights combining both paid work and care. Indeed, strategies concerning extensive leave schemes and public child-care provisions are most developed in Scandinavian countries, particularly in Sweden. Also, part-time work strategies are common in Sweden, particularly among women employed in the public sector.

In addition to the Swedish public child-care system and generous parental leave schemes, the universal system of social rights and the individualization of tax and social security contribute to a high level of security for individuals, together with the possibility to combine a working career with a family life. As a result, the life-cycle seems to be more balanced than in other welfare states, where paid work has been regarded as a much more exclusive activity. Or, as Esping-Andersen states, one might say that the life-cycles in Scandinavian countries have been most 'revolutionized', because women's life-cycle has come to resemble men's, whereas male life-cycles have to a certain extent become feminized (Esping-Andersen 1994: 180).[1]

For these reasons, the Scandinavian welfare state experience has often been mentioned as an example for other countries, especially in Continental Europe and particularly by the Left. Indeed, the Scandinavian route answers some of the needs of changing life-cycles. It responds, to a certain degree, to the need of combining paid work and care. Scandinavian policies have also stimulated education (through leave schemes and other arrangements with respect to life-long learning). However, it has also created new hazards. It heavily depends on paid work for all, and, therefore, places the right to work in the centre of social citizenship. People who are outside the labour force easily lack the opportunity to use social welfare, other than as a means to integrate in the labour market. This is reflected in policies concerning care and education. In other words, labour market participation is a *sine qua non* for citizenship in the Scandinavian welfare state regime. This is problematic at a time when full employment seems unlikely to return. In addition, because of high taxes, a dual income is a necessity for many families to uphold a high living standard. This makes partners easily dependent on each other's income. Moreover, the Scandinavian strategy may ensure a high level of social protection and thus fight income-poverty, but it may also engender a new form of poverty: time-poverty. Currently, citizens seem to prefer more time over more income and provisions, as strikes in 1998 in Denmark – which, we should note, is less work orientated than Sweden – clearly illustrated. Furthermore, while the Scandinavian route might be adequate from the perspective of the combination of paid work and care in adult life, it has problems in dealing with diversity and heterogeneity of the population, partly an effect of migration, and partly an effect of changing family and gender relations. Finally, the Scandinavian, and particularly the

Swedish, system is not flexible in its arrangement. Its universal, but standardized, character does not provide many possibilities for choice between various kind of solutions (for example with respect to the question of whether one wants to take care of a child at home, or prefers public child-care). From this perspective, the neoliberal Swedish critics of the welfare state had a strong argument when, in the late 1980s, they stressed the importance of recognising people's differing needs. They highlighted, as Mahon argues, some of the limitations of a system which strives for universality in the form of standardized 'one size for all' solutions (Mahon 1997: 15). Although there has been an emerging consensus since the 1990s about the problems of standardized solutions in current society, and some policies – for example concerning child-care – now offer more flexibility and variety in the kind of provisions available, the Swedish system still creates certain limitations from the perspective of diversifying life-courses.

Whereas Sweden has been *the* example of a generous modern welfare state for many in the 1980s, in the mid-1990s the Dutch welfare state gained international fame because of its economic modernization in combination with a relatively high level of social protection. The so-called 'Dutch miracle' has been particularly appreciated for its institutional reform of social security and wage-levels, resulting from long negotiations between employers, employees and the state – a modern form of corporatist politics. However, policies to stimulate new labour market patterns, particularly through part-time work and flexible work-schemes were also part of the game. The Netherlands has an exceptionally high proportion of part-time workers: 36.4 per cent of employees work part-time. Although there is still a high gender gap (65.9 per cent of employed women and 16.1 per cent of employed men work in part-time jobs; Eurostat 1996: 20–21) it is smaller than in other European countries, while both men and women are more likely to work part-time in The Netherlands than in any other country. The availability of part-time jobs has firmly contributed to the increase of female participation in the labour market; over the last decade female participation increased from 35 per cent in 1984 to 51 per cent in 1994. The part-time work strategy – together with a modest increase in child-care provisions (Bussemaker 1998) – has contributed to the development of new patterns of work and care. Many parents combine part-time jobs with taking care of their children. They both work 32 hours or less (especially women work in low-hours part-time jobs), and take care of their children on the other days. Child-care is often used for around 3 days, seldom for 5 days a week. The strategy of part-time work seems to be very successful, and men in particular indicate a preference for working fewer hours – which may be guaranteed through a new regulation to extend the rights of part-time workers in the near future. Part-time work is viewed as work of full-value, not as second-rank, as is the case in many other countries. Although part-time work is well regulated, this can not be said for leave-schemes. Parental leave has only existed since 1991 and includes a reduction of working hours for a period of 26 weeks. Civil servants receive 75 per cent of their wage, but for others compensation depends on collective labour agreements. Very recently, an arrangement for (rather modest) financial support during career-breaks has been accepted by Parliament. This includes leave for care or education for 2 to 18 months, under the condition that an unemployed person will replace the person on leave.

The Netherlands also shows a firm increase in flexible work. Most workers with temporary contracts are women. In some respects flexible working can help to create more balance in the life-course. But this is only the case when flexible work is regulated in such a way that it not only serves the interests of employers, but also those of employees. Recent legislation about 'flexibility and security' contributes to such a perspective. It grants more rights for flexible workers concerning pension and social security in exchange for a loosening of dismissal protection and longer probation periods.

Compared to the Scandinavian countries, and Sweden in particularly, the Dutch strategy seems to provide better conditions for variety in working hours (both as an effect of part-time work and flexible work), and creates better conditions to avoid the problem of 'time-poverty'. However, social care provisions (child-care, and care for the elderly) are less developed than in Sweden, as are leave schemes, which impedes strategies to combine work and care.

Both countries provide examples of redirections in social policy to cope with changing life-courses of citizens and, in addition, a redefinition of social citizenship. However, neither country gives a ready framework for other countries to follow in adjusting their policies. The concept of social citizenship underlying Swedish welfare policies comes close to the integration of work, welfare and care, but still assumes, to a certain extent, full employment, stable work and family careers, and, consequently, believes in standardized solutions. In addition, the model copes with problems resulting from increasing heterogeneity and internationalization. The Dutch experience gives some clues as to how to deal with variation in needs and flexibility and time-autonomy during the life-course, but is still poor in the integration of care in social policies. Moreover, the Dutch welfare state reform was certainly not the effect of a 'grand design' but in many respects more the result of 'accidents' (cf. Hemerijck and Van Kersbergen 1997), which makes it difficult to use as a policy example for other countries.

Alternative policy proposals

Currently, social citizenship concerns the complicated relationships between the diverse needs of work, welfare and care. The challenge is to redefine social citizenship in relation to welfare policies. Analysis of the Swedish and Dutch welfare policies indicates some directions to be taken in implementing such a concept of citizenship through concrete policies.

However, they certainly are not the only solutions one can imagine. Much more radical policy measures to deal with new combinations of work, welfare, and care, as well as with the need of flexibility and time autonomy, are being developed in theoretical work. Although they are not yet implemented in concrete policies, they certainly deserve attention. One of these more radical ideas concerns the introduction of a basic income. A basic income has been particularly discussed in some continental countries, among others, Germany and The Netherlands. Although there are a lot of variations in the way a basic income has been conceptualized, the central idea is that citizens have a universal, individual right to an income, irrespective of their former career, household, gender, age or any other factor. The relationship between work and income – crucial in most post-war welfare arrangements – is disconnected in a basic minimum income strategy. It no longer considers employment as the central criterion for citizenship, but instead argues that the concept of a basic minimum income, or 'citizenship income', better suits a post-industrial society.

A basic income would make citizens less dependent on employers for their income, since they would have an exit option, although the extent to which this would be successful would largely depend on the level of the basic income.[2] Proponents of a citizenship-income approach argue that citizenship cannot be enforced through duties, as in activation and workfare programmes, but can only evolve on a voluntary basis. Self-respect is more important than force (Van Stokkom 1992). It is precisely this free will which can promote full citizenship for all, since a guaranteed minimum income gives citizens the freedom to become involved in the social and political domain, for example by engaging in care or voluntary work.

However, the idea of a basic income creates a lot of hazards as well. To mention only a few: it may generate greater risk of social exclusion, because there would be less pressure on the government to take action. It may even be used as an argument to withdraw some public services, and it may increase gender inequality as long as men do not use the basic income to take up care responsibilities. Finally, it creates many problems from an international perspective (cf. Roche 1992: 178–89). Indeed, it is generally agreed that a radical citizenship income is undesirable and impossible (although there are still some strong advocates of a basic income, cf. Van Parijs 1992). However, less far-reaching alternatives such as a negative income tax, may be beneficial. A negative income tax system sets a minimum income level. Citizens with an income below this level receive benefits up to this level; citizens with an income above the minimum level pay taxes, because welfare benefits are deducted. The idea behind the negative income tax is that it will increase financial independence, and create a financial basis to temporarily withdraw from the labour market (as with a career-break interruption scheme). In proposals developed by Dutch trade unions and the Dutch Labour Party, the system would start slowly with a small negative income tax, which may, in the long term, become a real basic income (or a basic-entitlement if one wants to exclude people who earn more than the minimum wage).[3]

Another variation of a basic-income strategy has been introduced by Offe (1998). He developed the idea of a 'sabbatical account'. Offe wants to break with the formal (German) policy in which production and redistribution are closely related, through the introduction of a sabbatical account. This is cheaper, more reversible and more gradualist than a basic-income strategy. The idea of the sabbatical account is that every citizen is born with an account that gives the right to 10 years' break with an income compensation somewhat above social assistance level and at a flat rate. This should be a citizen's right, not a question of employment or status. The right can be effectuated any time after early adulthood (say 18 years) and before retirement age. Some conditions would be made for the minimum time one can 'opt out', in order to create real job vacancies for others. To avoid the possibility that citizens use up their whole account as soon as they can, Offe suggests including the condition that people make an education plan during early adulthood. In addition, he suggests that each year claimed when a person is under 30 should count double. Inversely, each year which is taken after the age of 45, should only count as 0.6 years (Offe 1998: 34). Such conditions may stimulate a balanced use of the account.

Another problem is the valuation of care. For, if the sabbatical account would be used as a substitute for care-leave schemes, it could easily increase gender inequality. This is even more problematic in relation to the age restrictions Offe proposes, because they would discourage women from becoming pregnant before the age of 30. However, the introduction of 'special discounts' for care for children or other dependents may relieve this problem.

The idea of a sabbatical account is attractive from the perspective of heterogeneous life-courses and life-styles, freedom of choice in time allocation, and valuation of activities other than paid work, varying from unpaid care, voluntary or community activities, to education and leisure time. Nevertheless, it is very unlikely that it will be introduced in any European country in the near future. However, there are a couple of recent initiatives in different countries which may be a viewed as a first, small step towards such a new definition of citizenship. The Dutch example of financial support for career breaks, mentioned above, is a very modest variant, but there are other examples as well. In 1985 Belgium introduced the possibility to take an 'Interruption of Occupational Career'. The duration of such an interruption varies from 6 to 12 months, and is subject to the employer's agreement. The interruption can be requested for various reasons, including child-care and education. Until 1991 benefits were at a flat rate; since then the amount of cash benefit paid is reduced after the first year, or at the second and subsequent breaks (Gauthier 1996: 179). Also in Denmark generous leave schemes exist, particularly since the Social Democratic–Centre government introduced temporary leave of absence schemes in 1994. The schemes include education, child-care, and sabbatical leave. They are thought to improve the qualifications of the work force, offer more combinations of paid work with care and family life, and to combat unemployment through the creation of jobs for the unemployed. From that perspective, they are related to notions of job sharing and job rotation (Siim 1998). The wage replacement rate for child benefit and sabbatical leave was 80 per cent of the unemployment rate of benefits, but the level was reduced to 70 per cent in November 1994, and to 60 per cent in 1997. The leave schemes have gained unexpected popularity, particularly among working mothers. Although the leave schemes are criticized, in part because they would not offer real new jobs and not stimulate economic growth, they seem to be a very good example of innovative social policy (Siim 1998).

Another alternative way to conceptualize new forms of welfare responding to changing and diversifying life-courses, is the idea of 'vouchers'. This idea has some similarities with the notion of a sabbatical account, although it has been particularly developed in relation to education, training and life-long learning policies (Bussemaker 1997b). The central idea is that education should not stop at a certain age; economic, technological and social developments call for more flexibility between education and employment. Life-long learning is the central concept; dual learning, leave arrangements and vouchers are the policy terms (European Commission 1994, 1995; OECD 1996; UNESCO 1996). After compulsory school age, citizens would receive vouchers to follow any form of education. It would be up to them whether they wanted to use them all directly after compulsory school age, or whether they wanted to have some breaks later in their careers. Vouchers would guarantee entry to education, as well as a basic level of income during this time.

However, as with the idea of a basic income and the sabbatical account, there are some problems with respect to the idea of vouchers. Among them are practical problems – many argue that it is too difficult to organize; the whole idea would not be feasible. More principled arguments concern the possible hazard of increasing inequalities between citizens because of unequal capacities to use these vouchers properly during the life-course. This is due to the fact that people would have to decide when they wanted to spend their vouchers, whereas the whole idea of the welfare state arose precisely from the unpredictability of risks and life-courses. What, for example should be the response to people who spend all their vouchers when they are 20 years old, without saving anything? Such problems may be solved in a similar fashion as with the sabbatical account, by introducing incentives for a balanced application of the vouchers.

If the idea of vouchers may not be desirable or attainable in the near future, there are still other, less far-reaching, policy options. For example, the same notion opens the possibility of granting people some vouchers to be used for a specific purpose. To mention only one example in relation to care: a Client-Budget System, introduced recently in The Netherlands, aims to provide care-dependants the ability to decide for themselves what sort of care they prefer. They receive coupons for use either in exchange for services (and the choice between services) or to pay (informal) care-givers. This Client-Budget System may maintain the independence of people who need care for themselves (frail, elderly, disabled people) as well as families who have to provide long-term care for a family-member, a disabled child for example. Such provisions might also be useful in other fields of welfare. One can think of a guarantee, created by a special set of coupons or vouchers, to use free public child-care services for children. One could decide at what moment one prefered to use it, and whether, for example, one prefered full public child-care for very young children, or working part-time and using after-school services when children are older.

The main advantage of a negative income tax, vouchers and sabbatical accounts is that they would increase the freedom of choice for citizens on how to spend their time over their life-course, and the value they attach to other activities apart from paid work. It seems that within European welfare states many people prefer freedom of choice, time autonomy and flexibility of arrangements above paternalism from the state. However, to guarantee this freedom, generous state provisions are still necessary. Therefore, these suggestions should be sharply distinguished from proposals to increase 'freedom of choice' and 'flexibility' through market-forces alone, because that would easily increase inequality and decrease the conditions of choice for the more vulnerable.

Conclusion

Marshall's concept of social citizenship has some shortcomings in the analysis of current developments, particularly concerning changes in the life-cycle. It is too much grounded in the idea of Fordist life-styles, which assumes predictable life-courses. Indeed, social citizenship rights, particularly in continental Europe, are more able to protect stable wage and family relations, rather than instable and diversifying life-course patterns.

Therefore, we need to redefine the concept of social citizenship. Social citizenship should not only concern the relation between work and welfare, but should also include care. In addition, it should not only take class relations into consideration, but also, gender, age and ethnicity. More generally, it needs to deal with diversity and heterogeneity, both among citizens and in the life-course of a citizen. Consequently, citizenship should not only concern the spheres of the state and the labour market, but also the family and civil society.

What should such a renewed concept look like? It needs to meet the basic needs of citizenship and should therefore – in an ideal situation – be universal, should provide a certain flexibility in social rights to assure time autonomy, and should incorporate care as a dimension of social citizenship (besides work and welfare). Universality is a necessary condition to come to terms with the basic idea of social citizenship as equality. Therefore, breadwinner arrangements and strong means-tested policies are problematic. Social rights should be independent of status, gender, age or class and should have a certain level of generosity which guarantees a 'human life standard'. In addition, the welfare state should not only provide protection from the old risks of unemployment and sickness, but should also give protection from new risks resulting from flexible labour market patterns and changing family structures (single parenthood, for example). Flexibility is a necessary condition to come to terms with different needs during the life-course, as well as to deal with the heterogeneity of the population and diversity in needs and wants among citizens. Flexibility of social rights must guarantee that people can easily shift from periods of work to periods of care, education or leisure time. At one time in life one might need more money (for example, when a person has just bought a house), at another time one might need more time (when one has young children, wants to update education or simply wants to travel around the world). This kind of flexibility should be sharply distinguished from economic flexibility, sometimes promoted by employers and right-wing parties, which diminishes the quality of social rights and freedom of choice for employees. The kind of flexibility I have in mind should serve the interests of citizens to combine different roles during their life and simultaneously if they wish. The integration of work, welfare and care is a necessary condition to make abstract social rights work and to incorporate changing family-relations and combat gender-inequality. Care as an issue of citizenship should include both the right to care and the right to receive care (Knijn and Kremer 1997).

A concept of social citizenship which starts from the integration of work, welfare and care, and which is universal and flexible at the same time, can help to develop an integrative perspective of social policies. The Scandinavian, especially the Swedish policy model, is universal in the sense that it grants rather generous entitlements to citizens, although there is a strong link to the labour market. It also meets, to a certain extent, the condition of the combination of work, welfare and care, especially through generous leave schemes and well developed public care services. To a limited extent, the system meets the condition of flexibility, particularly with respect to the combination of paid work and care. It is less flexible in the sense that it still assumes standardized solutions and assumes paid work as the basic activity in the life-course. In that respect, it has not really involved a change in the underlying assumption that citizenship is about work and welfare.

In contrast, recent Dutch policies may be less generous than the Scandinavian ones, but in some respects create more space for time autonomy and flexibility in the use of social citizenship rights, particularly through part-time work strategies and flexible work schemes, without undermining basic security rights. However, both strategies have their limitations. More far-reaching strategies are necessary. Proposals for a negative income tax, sabbatical accounts, vouchers concerning care, education and other welfare provisions, may help to develop such a strategy.

Currently, many western European countries are doing quite well from a financial and economic perspective. However, their social policies need adjustment to cope with changing and diversifying life-styles and life-courses. In the long run this is not only necessary to provide social protection and to adjust welfare states to new circumstances, but also to assure broad support for the project of the welfare state. This is particularly a challenge for the social-democratic parties which are now in power in many European countries.

Notes

1   That is not to say that Scandinavian countries are not confronted with gender inequality; women are over represented among the workers in the public services, work part-time more often than men and are in general much more dependent on the state, whether for employment or as a client of state-provided facilities (Siim 1993).

2   The notion of a basic income has been discussed by the Left as well as the Right; on the Left it has been viewed as a basic citizens' income which should be supplemented with generous social provisions. The Right has often viewed it as a minimum provision without supplements, fitting well in a strategy of marketization and the dismantling of the welfare state. Here, I am concerned with the Leftist option.

3   Although Roche (1982: 183–4) summarizes a lot of problems with American experiences with a negative income tax system, we may wonder whether this is because the system itself is not accurate, or whether this is because of the context of the American welfare system in which the experiences were embedded.

Bibliography

Bussemaker, J. (1997a) 'Citizenship, welfare state regimes and breadwinner-arrangements: various backgrounds of equality policy', in F. Gardiner (ed.), *Equality Policies in Europe*, London: Routledge.

—— (1997b) *Leren: geen afgesloten boek. Arrangementen voor levenslang leren in de context van arbeids- en verzorgingsregelingen in verschillende Europese verzorgingsstaten*, Den Haag: Staatsuitgeverij.

—— (1998) 'Rationales of care in contemporary welfare states: the case of childcare in the Netherlands', *Social Politics* 5, 1: 70–96.

Bussemaker, J. and Voet, R. (1998) 'Introduction. Theoretical approaches and historical legacies', *Critical Social Policy* 18, 3: 277–308 (special issue on vocabularies of gender and citizenship in Northern Europe).

Esping-Andersen, G. (1990) *The Three Worlds of Welfare Capitalism*, Cambridge: Polity.

—— (1994), 'Equality and Work in the post-industrial life-cycle', in David Miliband (ed.) *Reinventing the Left*, Cambridge: Polity Press.

—— (ed.) (1996) *Welfare States in Transition. National Adaptions in Global Economies*, London: Sage.

European Commission (1994) *European Social Policy – a Way Forward for the Union*, Luxembourg: Commission of the European Communities.

—— (1995) *White Papers on Education and Vocational Training*, Brussels.

Eurostat (1996) *Labour Force Survey Results 1994*, Luxembourg.

Fraser, N. (1994) 'After the family wage. Gender equity and the welfare state', *Political Theory* 22, 4: 591–618.

Gauthier, A. (1996) *The State and the Family. A Comparative Analysis of Family Policies in Industrialized Countries*, Oxford: Clarendon Press.

Hemerijck, A. and Van Kersbergen, K. (1997), 'A miraculous model? Explaining the new politics of the welfare state in the Netherlands', *Acta Politica* 32, 3: 258–80.

Knijn, T. and Kremer, M. (1997) 'Gender and the caring dimension of welfare states; towards inclusive citizenship', *Social Politics* 4, 3: 328–62.

Leira, A. (1989) *Models of Motherhood. Welfare State Policies and Everyday Practices: The Scandinavian Experience*, Oslo: Institute for Social Research.

Lewis, J. (1992) 'Gender and the development of welfare regimes', *Journal of European Social Policy* 2, 3: 159–73.

—— (ed.) (1993) *Women and Social Policies in Europe. Work, Family and the State*, Aldershot: Edward Elgar.

Lewis, J. and Ostner, I. (1994) *Gender and the evolution of European social policies*. Bremen: Centre for Social Policy Research.

Mahon, R. (1997) 'Child care in Canada and Sweden: policy and politics', *Social Politics* 4, 3: 382–418.

Marshall, T. H. (1964) *Class, Citizenship and Social Development*, Garden City/New York: Doubleday.

Myles, J. (1990) 'States, labor markets and life cycles', in R. Friedland and S. Robertson (eds), *Beyond the Market Place: Rethinking Economy and Society*. New York: Aldine/de Gruyter.

OECD (1996) *Lifelong Learning for All*, Paris: OECD.

O'Connor, J. (1996) 'From women in the welfare State to gendering welfare state regimes'. Special issue of *Current Sociology* 44, 2: 1–130.

Offe, C. (1998) The German welfare state: principles, performances, prospects. Paper prepared for the conference The welfare state at century's end: current dilemmas and possible futures. Tel Aviv, 5–7 January 1998.

Orloff, A. (1993) 'Gender and the social rights of citizenship: the comparative analysis of gender relations and welfare states', *American Sociological Review* 58: 303–28.

Pateman C. (ed.) (1989) *The Disorder of Women*, Stanford: Stanford University Press.

Roche, M. (1992) *Rethinking Citizenship. Welfare, Ideology and Change in Modern Societies*. Oxford: Polity Press.

Sainsbury, D. (ed.) (1994) *Gendering Welfare States*, London: Sage.

—— (1996) *Gender, Equality and Welfare States*, Cambridge: Cambridge University Press.

Sevenhuijsen, S. (1998) *Citizenship and the Ethics of Care. Feminist Considerations on Justice, Morality and Politics*. London: Routledge.

Siim, B. (1993) 'The gendered Scandinavian welfare states; the interplay between women's roles as mothers, workers and citizens in Denmark', in J. Lewis (ed.) *Women and Social Policies in Europe. Work, Family and the State*, Aldershot: Edward Elgar.

—— (1998) 'Vocabularies of citizenship and gender: the Danish case', *Critical Social Policy* 18, 3.

Taylor-Gooby, P. (1991) 'Welfare state regimes and welfare citizenship', *Journal of European Social Policy* 1, 2: 93–105.

Tronto, J. (1995) *In Care of Democracy*, Utrecht: University for Humanist Studies.

UNESCO (1996) *The Treasure Within. Report to UNESCO of the International Commission on Education for the Twenty-first Century*, Paris: UNESCO.

Ungerson, C. (1995) 'Gender, cash and informal care: European perspectives and dilemmas', *Journal of Social Policy* 24, 1: 31–52.

—— (1997) 'Social politics and the commodification of care' *Social Politics* 4, 3: 362–81.

Van Parijs, Ph. (ed.) (1992) *Arguing for Basic Income: Ethical Foundations for a Radical Reform*. London: Verso.

Van Stokkom, B. (1992) *De Republiek der Weerbaren*, Houten: Bohn Stafleu Van Loghem.

6 Towards a gender-sensitive framework for citizenship

Comparing Denmark, Britain and France[1]

Birte Siim

Introduction

The objective of this chapter is to involve gender issues in the study of citizenship, and to compare the recent changes in the fulfilment of women's citizenship in Denmark, France and Britain. The argument is that developing a gender-sensitive framework for citizenship necessitates a rethinking of the interplay between two aspects of citizenship, the social and the political. There are three key questions in the comparative analysis of gender and citizenship in Denmark, France and Britain. How is the meaning of key concepts of citizenship, such as the distinctions between public and private arenas and active and passive conceptions of citizenship, transformed when viewed from the perspective of gender?; What has been the relationship between welfare and political agency?; What are the implications of the on-going changes in women's social and political citizenship for gender relations and for the citizenship discourses in European welfare states in transition?[2]

The inclusion of gender in a comparative framework for citizenship

The modern understanding of citizenship has been inspired by T. H. Marshall's notion of civil, political and social rights (Marshall 1992). This model of citizenship did not include women, and there was no evolution *à la* Marshall from civil, to political to social rights for women. Women were second-class citizens, excluded from full citizenship in the economy and the state, and faced with a division between waged work and motherhood-structured welfare states (Pateman 1992). Today, women have been included as salaried workers and increasingly participate in politics, but they still have not gained a full and equal access to citizenship (Sarvasy and Siim 1994).

Lewis and Ostner found that the norm of a male breadwinner, that 'in its ideal form prescribes breadwinning for men and homemaking/caring for women', has been a crucial principle in all welfare states (Lewis and Ostner 1994: 17–19). There are, however, differences in the way the breadwinner norm has been implemented in social policy. They categorize European welfare regimes by differentiating between strong, medium and weak breadwinner states. Lewis and Ostner argue that the strength or weakness of the male breadwinner model 'serves as a predictor of the way in which women are treated in social security systems; the level of social service provisions, particularly in regard to child care; and the nature of married women's participation in the labour market' (Lewis and Ostner 1994: 17–19).

The model is useful, because it pinpoints a missing factor in Marshall's model, that is, women's relation to salaried employment. However, it is questionable whether the development of social policies and women's waged work can be reduced to one underlying logic – the male breadwinner norm. There is an interplay between women's waged work and social policies, but women's active citizenship cannot be deduced from the strength or weakness of the male breadwinner model.[3] The suggestion here is that a more dynamic framework of citizenship focusing on the interrelation between women's welfare and political agency is needed.

The Australian sociologist Turner (1992) introduced a framework for comparative research of citizenship on the basis of national histories of citizenship. In his framework two dimensions describe the interplay between citizens and political institutions, and the interplay between public and private arenas:

- The *active/passive dimension* expresses how the rights of citizens were historically institutionalised in modern democracies, for example through revolutionary movements 'from below' against the Absolutist state or through strategies 'from above' (for example by the state).
- The *public/private dimension* expresses whether the key to citizenship is connected with the public or the private sphere, with public or private virtues.

The two dimensions are the basis for a typology of four political contexts for the institutionalization and creation of citizenship rights. This ideal-type construction is later applied to specific historical cases. The objective of the typology is twofold:

> The point of this historical sketch has been partly to provide a critique of the monolithic and unified conception of citizenship in Marshall and partly to offer a sociological model of citizenship along two axes, namely public and private definitions of moral activity in terms of the creation of a public space of political activity, and active and passive forms of citizenship in terms of whether the citizen is conceptualised merely as a subject of an absolute authority or as an active political agent.
>
> (Turner 1992: 55)

Turner's principal addition to the previous comparative studies of the histories of citizenship lies in his attention to the structural relationship between the private and the public arena and their different cultural meanings for the understanding of the development of citizenship. The framework is preliminary and needs to be developed further through case studies. I suggest that it has the potential to understand gender relations, because it focuses on the interrelation between civil society, social movements and political institutions from different national contexts.

Turner does not observe that the structural relations between the private and the public, as well as their meanings, are essential components of the understanding of gender differences in modern democracies (Pateman 1988). Walby (1994: 383) notices that in Turner's framework the private arena can have two different meanings: (a) the autonomy of the individual in the family; and (b) individual freedom from state intervention. The feminist point is that individual autonomy in the liberal model does not apply to women, because women are both in theory and in practice subordinated as dependent wives (Pateman 1988). The 'private' arena is, both in practice and in theory, a contradictory term for women: a site of caring and mothering as well as a site of oppression and dependency (Walby 1994). The implication is that the different perceptions of the private and the public arena in political philosophy, as well as the construction of the border between the public and private arena, have gendered implications (Lister 1995). The feminist perspective illuminates the need for state regulation of families and for an expansion of public responsibilities for caring for children and the elderly that transcends the different models of citizenship (Knijn and Kremer 1997; Yuval-Davis 1996).

The gendered perception of the private arena is one problem with Turner's model. The other problem is the gendered character of the active/passive dimension. Throughout history women and minority groups have been excluded from active democratic citizenship. The active/passive dimension tends to be gendered, because the public/private divide was at the same time a construction of the separation between 'private' women and 'public' men (Pateman 1988). Active citizenship did not include women's political rights, and even during the French Revolution women were denied the right to speak in public, to form political meetings and to vote (Landes 1988). The feminist perspective illuminates the need to strengthen women's political agency through strategies that empower women in civil society and improve their presence in the public arena in order to transcend the different models of citizenship (Young 1990; Phillips 1995).

The discourse of citizenship in Denmark, France and Britain

The comparison between Denmark, Britain and France is interesting, because the three countries in many ways represent different systems and discourses of welfare, citizenship and gender. In terms of the active/passive dimension, France expresses an active republican, Britain a passive liberal and Denmark a mixed social–democratic model. In terms of the public/private dimension the three cases also express different visions, histories and structures that have implications for social policy. Britain has a tradition of a passive state and a political culture that emphasizes the private virtues of citizens, whereas France has a tradition of an interventionist state and a political culture that emphasizes public virtues. The argument is that Denmark is a mix between Continental and Anglo-Saxon traditions that expresses an active state and a political culture with a balance between the public and private spheres. Finally, from a feminist perspective, it can be argued that Denmark represents a weak, Britain a strong and France a medium, male breadwinner model. In the following, Turner's framework is used as an inspiration for a comparison of the different perceptions of citizenship and gender in the three countries. The focus is on the interplay between women's welfare and political agency and on the implications of the recent shifts in discourses and practices of citizenship.

Gender and citizenship in Denmark

In the Danish discourse, neither social rights nor political participation has explicitly been phrased in the language of citizenship: social citizenship has until recently been based on political consensus about the universality of social rights, i.e. the equal right of all citizens to welfare, independent of income, which has permeated both the political culture and political institutions. Ideals and norms of self-organization, participation and incorporation of social groups are key aspects of the political culture with roots in both the Radical, the Liberal and the Social Democratic Parties (Kolstrup 1997).

The Danish, and indeed Scandinavian development of citizenship has been described as a mix of Continental and Anglo-Saxon traditions – of active and passive citizenship (Nielsen 1992: 81): on the one hand, civil and social rights were introduced gradually 'from above' during the eighteenth and nineteenth centuries, and democracy was granted peacefully by the King in 1849, not through a violent revolution. On the other hand, the political culture expresses a pragmatic perception of the state as a tool to solve social problems that rests on a balance between citizens and the state, between the public and private spheres (Nielsen 1992: 80). There is a tradition of involving ordinary citizens in politics that dates back to the political and cultural self-organization of the farmers in the nineteenth century as well as to the ideas of the workers' movement in the twentieth century.

The political culture has also been influenced by a paternalist social democratic vision aimed at regulating society and the lives of citizens 'from above' (Finneman 1985). Since the 1930s, a high degree of institutionalization and incorporation of economic class organizations, and indeed all interest groups have marked political development. Corporatism has enabled centralized and male-dominated economic and political organizations to play a major role in politics. The Social Democratic Party has combined a paternalist perception of women as the objects of social policies, with ideals about social equality, workers' participation and equality of women and men (Hernes 1987).

Shifts in gender relations

From the perspective of gender, the meaning and practice of citizenship in Denmark has changed dramatically as women have increased their participation in the labour market and in politics. Denmark, and the other Scandinavian welfare states, have been characterized as weak male breadwinner models (Lewis and Ostner 1994), or potentially women-friendly states, that have given women opportunities to provide for themselves through waged work with support from a large public service sector (Hernes 1987; Siim 1988).

Since 1960, universalism has been the key element in health, education and social policy, and social services and benefits have been directed toward all citizens, independent of income. The growth of the welfare state and the large public sector, financed by taxes, has been followed by a parallel integration of women as the majority of salaried workers in the public sector (Schmied 1995). The basic unit in social legislation has, since the beginning of the 1970s been the individual, not the household or the family. The change to a dual breadwinner model implies that all individuals, women and men, have a duty to provide for themselves through paid employment. At the same time public policies have helped families to reconcile working and family life, for example through child-care centres and child/family benefits.

During the 1980s the increase in married women's salaried work and the growing interplay between everyday life and politics have resulted in political consensus on the need for public responsibility in the provision of care for the elderly and child-care. The implications are that women have gained new economic and social rights as paid employees and mothers. There is, however, public debate about the time constraints families with young children face in their daily lives when reconciling employment and care, and about the economic polarization between employed and unemployed families. Time constraints have been especially acute for single mothers and for working mothers, and unskilled women generally have higher unemployment rates than unskilled men (Siim 1997).

During the last 25 years, there has been a change both in the meaning of motherhood and in women's roles in public, political life. Women have increased their presence in political institutions, although there is no equality in political power between women and men. Research has shown that motherhood is no longer a barrier for women's political participation; instead motherhood, and indeed parenthood, has become a potential for citizenship (Siim 1994). Parents have become increasingly active citizens gaining new rights in relation to schools and child-care institutions, and both the mothers and the fathers of children under 9 years of age have (since 1993) gained the right to child-care leave. Women make up the large majority of the parents on parental leave, and there is a growing debate about the need to make child-care leave more attractive to fathers (Siim 1998).

Feminists have agreed that the universalist welfare state has been beneficial for women, because it has made it easier to reconcile motherhood with salaried employment. Feminist historians have noticed that the structural split between the private and the public sector has not been as acute in Denmark as in countries with a strong bourgeoisie. Women's organizations have formed alliances and networks in order to advance equal rights between women and men in the labour market (Rosenbeck 1989; Ravn 1995).[4]

It is more difficult to explain the change in women's political roles. It can be argued that the political cultural values of 'democracy from below' have created a space for women's social and political activities that has made it easier for organized women to gain access to the public arena. Until the mid 1980s feminist scholars, generally interpreted corporatism as a barrier for gender equality in political and administrative decisions (Hernes 1987), and some scholars still interpret corporatism as the main barrier for gender equality (Hirdman 1990). However, since the introduction of the equality law in public committees and commissions in 1986, it can be argued that the combination of state feminism and corporatism has become a means for the integration of women in politics (Bergquist 1994; Borchorst 1997).

To conclude, in Denmark there has been a complicated interconnection between women's welfare and political agency. Women were the objects of social policy before they became the subjects in the political process. In that sense, welfare seems to have been the *cause* rather than the *effect* of political agency, but women's agency has also managed to influence political decisions. Today, women have gained access to the political élite, and one of the crucial questions is whether women have the ability and the will to transform the political agenda as feminists hope, or whether political institutions will change women. Another question concerns the implications of the growing gender division of work with men employed in the private sector and women employed in the public sector. Will there be a growing conflict in political values between privately employed men and publicly employed women, or will political cultural values of men and women continue to converge?[5]

Gender and citizenship in Britain

Britain is an example of a passive democracy where the emphasis on the freedom of the individual from state oppression has simultaneously been interpreted as the freedom of the family from state intervention. The liberal tradition has given high priority to individual rights, and civil and political rights have traditionally had priority over social rights. British women obtained civil and political rights relatively early, compared to countries like France (Sineau 1992). The passive conception of citizenship and the lack of political will to use the central state as a means to combat social inequalities as well as inequalities between women and men has, however, been a problem for women.

Britain has had a distrust of centralized government and a traditional reliance on local and private forms of welfare provisions (Koven and Michel 1993). Voluntary organizations already in the pre-World War I period played a central role in the administration of welfare. The British state has been characterized as a weak or 'minimal' state, and it has been argued that 'weak' states like the United States, and to a lesser extent Britain, opened a space for women's political activities on the local level that allowed women's voluntary associations to flourish. However, British women, in contrast to their American counterparts, never managed to gain a foothold in the central state (Koven and Michel 1993: 21; Lewis 1994: 40).[6]

In terms of social policy, Britain has been characterized as a strong male breadwinner model where married women were perceived in social policies either as mothers or dependent wives, not as breadwinners (Lewis and Ostner 1994). What has been the relation between welfare and political agency in Britain? The liberal policy of non-intervention in family affairs has historically been a problem for women. There tends to be a contradiction between the general principle of *autonomous* individuals and the discourse on social policy that is based upon a hidden assumption that married women are *dependent* on their husbands (Orloff 1993).

It was not until after World War II that the Labour movement came to play a dominant role in the British welfare state. Since the late 1930s, the welfare state has been inspired by Marshall's ideas about social rights institutionalized in William Beveridge's proposals for universal social policies in two key areas: health care and education. Beveridge noticed the unpaid work of married women, but wives and husbands were treated differently under the National Insurance Act of 1946. Social policies have generally treated women primarily as mothers or dependent wives (Lewis 1994), and until recently there has been a strong political opposition to policies in support of working mothers, for example through child-care centres. The private notion of citizenship focusing on freedom from state intervention has impeded women's autonomy in the family. Until recently, there has been a remarkable political consensus about the necessity of leaving the responsibility for children to parents which contrasts with the strong political struggle about nationalization of industries between right and left.

During the latest twenty years, established social rights have increasingly come under strong pressure from neoconservative political forces, especially in relation to education and health care. At the same time neoliberal economic policies of privatization have substantially weakened the established social rights of citizens. The perception of a relatively passive state in times of mass unemployment has generally been a problem for weak groups, and it has increased the general problems of families, children, and indeed lone parents, through marginalization and poverty.

Shifts in gender relations

During the last twenty years women's participation in the labour market has increased, and it is remarkable that there are still no child-care centres to help working women take care of their children. This raises the question why Britain

never succeeded in developing public child-care policies. Lovenduski and
Randall (1993: 286) are not satisfied with the usual reference to the liberal
family tradition of non-intervention. They emphasize that the political–
ideological climate since World War II has strengthened the liberal vision of
the family. In addition they point to other factors, like the lack of a public
institution to oversee child-care, and more interestingly to a split in the
feminist discourse on the role of the state in child-care.

Lovenduski and Randall (1993: 266–69) discuss the contradictory effects of
family policy under Mrs Thatcher. On the one hand Thatcher intervened in the
family to support traditional family values. An example of this is the 1991
Child Support Act, which sought to compel absent fathers to contribute to the
upkeep of their children. On the other hand, the Government formulated
policies that were much less dogmatic, like the 1987 Family Law Reform Act,
aimed at eliminating the legal disadvantages associated with illegitimacy, and
the Children Act.

The dominant liberal values of non-intervention in family matters were
seriously challenged by the 1994 Report from the Commission of Social Justice.[7]
The report introduced a radical programme for social and economic reforms
that represents a political alternative to both the passive (welfare) state and the
male breadwinner model (Sassoon 1996). The report became an inspiration for
Labour's political debate about a renewal of the British welfare state and about
the need for an active welfare state that combines individual responsibility with
collective solidarity. The vision is to prevent poverty through public policies
that enable citizens to combine life-long education with paid employment and
care for the weakest social groups (*Social Justice* 1994: 223).

In terms of political citizenship, women have increased their participation in
politics and today there are only small differences in women's and men's
participation on the mass level (Parry *et al.* 1991). The problem has been how to
transform women's influence on the local level, in voluntary organizations and
on the grass roots level to an influence on national policies. Feminist scholars
have suggested that there is a strong masculinity in the British labour
movement, which has contributed to the exclusion of women from political
institutions. During the 1980s feminists have increasingly attempted to
influence the Labour Party, and during the 1990s, there has been a widespread
acceptance of quotas for women in Labour Party (Lovenduski and Randall
1993: 141–42). However, in 1992 only 13 per cent of Labour MPs in the
British parliament were women, and in the same election the gender gap re-
emerged among women over 35 years old, who voted Conservative in a
significant greater proportion than men (Lovenduski and Randall 1993: 157).
The results from the last elections (in May 1997) indicate that Labour is
changing its image among the electorate, and today 25 per cent of the new
Labour group in Parliament are women.

Political and cultural support for the principle of cultural diversity and
pluralism can be interpreted as a potential for the self-organization of citizens
that has strengthened women's abilities to influence the local welfare state,

although there has been no spill-over effect to women's influence on the central state. In contrast, political cultural norms and values advocating a separation between the public and the private sphere can be interpreted as an institutional and cultural barrier for further progress in women's material welfare. The conclusion is that during the last 20 years state welfare programmes have not substantially improved the social and economic situation for ordinary women. Women have gradually increased their paid employment, but many work part-time or for low wages, and there has been no substantial improvement of crèche provisions or maternity leave. Women have not done well either in terms of welfare or in terms of political influence and power. The strategy of the New Labour government towards a more active state will undoubtedly help working mothers, but it will also strengthen the tendency to treat lone mothers as workers (Lewis 1997).

Gender and citizenship in France

France is a combination of an active model for citizenship, where citizens have fought for political rights 'from below' through a revolution, and a political culture with a strong emphasis on the public sphere and on public virtues. The French republican model attaches high value to political equality as well as to solidarity/brotherhood and collective responsibilities of citizens (Jenson and Sineau 1994). The French state is an active, centralized state with the objective to regulate both the economy and the family. Public policies have been described as 'socialism from above', because the state has collectivized social problems and social costs with the help of 'insurance technologies' (Schmied 1995).

The universalism in French political culture has proved to be a strong institutional and cultural barrier for the development of voluntary political organizations and independent organizations in civil society (Rosenvallon 1992). The separation in the republican discourse of public and private has, in practice, often led to a subordination of interests of individual citizens and organizations under the abstract common good, and it has made it difficult to legitimize the vision of cultural and political diversity. Rosenvallon (1992: 83) has pointed to a split in the political culture between a universal vision of radical political equality and an emphasis on women's difference from men in the family. He suggests that the French model of political citizenship based on abstract individualism could explain why French women got the vote very late compared to British women. The Anglo-Saxon model of citizenship, based on interest representation, emphasized women's difference as the basis for their citizenship. When women finally gained the right to vote in France (in 1945), it was in connection with their activities and work during World War II.

The French vision of republican motherhood, which has historically been influenced both by the Catholic ideal of the virtuous mother and by the socialist ideal of working mothers, can be seen both as offering potential for, and as a barrier to, the advancement of women's rights. France has historically adopted a nationalist population and family policy that has given women social rights as mothers long before they obtained fundamental civil and political rights. During the 1930s, there were disagreements about family policies not only between women's organizations and political men, but also between Christian feminist organizations, like the *Union Féminine Civic et Sociale* (UFCS), and the feminist organizations such as the *Union pour le Suffrage de Femmes*. In 1938 the French government introduced an additional family allowance as a supplement for unwed mothers (*allocation pour la mère au foyer*) with the support of the UFCS. The adoption of the new social rights of mothers contrasted with the backlash against married women's employment in the 1930s. Pedersen (1993: 265) concludes that 'motherhood was to be "endowed" but women's choice to participate in the new state project was to be simultaneously curtailed'.

Modern feminist scholars disagree about the interpretation of French family policies and their implications for women. Some emphasize the positive implications of French family policy during the Fourth Republic (1946–58) when it was generally taken for granted that women as mothers, whether married or single, would receive government assistance through an elaborate system of family benefits (Offen 1991: 151). The politics of motherhood resulted in the adoption of a medical parcel that included a full-scale system of state-supported maternity allowance paid to women themselves, as well as free maternity care. There is no doubting the substantial economic importance of financial support in maternity and family allowances for poor women. However, other feminists point out that there was an underlying contradiction between the Constitution of 1946 that guaranteed the individual right to employment and the French Civil Code that strongly supported a male breadwinner model in which the wife was assumed to stay at home with three or more children. Consequently, public policies tended to support women as workers and mothers, but at the same time married women's legal dependency on their husbands did not change substantially until the introduction of new family laws in the 1970s (Offen 1991: 150).

Shifts in gender relations

Lewis and Ostner (1994) have characterized France as a medium breadwinner model, because social policies have, since the 1970s, supported women's dual position as mothers and workers. It can be argued that Mitterand's Presidency in many ways represents a shift in the dominant discourse about gender and citizenship. Jenson and Sineau (1994) analysed the new discourse about state feminism introduced by Mitterand as part of his policies aimed at modernizing French society. They show that from the beginning of his presidency (1981–94), public policies consciously tried to strengthen women's position in the labour market through equality policies to support their roles as working mothers. Policies to expand child-care centres were combined with relatively generous benefits for families with children.

As a result, French policies toward married women and the family have been modernised, and today French women have gained full formal civil and political rights. In terms of social rights and equality between men and women in the labour market the situation is ambiguous and feminist scholars have contrasting interpretations of the French case. The American historian Offen (1991: 153) is extremely positive toward the French state which she describes as a 'mother-state' (*état-mère-de famille*) where women have finally achieved 'equality in difference'. This point of view can be supported by the fact that, in terms of women's labour market participation, France is today the country in the European Union that most resembles Denmark (Hantrais 1993).

Jenson and Sineau are more sceptical about the effect of public policies. They discuss the rather advanced discourse of state feminism introduced by Mitterand, but their evaluation of the outcomes indicates that the ambitious policies failed. Women have obtained access to formal civil rights, but women's position in the labour market has not improved in relation to men's. The right to abortion is still threatened, plans for the creation of 300,000 new places in day care centres were forgotten, and finally, there has not been any real progress regarding women's political presence and power. They conclude that the strategy of state feminism 'from above' has failed. They suggest an alternative strategy to influence public policies based on women's presence at the political level. Furthermore, they argue that, especially in periods of economic recession, labour market policies have serious implications for women. Finally, they hold that the right to abortion ought to be perceived as a fundamental civil right (Jenson and Sineau 1994: 341–43).

To conclude, there is a contradiction in France between women's welfare and women's political presence. I suggest that the strong emphasis on the 'public good' has been a potential for social policies supporting working mothers, but the political élite has, throughout history, subordinated women's civic, social and political rights to national needs. Political institutions represent a separate barrier for the advancement of political equality between women and men. Women are still marginalized politically, and proposals to improve women's political representation through quotas for women in Parliament have been declared unconstitutional by the Constitutional Council (Jenson and Sineau 1994). The result is a growing gap between women's empowerment in their daily lives as workers and mothers and their lack of political representation, influence and power. During the last elections (in June 1997) there was a growing awareness of women's under-representation and the number of women representatives in the National Assembly increased for the first time in many years from 6 to 12 per cent. It is, however, too early to say to what extent this is the beginning of a change in French political culture.[8]

Gender, citizenship and the transition of European welfare states

There is a need for a comparative framework of citizenship that analyses the dynamic interrelation between the civil, political and social aspects of citizenship from a gender perspective. The cases illustrate that Denmark, Britain and France represent different principles, norms and visions about private and public virtues as well as different institutional practices that rest on gendered assumptions and have gendered implications. The different dynamics between women's social rights and political participation in the three cases indicate that there is no determination between the evolution of women's social rights and their political participation.

This chapter suggests that the shifts in gender relations in European welfare states during the last 20 years have deep-going implications for women's citizenship. In Denmark, universal social policies have been the basis for the expansion of women's social rights, and the active perception of citizenship has stimulated women's political participation. The question is what difference women's political presence will make for the transition of the Danish welfare state and for democracy? To what extent do women, as some feminists believe, have potential, as newcomers, to change the political agenda and public institutions, and to what extent will political institutions change women? Will women be able to develop a common vision on the transition of the welfare state, or will there be a growing polarization among educated/employed and unskilled marginalized women in the labour market and in politics?

Britain developed a universal welfare state, in terms of health and education, relatively early, and it is interesting to question why social policies in Britain and Denmark have developed in a completely different direction since 1960. Why did Britain move so strongly in the direction of a liberal welfare state and Denmark in the direction of a universal welfare state during the last 20 years in which both have been hit by mass unemployment and influenced by Conservative governments? And what has been the role of the Labour Party and of women's organizations?

In the British case, the passive discourse of citizenship and the strong ideology of individual self-determination, advocated by both Conservatives and Labour, has been the basis for a politics of non-intervention in family life that has been harmful for all women, especially for non-privileged women from marginalized social groups. The policies of Thatcherism have been ambivalent towards gender and the family. During the 1980s and 1990s women have increasingly become integrated as salaried workers and their unemployment has actually been lower than men's. At the same time poverty, marginalization and exclusion of large groups of unskilled women and men, including single parents, has grown. One important challenge is therefore to introduce state welfare provisions, including social services for children and families, that will improve the situation of poor women and working mothers. The Labour Party recently introduced a notion of an active state to support working women. In addition, a notion of active citizenship has been developed that includes women, and the Labour Party is in the process of changing its male image to convince women to support their policies.

In the French case, the republican discourse and the political élite have supported active citizenship and public regulation of family life. During the

Fifth Republic, public policies gave working women, including single mothers, relatively strong opportunities for self-reliance. During Mitterand's presidency public policies were modernized by ambitious programmes for gender equality in the labour market. State feminism has increased women's position in the state apparatus. However, the strong republican tradition of universal public values and the fear of a fragmentation of the 'common good' has made it difficult for women, as well as for marginalized social groups, to organize separately and to gain a presence 'as women' in political institutions. Today it is a challenge for women to increase their presence in the public arena through political organization with the objective to gain political equality, influence and power.

In terms of social citizenship, the move toward a dual breadwinner norm is most advanced in the Danish case, while Britain is the laggard. Conservative governments have been ambivalent towards a modernization of family and social policy. Women's paid employment has increased, but there has been no real expansion of social service provisions for working mothers. Recently, the Labour government has introduced a new vision on social politics intended to help working women by expanding public services but it is not yet clear what the policies towards single mothers will involve.

In terms of political citizenship, there has been a general tendency towards a more active citizenship for women. Women have increased their political participation in modern democracies, and they have gradually moved from the Right to the Left. The changes toward an active citizenship for women are most visible in Denmark, where women's political representation has increased dramatically since the 1980s to 37 per cent in the last elections in 1998. The British discourse on women and politics is also changing, and the new Labour government is committed to advancing women's presence and power in the political élite. In terms of political presence and power for women, France is still the laggard, in spite of recent changes in French politics.

Notes

1 This chapter is a revised version of a paper presented in the workshop: 'Citizenship and the Transition of European (Welfare) States', the ECPR Joint Session of Workshops in Bern, February 27–March 4, 1997, and discussed at the second seminar of the thematic network: 'Gender and Citizenship: Social Integration and Social Exclusion in the European Welfare States', at Turino University, April 4–6 1997. I want to thank participants in the two workshops for stimulating discussions and useful comments, especially Selma Sevenhuijsen, Giovanna Zinkone and Jet Bussemaker. The original paper is published in the Scientific Report from the seminar: 'The Causes of Women's Oppression; Actors, Processes and Institutions', Aalborg University, 1997.

2 In my definition of discourse I am inspired by Nancy Fraser's distinction between the discursive and practical dimensions of social welfare programmes. Fraser defines the discursive or ideological dimension 'as the tacit norms and implicit assumptions that are constitutive of practice' (Fraser 1989: 146).

3 In some countries, like France, women combine high activity rates on the labour market with low representation in politics. In other countries women combine

relatively high representation in politics, like in Norway in the 1970s (and The Netherlands in the 1990s) with a relative low activity rate for married women on the labour market (Leira 1992).

4   One example is the unique alliance between women in the trade union movement and women in the Women's Rights Organization (*Dansk Kvindesamfund*) that prevented attempts to adopt proposals to limit married women's waged work during the 1930s. Alliances between women may also explain why protective legislation in the form of a prohibition on night work for adult women was never adopted in Denmark (Ravn 1995).

5   Results from the Danish Investigation of Citizenship show that in spite of a general tendency towards homogenization in political values, there is a growing polarization in the values of young citizens in the sense that young women tend to be more positive towards the welfare state than young men. This can be interpreted as a growing split between women's solidaristic values and men's liberal values, or as a split between new forms of collectivism and individualism (see Christensen 1997).

6   There is an interesting debate about the role of women's agency in the building of the British welfare state. Lewis (1994) is sceptical of women's influence, arguing that women have played little part in the construction of the core elements of the British welfare state. Thane is more positive about women's role in influencing social policies, and she stresses that women had a share of the making of the post-World War II British welfare state through their activities in the Labour Party (Thane 1993: 351).

7   The Commission of Social Justice was set up by the Labour Party in 1992 with the goal of analysing the need for economic and social reforms in the UK. The analysis was carried out by a group of independent experts from the 'Institute for Public Policy Research', an independent think tank Left of the Centre (*Social Justice* 1994: preface).

8   The Socialist Party, which won a majority in the new National Assembly with the Green party and the Communists, adopted a quota of 30 per cent of women candidates, and as a result 17 per cent of the elected representatives for the Socialist Party are women.

Bibliography

Andersen, B. R. (1993) 'The Nordic welfare state under pressure: the Danish experience', *Policy and Politics* 21, 2: 109–21.

Andersen, J., Christensen, A. D., Langberg, K., Siim, B. and Torpe, L. (1993) *Medborgerskab. Demokrati og politisk deltagelse*, Herning: Systime.

Andersen, J. and Torpe, L. (eds) (1994) *Medborgerskab og politisk kultur*, Herning: Systime.

Bergquist, C. (1994) *Mäns makt och kvinnors intressen*, Uppsala: Acta Universitatis Upsaliensis.

Bock, G. and Thane, P. (eds) (1991) *Maternity & Gender Policies. Women and the Rise of European Welfare States 1880s–1950s*, New York/London: Routledge.

Borchorst, A. (1997) *State of Art Study of Research on Women in Political Decision-making*. GEP Working Paper no 2, Aalborg: Aalborg University.

Christensen, A. (1997) 'De politisk–kulturelle betydninger af køn', in A. D. Christensen, A. B. Ravn and I. Rittenhofer (eds) *Det kønnede Samfund*, Aalborg: Aalborg Universitetsforlag.

Finneman, N. O. (1985) *I broderskabets ånd. Den socialdemokratiske arbejderbevægelses idéhistorie 1871–1977*, København: Gyldendal.

Fraser, N. (1989) *Unruly Practices: Power, Discourse and Gender in Contemporary Social Theory*, Minneapolis: University of Minnesota Press.

Hantrais, L. (1993) 'Les francaises et l'émploi. Portrait type ou prototype européen?' in *Femmes et Historie*, Paris: Plon.

Hernes H. (1987) *Welfare State and Women Power*, Oslo: Norwegian University Press.

—— (1988) 'Scandinavian Citizenship', *Acta Sociologica* 31, 3: 199–215.

Hirdman Y .(1990) 'Genussystemet', in *Demokrati och Makt i Sverige*, Maktudredningen huvudrapport, SOU 44.

Jenson, J. and Sineau, M. (1994) *Mitterand et les Françaises. Un rendez-vous manqué*, Paris: Presse de Science PO.

Knijn, T. and Kremer, M. (1997) 'Gender and the Caring Dimension of Welfare States', *Social Politics. International Studies in Gender State and Society* 4, 3: 328–62.

Kolstrup, S. (1997) 'Fra kommunesocialisme til velfærdsstat', *Social Kritik* 49: 5–21.

Koven, S. and Michel, S. (1993) 'Introduction', in S. Koven and S. Michel (eds) *Mothers of a New World. Maternalist Politics and the Origin of Welfare States*, New York/London: Routledge.

Kymlicka, W. (1990) *Contemporary Political Philosophy*, Oxford: Clarendon Press.

Landes, J. (1988) *Women and the Public Sphere in the Age of the French Revolution*, Cornell: Cornell University Press.

Leira A. (1992) *Models of Motherhood. Welfare State Policy and Scandinavian Experiences of Everyday Practices*, Cambridge: Cambridge University Press.

Lewis, J. (1994) 'Gender, the Family and women's agency in the building of welfare states: The British case', *Social History* 19, 1: 37–55.

—— (ed.) (1997) *Lone Mothers in European Welfare Regimes. Shifting Policy Logics*, London: Jessica Kingsley Publ.

Lewis, J. and Ostner, I. (1994) *Gender and the Evolution of European Social Policies*, Bremen: Zentrum für Sozialpolitik, Arbeitspapier, No. 4/ 94.

Lister, R. (1995) 'Dilemmas in engendering citizenship', *Economy and Society* 24, 1: 1–40.

Lovenduski, J. and Randall, V. (1993) *Contemporary Feminist Politics. Women and Power in Britain*, Oxford: Oxford University Press.

Marshall, T. H. (1992) 'Citizenship and social class' (originally published in 1950), in T. H. Marshall and T. Bottomore (eds) *Citizenship and Social Class*, London: Pluto Press.

Nielsen, H. K. (1992) *Demokrati i bevægelse. Sammenlignende studier af politisk kultur og nye sociale bevægelser i Vesttyskland og Danmark*, Aarhus: Aarhus Universitetsforlag.

Offen, K. (1991) 'Body politics: women, work and the politics of motherhood in France 1920–1950', in G. Bock and P. Thane (eds) *Maternity & Gender Policies. Women and the Rise of European Welfare States 1880s–1950s*, New York/London: Routledge.

Orloff, A. (1993) *Gender and the Social Rights of Citizenship: The Comparative Analysis of Gender relations and the Welfare States*. IRP Reprint Series, Madison: University of Madison.

Østergård, U. (1991) *Europas ansigter. Nationale stater i en ny og gammel verden*, Copenhagen: Rosinante.

Parry, G., Moyser, G. and Day, N. (1991) *Political Participation and Democracy in Britain*, Cambridge: Cambridge University Press.

Pateman, C. (1988) *The Sexual Contract*, Stanford: Stanford University Press.

—— (1992) 'Equality, difference and subordination: the politics of motherhood and women's citizenship', in G. Bock and S. James (eds) *Beyond Equality and Difference*.

Citizenship, Feminist Politics and Female Subjectivity, London/New York: Routledge.

Pedersen, S. (1993) 'Catholicism, feminism and the politics of the family during the late Third Republic', in S. Koven and S. Michel (eds) *Mothers of a New World. Maternalist Politics and the Origin of Welfare States*, New York/London: Routledge.

Phillips, A. (1993) *Democracy and Difference*, London: Polity Press.

—— (1995) *The Politics of Presence*, London: Polity Press.

Ravn, A. (1995) 'Discourses of gender and work. the Danish case', paper to the First German–Nordic Conference on Gender and History. Construction of Gender in the Long Nineteenth Century: German–Nordic Comparisons, Stockholm 21–4, 1996.

Rosenbeck, B. (1989) *Kvindekøn. Den moderne kvindeligheds historie 1880–1940*, Copenhagen: Gyldendal.

Rosenvallon, P. (1992) *Le Sacre du Citoyen. Historie du Suffrage Universel en France*, Paris: Gallimard.

Sarvasy, W. and Siim, B. (eds) (1994) 'Introduction', in *Social Politics. International Studies in Gender, State and Society* 1, 3: 249–55.

Sassoon, A. S. (1996) 'Beyond pessimism of the intellect: agendas for social justice and change', in M. Perriman (ed.) *The Blair Agenda*, London: Laurence & Wishart.

Schmied, H. (1995) 'Velfærdsstatens solidaritetsformer', *Dansk Sociologi* 3: 30–54.

Siim B. (1988) 'Towards a feminist rethinking of the welfare state', in K. Jones and A. Jonasdottir (eds) *The Political Interests of Women. Developing Theory and Research with a Feminist Face*, London: Sage.

—— (1994) 'Engendering democracy – the interplay between citizenship and political participation', *Social Politics. International Studies in Gender, State and Society* 1, 3, 1994: 286–306.

—— (1997) 'The dilemmas of citizenship in Denmark: lone mothers between work and care', in J. Lewis (ed.) *Lone Mothers in European Welfare Regimes*, London: Jessica Kingsley Pub.

—— (1998) 'Vocabularies of citizenship and gender: the Danish case', *Critical Social Policy* 18, 3: 375–96.

Sineau, M. (1992) 'Droits et democratie', in G. Duby and M. Perrot (eds) *Histoire des Femmes en Occident, le XX Siecle*, Paris: Plon.

Social Justice. Strategies for National Renewal (1994) *The Report of the Commission on Social Justice*, London: Vintage.

Thane, P. (1991) 'Visions of gender in the making of the British welfare state', in G. Bock and P. Thane (eds) *Maternity and Gender Policies. Women and the Rise of European Welfare States 1880s–1950s*, New York/London: Routledge.

—— (1993) 'Women in the British Labour Party and the construction of the welfare state 1906–1939', in S. Koven and S. Michel (eds) *Mothers of a New World. Maternalist Politics and the Origin of Welfare States*, New York/London: Routledge.

Turner, B. (1992) 'Outline of a Theory of Citizenship', in C. Mouffe (ed.) *Dimensions of Radical Democracy. Pluralism. Citizenship and Community*, London: Verso.

Walby, S. (1994) 'Is citizenship gendered?', *Sociology* 28, 2: 379–95.

Young, I. M. (1990) *Justice and the Politics of Difference*. Princeton: Princeton University Press.

Yuval-Davis, N. (1996) 'Women, citizenship and difference – citizenship as a multitier construct'. Working Paper, London: Greenwich University.

7 The heterogeneity of Spanish social citizenship

Elisa Chuliá and Berta Álvarez-Miranda[1]

Introduction

In Spain, the public debate on reform of the Spanish welfare state gathered momentum approximately one decade later than in neighbouring European countries. In the mid-1970s, when other Western countries were confronting the need for cutting back on social welfare as a result of the world economic recession caused by the oil crisis, Spain was dealing with a far more pressing problem: the transition to democracy from the authoritarian regime set up some 40 years before.

However, the difference between Spain and her neighbours as regards the debate on the welfare state was not only one of priorities but of objectives. While western European countries had entered the 1970s with powerful, comprehensive welfare states, Spain was emerging from the Franco regime with a far less well-developed public system of social protection. Economic benefits were provided for fewer members of the population and they were less generous, while social services were either ineffective or non-existent, as well as being somewhat discredited. In 1975, public social expenditure came to a little more than 13 per cent of GDP, while average spending in the European Community was around 24 per cent.

Taking European countries as their political model, and seeking to legitimate the new democratic regime, the first governments to emerge from the general elections of 1977 and 1979 decided to increase the funds allocated from the budget to cover social benefits. This strategy, together with the rapid rise in unemployment, which went up from 5 per cent in 1975 to 17 per cent in 1982, led to an enormous increase in state social spending. Between 1975 and 1982, state transfers in social benefits rose from 9 per cent to 14 per cent of GDP and social expenditure, which had been below 15 per cent, rose to almost 22 per cent (*Papeles de Economía Española* 1988: 26–7).

In 1985, the Socialist government of Felipe González approved the first restrictive reform of social benefits since the establishment of democracy. This entailed a reduction in state pensions for new pensioners. Since then, with the ups and downs typical of the political cycle, and the intermittent scrutiny of public opinion concerned mainly with the persistent problems of Basque separatist terrorism and unemployment, the subject of the financial viability of the welfare state has not ceased to be a constant in Spanish political and academic debate.

The concept of social citizenship, as defined by T. H. Marshall, has had little impact on the Spanish welfare reform debate. In the discourse of those who support the maintenance of public social protection, arguments of 'solidarity' or 'distributive justice' have been far more plentiful than justifications based on the 'social rights' that adhere to the individual as a citizen of a democratic community.

Workers rather than citizens

There are historical–political and institutional reasons which explain why, in this debate, cuts in benefits are not related to a diminution of citizenship or, in other words, to an impairment of the capacity to take decisions on matters of interest to the political community of which one is a member. In effect, the nature of the political regimes which laid the foundations for the construction of a public system of social protection and the model of the welfare state which was created were essentially incompatible with a discourse which emphasized the capacity of citizens to exercise their rights, individually and collectively, in defiance of the public powers.

The Spanish welfare state is the result of a long historical process in which we can identify three principal phases. The initial impetus (the phase of creation) occurred in the early decades of the twentieth century when state agencies were set up for the purpose of promoting social insurance, and the first legal measures for worker protection were approved. The second major development (the phase of institutionalization) took place in the 1950s and 1960s and led to the creation of the social security system. The most recent advance (the phase of intensification) came after democracy was established and coincided with a rapid increase in social spending by the state at a time when, in other countries, spending tended to remain stable or had already been cut back.

The earlier phases took place under different kinds of political regime: the first was presided over by a formal parliamentary democracy (the system of the Restoration) which manipulated the electoral results for the benefit of the political élite; the second occurred under a dictatorship. However, in both systems the rulers enjoyed wide margins of independence in relation to the population. As a result, the measures for social protection taken during these two phases did not correspond to social demand or to any wish to empower citizens.

The social policy designed in the early years of the century, which resulted in the so called *Seguro Obrero Obligatorio* (compulsory worker insurance) and voluntary insurance subsidized by the state, materialized out of the ambition of the political élites of the Restoration to put into practice in Spain the new ideas which were already fashionable in other European countries. These were ideas promoting the achievement of social harmony through reform 'from above' (Guillén 1990). In contrast, social policies under Francoism amounted to little more than a strategy to appease the population in general, and the working class in particular. It was hoped there would be acquiescent behaviour in return for public order and social benefits. The recipients of social benefits were not known as users, but as 'beneficiaries' because, in line with public discourse, they 'benefited' from the generosity of the regime. Although the term 'social rights' could be heard in discourse from time to time, it was unconnected to any concept of citizenship. It could hardly have been otherwise in a political system that did not recognize political rights and arbitrarily limited civil rights.[2]

However, neither was this concept in frequent use during the transition to democracy. The political programmes of the parties which called themselves 'progressive' (that is, the Socialist and the Communist Parties) approached the question of the welfare state with a rhetoric that emphasized more the defence of workers, who apparently had been the most disfavoured part of society during Francoism, than from any claims for democratic citizenship. Perhaps this was because if they linked public social services and benefits to the condition of citizenship, the politicians of the transition would have had to acknowledge some effort on the part of the preceding regime to endow Spaniards with that condition.

To these historical–political reasons must be added another, of an institutional nature, which also served to obscure an examination of the Spanish welfare state from a Marshallian point of view. The system inherited by the politicians of the transition had been consolidated as a professionalized system which established a clear distinction not only between workers and non-workers, but also between workers themselves. The system distinguished six kinds of workers' regimes (one general regime and five special regimes for farmers, seamen, miners, self-employed and home employees) plus the specific regime for public officials, each with different rates of social security contributions and different social benefits. The fragmentation and discrimination implicit in the system necessarily hampered public discourse based on the concept of citizenship which, it is clear, is grounded in the idea of universality and equal treatment.

It is true that Social Security appears under the first Title headed 'On fundamental rights and duties' in the Constitution of 1978. However, it is significant that the corresponding Article was not included in the chapter on 'Rights and freedoms' but in the one entitled 'On the guiding principles of social and economic policy'.

Curiously enough, the text of the afore-mentioned Article seems to indicate the intention of the fathers of the Constitution to move in the direction of a system of universal social protection based on citizenship: 'The public powers will maintain a public regime of Social Security for all citizens . . .'. None the less, this prescription has not been fulfilled. At present, recipients of economic benefits from the welfare state are basically workers in the legal sector of the economy[3] who are eligible for unemployment benefits and contributive retirement pensions. The introduction of non-contributory benefits in 1991, which provide for the retired, the unemployed and invalids living below a minimum level of subsistence, has attempted to mitigate the non-existence of a national system of minimum income. However, the amounts involved are very small and this coverage is used increasingly for workers who do not meet the minimum legal requirements in order to obtain unemployment benefit or a contributive pension.

In short, the public system of economic benefits revolves around the worker. As regards the health and social services, the situation is different. Since the *Sistema Nacional de Salud* (National Health System) was set up in 1986, health care has been universal; and even prior to that date, the public health service offered care to over 85 per cent of the Spanish population, which had been progressively incorporated in their capacity as relatives dependent upon the worker (Freire 1993: 86).

The social services, on the other hand, are the weakest element of the Spanish welfare state. To a paucity of programmes must be added the lack of resources necessary to make them accessible to all applicants. This means that, although all those who wish to apply for them may do so, the supply of public services is so inadequate that it is impossible to talk of universally available benefits. Furthermore, inequalities are produced among recipients because of the complexity of the organizational design in which three administrative levels are involved: the central state, the autonomous communities (regional units with political and administrative competence) and the municipalities.

In summary, if we leave aside the question of education and concentrate on the main programmes of the Spanish welfare state, we must conclude that their 'target' has been the working population. The incorporation of the non-working population into the state system of social protection has occurred formally and informally through the family. Thus, in the case of health care, non-workers were legally included in the public system as dependants of the entitled person, that is the worker. On the other hand, in the case of economic benefits, which the state transfers to the individuals, the family operates in fact as the addressee, inasmuch as it constitutes the unit which assigns among its members these public resources.

The family plays an essential role in the welfare of the Spanish citizen, a role that appears to be acknowledged by the Constitution when it attributes the duty of ensuring social protection of the family to the public powers. Given that Spain is, at present, the European country in which families receive least support from the state as regards child care, this constitutional mandate for the social protection of the family cannot be interpreted in a strict or limited sense. Rather, it should be understood as an express commitment to the maintenance of an institution which, as well as contributing to finance the welfare state, compensates for some of the latter's deficiencies in the redistribution of income, the search for employment and the provision of personal care.

The family and welfare in Spain

In the most recent bibliography on welfare states in western Europe, there seems to be a consensus regarding a peculiarity of the countries which make up the 'Latin rim'. This peculiarity resides not only in the fact that all these countries were latecomers to developing systems of social protection, but that their systems share particular institutional characteristics (Rhodes 1996). The series of features which define the welfare states of Italy, Spain, Portugal and Greece would justify their interpretation as belonging to a model different from the three dominant models in the European sphere, that is, the liberal–Anglo-Saxon model, the corporatist–continental model and the social democratic–Scandinavian model (Esping-Andersen 1990). In comparison with these classic regimes, the southern European model is characterized by comparatively moderate levels of social expenditure by the state,[4] the implementation of systems of contributive income maintenance which are conspicuous for their relative generosity in terms of the high substitution rate between the last salary and the amount of the pension or unemployment benefit, the asymmetric development of economic benefits and social services favourable to the former, and the importance of informal mechanisms of solidarity to the supply of social benefits.

As regards the latter characteristic, it has also been observed that the family is pivotal to those forms of solidarity not subject to, or regulated by, public procedures. The family constitutes a key component of the welfare mix observable in the societies of southern Europe. Its strength lies in cultural traditions reinforced by institutional factors. In fact, the very configuration of welfare states in southern Europe, which protect some sectors of the population to the detriment of others, which lack a universal system of minimum incomes, and which have never fully developed the social assistance dimension, has allowed families to maintain their prominence within these systems.

In the Spanish case, it has been observed that the family shares out the economic resources forthcoming from different sources in order to avoid any one member suffering extreme hardship. A family's economic resources are primarily income from the labour market and the welfare state.

The Spanish labour market provides employment for approximately four fifths of its citizens who claim to want to work. The remaining 20 per cent have to get by on social benefits, resort to the underground economy or turn to their family for help (Pérez-Díaz and Rodríguez 1995). The welfare state, for its part, takes very good care of those who have retired from the labour market through old age (that is, pensioners) and approximately half of the unemployed.

The most vulnerable are, therefore, the unemployed who are not eligible for social benefits, and the majority of this group is made up of young people. On the one hand, they have the highest rate of unemployment of any age group: among Spaniards aged between 15 and 24, 37 per cent of men and 48 per cent of women were unemployed in 1996 (Eurostat 1997: 115). On the other, they suffer the consequences of a dualistic labour market which divides the working population into workers in secure employment, with contracts stipulating broad social rights, and young people taken on for short periods under less advantageous conditions. In effect, protection from unemployment is based on a prior working career. Those who have worked for a prolonged period (for longer than a year) have generated unemployment benefits proportional to their wages. Those who have worked for shorter periods get a far less generous unemployment 'subsidy'. Finally, those still in search of their first job are ineligible for any specific assistance although, in the last resort, they can apply for certain kinds of social wages from the autonomous communities.

Given that the labour market does not offer sufficient opportunities for all those seeking employment, and that those who profit most from the welfare state in its present form are pensioners, it is understandable that the elderly have proved an increasingly important source of economic assistance within the family in recent years. This circumstance has served to partially invert the relationship of support between generations of the same family.

Traditionally, as children grew up and found a job, economic help from their parents would gradually diminish until it practically ceased when they left their parents' home to set up their own home. Then, once this 'mitosis' of the family nucleus had been consolidated, working children would attend to their parents as they grew older, providing them with economic help and personal care if and when necessary. At present, however, the protection of the welfare state and the good health that many pensioners now enjoy in their old age have meant that the elderly have come to play a more active part in the social protection of the family. On the one hand, they often help their children by taking care of small grandchildren and by running errands that their children have no time for. According to data from a survey in the early 1990s, approximately half of elderly Spaniards look after their grandchildren (54 per cent) and/or help their children with other tasks (52 per cent) (Miguel 1994: 819–20).

On the other, it is no longer unusual for the elderly, many of whom have no financial commitments like mortgages because they already own their homes (Castles and Ferrera 1996), to provide their children with economic assistance. In a survey carried out in 1993, almost 22 per cent of those over 64 years of age said that they helped their children or some other family member financially (INSERSO 1995a). Two years later, another survey revealed that 20 per cent of pensioners (or spouses of pensioners) helped their children financially. The percentage of those who declared that they gave this assistance was slightly higher than the percentage who admitted to receiving financial help from their children (Herce and Pérez-Díaz 1996).

As a result, it would seem that the elderly were taking up the burden of assistance for their families if it were not for the fact that they are also, under certain circumstances, the recipients of essential family support for which the Spanish welfare state does not make adequate provision. In 1993 expenditure on social services through the *Instituto Nacional de Servicios Sociales*, the public institution depending on the central government which is in charge of offering care and entertainment programmes specially for old people, only represented under 3 per cent of the total social expenditure (CES 1994: 243). Thus, the care that parents receive from their children is crucial for them when their health or faculties begin to fail. Such care comprises mainly household tasks and personal hygiene, but may also involve keeping them company on a daily basis (INSERSO 1995a: 53–62).[5] Because of its routine nature, care of the elderly requires a regular effort; 85 per cent of the routine tasks have to be carried out every, or almost every, day; and almost three-quarters of them require a minimum of 3 hours work a day (INSERSO 1995b: 231–33).

It is obviously easier for children to provide their parents with the care they need if they live nearby. According to a survey in 1993, 26 per cent of those aged over 65 with children live in the same building as one of them; 28 per cent live in the same suburb or village; and an additional 25 per cent have at least one child living in the same city. Thus, approximately eight out of every ten elderly people with descendants, and six out of every ten elderly people, with or without descendants, can count on the presence of one or more children in the same district (Miguel 1994: 805).

Nevertheless, the burden of providing care is not shared equitably within families. To a large extent, it is women who attend to the elderly. The main burden of caring for elderly parents falls most heavily on daughters, particularly if they do not work outside the home.

In summary, young unemployed people and housewives are the two collectives that are least protected by the welfare state; a state which relies on family solidarity and sentiments of moral obligation towards parents in order to achieve levels of social welfare similar to those of other western countries with better developed public benefits. Precisely because the pillar of the family is so extraordinarily solid, Spanish politicians have enjoyed a certain latitude for reform of the welfare state with a view to improving economic competitiveness and European economic convergence.

Limited reform on the welfare state and recourse to private institutions

Reform of the welfare state has been gaining in importance in the Spanish public debate ever since the mid-1980s, in the midst of a generalized discourse, ongoing since the democratic transition, that has centred on achieving the Community average in levels of social expenditure and the quality of social services. In terms of public discourse, the cautious proposals for cutting back on some benefits have acquired high visibility in the media because of the electoral and union opposition which they have engendered. As a result, both the preceding socialist government as well as the present *Popular* government have tended to combine demands to limit spending on some specific aspects of their welfare policies with promises to maintain or increase their social policy in general. In terms of public policies, this strategy of expanding coverage and creating new programmes has been employed in combination with specific, limited cutbacks in other spheres of the welfare state.

Over the last two decades, social spending as a whole has followed an upward trend, with growth higher than the Community average. The socialist governments (1982–96) brought the Spanish welfare state closer to the universal model by introducing measures which extended the coverage of existing major policies and which developed assistencial service programmes. The *Partido Popular*, which has been in government since 1996, has tried to prove that the repeated accusations of neoliberalism made by the left in electoral campaigns throughout the 1990s are false, by promising to maintain and improve basic welfare programmes, and by being extremely cautious over their decisions to moderate costs.

As regards measures for extending coverage, since 1986 practically the whole of the population has finally been included in a single public health system. The period of compulsory education for young people in school has been extended in 1990 by raising the school-leaving age from 14 to 16 years of age. Also, reinforcement of the assistencial dimension of the welfare state, though modest, has broken the traditional mould of Spanish social policy, according to which access to social protection has always depended on access to work. The decisions to provide very low income families with non-contributory pensions in 1991, create regional programmes of social wages, and increase unemployment subsidy all work in this direction.

In addition to the extension of coverage and the creation of new programmes, social spending has tended to increase because of the more generous sums now paid out in some social transfers. For example, maternity benefit has increased from 75 to 100 per cent of wages, and the required contribution may now be made over a period of 5 years instead of one, which provides access to women in successive fixed-term jobs. Of greater impact is the cost generated by the annual indexation of pensions, which has remained constant (although since 1994 it has been linked to predicted inflation instead of the real inflation of the preceding year), while other European countries occasionally froze them.

Simultaneously, however, the governments of both parties have gradually been accumulating measures for reform which involve cutting costs, with the declared objective of guaranteeing the viability of social insurance in the long term, and reducing the public deficit in order to stabilize the Spanish economy and integrate it into the European Monetary Union. Successive reforms of the contributive pensions system, in 1985 and 1996, have tended to trim the rights of future pensioners while today's pensions continue to be indexed. The key component of the cuts is based on extending the contribution period included in the pension calculation, so that the early years in a job, in which salaries are generally lower, are included (and given more weight in the calculation formula): in 1985 this period was extended from 2 to 8 years, and in 1996 a step-by-step prolongation of up to 15 years was decided upon. This strategy of the progressive increase in the proportionality between salary and pension was consolidated in a pact signed by all political parties with parliamentary representation in 1995. One year later, the unions withdrew their former opposition to the reform and accepted its philosophy by joining in a pact with the government.

Contributive insurance against the risk of unemployment has also been cut back so that, since 1992, the contribution period necessary in order to claim unemployment benefit has been extended (to a year instead of 6 months) and the time for which it can be claimed, reduced (only one third of the working period instead of half, and up to a maximum of 2 years as before). At the same time, the proportion of salary to benefits in the first year, when insurance is more generous, was also reduced. Moreover, since 1994, unemployment transfers have been subject to tax.

In the field of health care, both the socialists and the *populares* have tried to limit the growing cost of subsidizing medicines prescribed by doctors in the public system at 60 per cent of the retail price for the majority of the population, 70 per cent for public officials and 100 per cent for pensioners (excluded retired public officials who pay 30 per cent of the price of the medications). The method selected by both parties in the mid-1990s, apart from negotiation with the pharmaceutical industry, was to exclude a list of medicines from state subsidies, while relinquishing other, even more politically conflictive proposals such as a flat payment of the cost per prescription.

The decisions taken as regards reform of the welfare state do not seem to bear much relation to the visibility which this matter has acquired in the public debate, particularly on the question of the future viability of the social security system (Herce and Pérez-Díaz 1995: 56–90; Pérez-Díaz *et al.* 1997: 13–24). The sensitivity of public opinion on this subject has changed it into an electoral issue of the first magnitude and given rise to political practices, such as the tendency to deny the problems or to criticize the restrictive solutions of successive governments from the opposition, that do nothing to enable a solution to problems of the design, management and financing of social policies to be found. The kind of debate that takes place in Spain on the subject of reform of the welfare state risks alarming the public without informing them in a reasoned manner, though it serves to alert them to the costs of the welfare state and the limits to its expansion.

At a time when Spaniards are becoming aware of the need for reform of the state welfare system, experience of the deficient quality in some spheres of the education and health services, uncertainty about the level of future retirement pensions, and the lack of social services, are leading families with the economic means to turn increasingly to private insurance and provision. According to business associations in this sector, growth in over the last few years has been remarkable, although private insurance is still not habitual and usually provides dual coverage rather than acting as an alternative resource. Between 1987, when private pension funds were regulated and granted tax incentives (which were later increased by the *Popular* government), and 1997, almost three and half million Spaniards (7 per cent of the whole population) had subscribed to a savings fund for their retirement. This last year, approximately six million Spanish citizens (15 per cent) were covered by private health insurance.

The people who resort to private welfare institutions demand not only better benefits, but also more capacity to choose differently from those in the public welfare system. They often circumvent this system because they want to be treated with celerity, and in an individualized and polite manner, as clients, not as users of 'public goods'. But the resource to private services is another source of distinction in the access to welfare benefits, which, added to the multifarious fragmentation implicit in the public system, explains the existence of a rather heterogeneous Spanish social citizenship.

Conclusions

The current debate on the reform of the welfare state is pervaded with objectives such as 'solidarity' with those in need, comprehensive but not necessarily homogeneous coverage, and some type of social justice in the distribution of income. These guiding principles, among others, seem to overlap, alternate or complement one another according to the argument, but are seldom clearly defined or prioritized. In any case, equality and solidarity have become keywords in this issue to a much greater extent than citizenship.

If the concept of social citizenship has not been heard more frequently in the debate on reforms of the welfare state in Spain, it is probably owing to the fact that social benefits have never been linked in either the public sphere or the collective imagination to the concepts of universality and democracy. It is true that, in recent years, some efforts have been made to move the Spanish welfare state in the direction of universalization. However, in the distribution of economic benefits, at which the welfare state is more effective, it continues to avoid the principle of basic homogeneity in its treatment of citizens because the whole system is based on employment and, moreover, distinguishes between numerous job variants.

Furthermore, given that the Franco regime always tried to maintain a high profile in social policy and championed worker protection, social rights have not been perceived as an intrinsic part of democracy. The idea of democracy is more closely related to the recuperation of the political rights that the Spanish population had been deprived of for 40 years, than with an improvement in the social rights that, though not well-developed quantitatively or qualitatively, they already enjoyed under the dictatorship.

It is, however, indisputable that democracy has brought with it a visible improvement in state social benefits. Likewise, it has entailed a significant change in thinking on the part of benefit recipients: they have gone from beneficiaries of services offered by a paternalistic state that avoided advertising the costs of protection, to being the users of a supply. Also as users, their opinion matters to governments and public administrations, above all because it can be reflected in the ballot box.

It is precisely this electoral dependence on matters relating to reform of the welfare state that constitutes an element favourable to maintaining the system in its present form. In effect, the question of pensions, which are the benefits that absorb most social resources (approximately 40 per cent of total social expenditure), has taken high priority in the elections during this decade. The political parties take good care of the electorate of approximately seven million people who draw state pensions. Their way of caring is to guarantee pensioners their purchasing power. Thus, instead of aspiring to introduce new claimants into the public system, politicians concentrate their efforts on reinforcing the protection of those already benefiting from it. In this way, the differences between the protected and the unprotected are accentuated and the heterogeneity of social citizenship consolidated.

We have identified several sources of heterogeneity in Spanish citizenship with regard to the welfare state. These begin with the legacy of the origins of Spanish social policy, conceived of as benefits which the state granted to industrial workers to increase their security against the risks of accident, sickness or old age. In accordance with this conception, this century has witnessed a progressive accumulation of different kinds of social insurance for different sectors and professions. Although all types of insurance were unified under a single Social Security in the 1960s, the fragmentation of the system and inequality of levels of protection were maintained, and even increased from that time on due to the inclusion of new professional regimes.

Nevertheless, in the last 25 years, we have witnessed an even greater cleavage deriving from that conception of social policy. To the extent that the active population increases, but the number of jobs does not, the obstacles to finding employment are becoming all but insuperable for younger Spaniards, and women of all ages, who are joining the labour market for the first time.

Though the main rationale of the Spanish welfare state is professional, the most recent reforms have tended to incorporate the remainder of the population by two very different means, which have also contributed to the heterogeneous situation of citizens. On the one hand, the health and education services have tended towards universalization, extending the coverage of what were originally more limited social programmes. On the other, programmes have been created that are means tested, that is, not open to all of those who wish to apply for them (or even those who do not, as in the case of education) but only open to the lowest income groups. Spaniards have access to state social protection through two different formal channels: work and level of income.

To these two formal access channels (to which, today, we could still add nationality) there is a third, more informal one that is particularly important in Spain: the family. The redistribution of economic resources, rights and care in the home is an extended, flexible form of support when facing up to the risk of illness, old age or unemployment. The adaptive capacity of Spanish families has been proven over the last two decades as the problem of unemployment and job insecurity has risen to previously inconceivable levels. The hard situation of young people in the labour market and, thus, in the welfare state, has led the older generations of the family to protect the younger ones. Young people now remain in the parental home for a longer period, postponing their emancipation until the age of 25–30. They find a remarkable number of jobs through family connections and, with increasing frequency, they receive economic help from the older members of their family.

Finally, recourse to private insurance is becoming increasingly common. However, although this component of the 'welfare mix' is growing in importance, private policy-holders are still in minority. The trend in recent years seems to indicate that there will be a progressive expansion in the role of private insurance companies, as policies promoting private insurance by means of tax deductions continue, and an increasing number of Spaniards subscribe to them.

In short, the relationship of Spanish citizens to their welfare state is not one of equality but of diversity. The heterogeneity of protective measures with which the welfare state has been burdened since its foundation has been maintained with few modifications even when, in the democratic period, specific measures of universalist nature have been superimposed. The diversity of the treatment accorded citizens by reason of their different job and income categories, that is especially evident in state economic benefits, leads to huge normative dispersion and excessive complexity in the legal regime of social security. On the other hand, it does, however, introduce elements of individual responsibility and personal choice that, in more egalitarian welfare regimes seem to be less present.

Likewise, the fragmentation of the system offers politicians wider margins for carrying out partial and, therefore, less costly reforms from a social and political perspective. This is a comparative advantage that Spanish politicians have over those of other countries in the European Union; an advantage that, depending on the objectives and criteria with which it is applied, may be differently judged.

Notes

1   This paper is linked with a research on the family and the welfare system in Spain under the direction of Professor Víctor Pérez-Díaz, head of the research institute Analistas Socio-Políticos (ASP). We wish to thank our colleagues for their useful comments.

2   The Franco regime did not adopt a more liberal policy on rights of association, information and religion until the 1960s. Only after the death of General Franco could free political parties and labour unions be erected.

3   The underground economy is a phenomenon of considerable importance in Spain. Although verifiable figures are lacking, it has been estimated that this sector may be generating wealth equivalent to one-quarter of GDP.

4   In 1994, total expenditure on social protection was 23.6 per cent of GDP in Spain, 25.8 per cent in Italy, 21.7 per cent in Portugal and 14.5 per cent in Greece. The European average was 29.1 per cent (Eurostat 1997: 243).

5   Old people's homes and home helps provided by social services make up a very small proportion of the total: at the beginning of the decade, fewer than 3 per cent of those over 65 lived in a home, compared to a European average of 5 per cent (Guillemard 1992: 37); home helps assisted 1 per cent of this population.

Bibliography

Castles, F. G. and Ferrera, M. (1996) 'Home ownership and the welfare state: is southern Europe different?', *South European Society & Politics* 1, 2: 163–85.

CES [Consejo Económico y Social] (1994) *España, 1993. Economía, Trabajo y Sociedad. Memoria Sobre la Situación Socioeconómica y Laboral.* Madrid: CES.

Esping-Andersen, G. (1990) *The Three Worlds of Welfare Capitalism.* Cambridge: Polity.

Eurostat (1997) *Anuario '97. Visión estadística sobre Europa 1986–1996.* Luxemburg: Eurostat.

Freire, J. M. (1993) 'Cobertura sanitaria y equidad en España', in *I Simposio Sobre Igualdad y Distribución de la Riqueza*, Madrid: Fundación Argentaria.

Guillemard, A. M. (1992) *Análisis de las Políticas de Vejez en Europa*, Madrid: INSERSO.

Guillén, A. M. (1990) 'The emergence of the Spanish welfare state: the role of ideas in the policy process', *International Journal of Political Economy* 20, 2: 82–96.

Herce, J. A. and Pérez-Díaz, V. (1996) *The Reform of the Spanish Public Pensions System.* Barcelona: La Caixa.

INSERSO (1995a) *Las Personas Mayores en España. Perfiles. Reciprocidad Familiar*, Madrid: Ministerio de Asuntos Sociales.

INSERSO (1995b) *Cuidados en la Vejez. El Apoyo Informal*, Madrid: Ministerio de Asuntos Sociales.

Miguel, A. de (1994) *La Sociedad Española, 1993–94.* Madrid: Alianza Editorial.

Papeles de Economía Española 37 (1988).

Pérez-Díaz, V. and Rodríguez, J. C. (1995) 'Inertial choices: an overview of Spanish human resources, practices and policies', in R. Locke, T. Kochan and M. Piore (eds), *Employment Relations in a Changing World Economy*, Cambridge, MA: The MIT Press.

Pérez-Díaz, V., Álvarez-Miranda, B. and Chuliá, E. (1997) *La Opinión Pública ante el Sistema de Pensiones*, Barcelona: La Caixa.

Rhodes, M. (1996) 'Southern European welfare states: identity, problems and prospects for reform', *South European Society & Politics* 1, 3: 1–22.

8 Profiles of citizenship
Elaboration of a framework for empirical analyses

Markku Kiviniemi

Introduction

Recent changes in national and international political and socio-economic orders have engendered renewed interest in the analysis of citizenship. Citizenship serves as an integrative perspective for understanding relations between individuals and larger social systems. Intellectual reflections must confront several conceptual elements of citizenship: ideological, institutional and operational. There are interrelated problems of principles, organizing systems and concrete practices of citizenship. Thus, the reference area of citizenship seems to develop as a key analytical principle. Meehan (1994: x) has noted the relatively peripheral position of citizenship studies in political science. This inherited peripheral position implies a certain 'underdevelopment' of research frameworks and analytical settings. However, citizenship themes are closely related to issues of democracy and participation as well as human rights, social justice and equality. Citizenship thus sits at the crossroad of these 'central concepts'.

A consciousness of the varieties of citizenship is one starting point for comparative studies. The tradition of comparative studies on citizenship is not very extensive. Most empirical studies have focused on relatively specific issues. In wide historical analyses, the approach has been mostly illustrative and of an ideal-type character (e.g. Weber 1950; Durkheim 1992). The realities of citizenship have been considered through broad examples and plausible generalizations. The immense coverage of issues in empirical terms is an explanation for the prevailing style of analysis. There are, however, conceptual elaborations which offer intellectual direction towards comparative frameworks. These include the work of T. H. Marshall (1964), Derek Heater (1990) and Bryan S. Turner (1990).

The aim here is to develop a tentative analytical framework for empirical analyses of citizenship. This will be done by utilizing the above-mentioned studies and analysing the relationship between key conceptual elements. On the one hand, the varieties of citizenship can be made comprehensible by reference to their contexts (for the concept of 'context', see e.g. Riggs 1980: 107–8) as meanings of citizenship are socially contextual (Heater 1990: 163;

Meehan 1994: 4). On the other hand, the defining characteristics of citizenship should be identified for use in analysing empirical cases. There are several alternative ways of doing this. The studies by Marshall, Heater and Turner offer orientations for identifying essential defining characteristics here called 'profiles' of citizenship. A 'profile' is a definable form based on certain selected dimensions.

In the first section of this chapter, conceptual dimensions of citizenship are formulated in terms of certain basic elements. These elements will then be introduced in a conceptual framework. In the following section empirical references about the development of citizenship in Scandinavia, particularly in Finland, will be presented as an illustration of the framework. Finally, some points of discussion are presented about the research area, particularly concerning the possibilities for comparative empirical research.

A framework of citizenship

To develop a framework for the study of citizenship an understanding of the concept is required. This should enlighten us as to the nature of citizenship and introduce its context into the analysis. Paul Close has offered a systematic and summarizing list of the conceptual meanings of citizenship (Close 1995: 1–2). Three essential defining elements can be drawn from this list, defining the concept at the most general level: citizenship is (1) a relationship between the individual and the collectivity; (2) including membership in that collectivity, and (3) delineating a status. Of course, several other attributes can be added; however, these vary according to time and place.

Why speak abstractly about some collectivity instead of defining the nature of the collectivity more precisely? The reason is that citizenship collectivities vary in time and place. In modern times the usual citizenship collectivity is the nation state. However, the historical origins of the concept of citizenship lie in the Greek *polis*, and later in medieval towns and cities (Weber 1950; Heater 1990; Marshall 1964: 77). Furthermore, the notion of citizenship has been transferred to international and interstate level, with European citizenship as a modern example. In addition dual and multinational citizenship is quite possible (Meehan 1994: 7–8). While recognizing these variations it can be stated that, in empirical terms and in this century, the collectivity typically involved in citizenship relations is the state.

From the viewpoint of individuals citizenship refers to belonging. From the viewpoint of collectivities it refers to the composition of these collectivities themselves (e.g. Habermas 1996: 25). The nature of citizenship as a social relationship is defined by norms implying a regulation of citizenship. The roots of this kind of regulation go back to ancient Athens, Pericles being one of the first figures who defined citizenship in normative terms. In the late eighteenth century, the first 'modern' declarations of citizens' rights emerged. *The Bill of Rights* in the United States (1791) was based on the assumption that the rights of the individual pose limits to the legislative power of the state. The French

Déclaration des droits de l'homme et du citoyen (1789), on the contrary, was based on the notion that the rights of the individual should be guaranteed and implemented by law (Viljanen 1988: 22–6). There have, thus, been different conceptions about the nature of the relationship between the individual and the collectivity. In the late 1990s, issues of citizenship legislation have again gained an important position on the political agenda.

The relationship between the individual and the collectivity is further specified by its membership quality. Citizens are members of their citizenship collectivity, e.g. the state. The membership characteristic creates a differentiation within the human population by including citizens and simultaneously excluding other individuals, non-citizens. Membership carries the meaning of belonging to something or – alternatively – a sense of not belonging.

The meaning of belonging is further articulated by citizenship's implication of a specific status, implying a set of rights and duties. Rights and duties are considered to be central characteristics of citizenship. I will return to this characteristic later. Meanwhile, it should be added that citizenship may also function as a basis for individual understandings of identity.

> The nation of citizens does not derive its identity from common ethnic and cultural properties but rather from the praxis of citizens who actively exercise their civil rights. . . . This socio-psychological connection does not mean to say that the two are linked in conceptual terms. . . . Citizenship was never conceptually tied to national identity.
>
> (Habermas 1996: 23)

Cultural and socio-economic factors may counter the relevance of citizenship as a basis of identity and give room for alternative bases (e.g. language, religion, subculture). However, citizenship should be distinguished from the concept of nationality which refers primarily to relations between states (Close 1995: 101).

Since the nature of citizenship is normative, it is a basic political issue in the proper and traditional sense. In the course of history different traditions of citizenship have emerged (see Heater 1990: 318; Turner 1990). These traditions relate to different political doctrines and ideologies. Heater (1990) distinguishes six different traditions (republican, cosmopolitan, nationalist, liberal, totalitarian and socialist traditions), while Mann (1987) describes five 'strategies' of citizenship (liberal, reformist, authoritarian monarchist, fascist and authoritarian socialist). The existence of different traditions points to the importance of long-term processes in citizenship formation (Turner 1990: 197). Political ideologies are influential contextual factors which leave their traces on developments in citizenship practices. Elements of political ideologies may be introduced into existing patterns of citizenship as 'internalized' aspects.

Different ideologies have different views of the individual, the collectivity and their mutual relationship. As contextual factors political ideologies do not usually define citizenship in practical terms. Rather, different ideologies offer starting-points and premises for the formulation of citizenship at a more concrete level.

Another aspect of analysis which can be distinguished is the regulated system of citizenship. By this I mean citizenship's quality as an institutional and normative relationship, as a system of rights and duties. Modern systems of citizenship are based on national legislation involving a vast number of potential, often implicit, effects. The system of rights and duties as such does not, however, delineate all the concrete consequences of citizenship. The final outcome also depends on the way in which rights and duties are implemented in public policies. The system of rights and duties presents a formal level of citizenship which differs from social realities (Campbell 1986). The practicalities of citizenship are created through government activities, i.e. the policies and practices of governmental systems, in interaction with the activities of their citizens.

To summarize, the accumulation of several defining features of citizenship engenders varying qualities which can be found at the empirical level. These features are collected in Figure 8.1. The figure incorporates those elements of citizenship which are socially dynamic, i.e. those varied influential factors which contribute to the development of citizenship collectivities, i.e. normative and institutional aspects, cultural and ideological aspects and citizenship practices. Contextual influences are also included in the scheme as models,

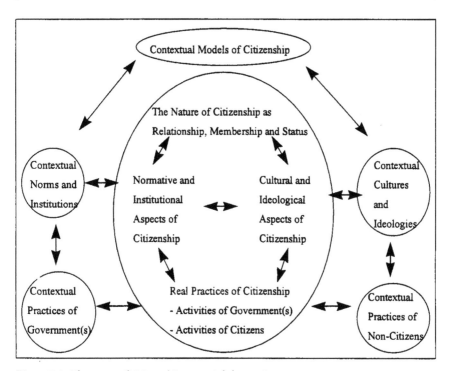

Figure 8.1 Elements of citizenship as social dynamics

norms and institutions, cultures and ideologies, and practices in the environment of the collectivity. Particularly modern contextual factors include relations with other states and interstate agreements.

Towards profiles of citizenship

In this section various characteristics of citizenship as presented in Figure 8.1 will be elaborated upon, with particular reference to the question of rights and duties.

The rights and duties of citizens are embedded within the normative and institutional framework that defines the relationship between the individual and the community. In modern states rights and duties are usually expressed in written constitutions and/or ordinary laws. Constitutional and legal rights and obligations are the manifestation of the principles of citizenship. They can be called 'formal' rights and obligations whose realization remains dependent on several political, social and economic factors.

In this century, international influences on citizens' rights and duties have become more and more decisive. This trend has been called the 'globalization of citizenship' (Turner 1990; 1993). Citizenship issues have developed with increased interaction between states and proneness to contextual factors. The 'human rights tradition', based on the Universal Declaration of Human Rights and other Conventions, now has fifty years' history. These international 'models' offer contextual patterns for different formal systems of citizens' rights. Whether and to what extent formal rights as defined by states have converged is a question for empirical study.

Formal citizenship rights are articulated in various social contexts, with the rise of the welfare state being of particular importance. Here, we should turn to T. H. Marshall's famous analysis of citizens' rights. His classification of citizens' rights into civil, political and social rights has acquired a certain intellectual status. Marshall's studies also include analysis of the developmental stages of industrial society in terms of citizens' rights. Globally seen, the fact that he takes Britain as his only empirical example could be considered a serious limitation. However, 'by 1950 . . . a cross between Marshallian citizenship and American liberalism dominated the West . . . it still dominates today' (Mann 1987: 351). Marshallian citizenship is tied up with modern Western nation states. It presents the bones of the development of welfare states in citizenship terms. Developmental routes to this Marshallian citizenship mixed with liberalism have varied within different ideological traditions (Mann 1987; Turner 1990).

One of several criticisms of Marshall's analysis is the lack of comparative historical material (Turner 1990). Giddens (1982: 171–3) has criticized Marshall for employing an evolutionary perspective which could imply a kind of developmental irreversibility. Turner disagrees, however, with this interpretation of Marshall's analysis as an evolutionary scheme, pointing to developments of the last decades which show that social rights can be reversible. 'There is . . . no necessary parallel or even development of different rights' (Turner 1990: 192).

Giddens (1982; 1985) also noted that the Marshallian categories of rights each have a different basic character and that they cannot be fully understood in isolation from their historical context. The categories are not so unitary as Marshall's analysis seems to suppose. Giddens argues that civil rights are not a homogeneous type of rights, and that 'economic civil rights' should be distinguished from 'individual civil rights'. This argument has found wider acceptance (Close 1995: 155–7). In fact, the term 'economic, social and cultural rights' is often used to describe Marshallian 'welfare rights' (e.g. Kartashkin 1982).

Sub-categories of 'welfare rights' can also be defined. Kartashkin includes the right to work, the right to just and favourable conditions of work and trade union rights in the category of 'economic rights'. He defines the rights to social security; protection of and assistance to the family, mothers and children; an adequate standard of living and to the highest attainable standard of physical and mental health as 'social rights'. The rights to education and other cultural rights exist on top of the aforementioned categories (Kartashkin 1982).

Alternative descriptions of citizens' rights have been developed by political scientists. David Held (1995: 191–200) elaborates a sub-categorization of rights, the implementation of which he argues to be a necessary precondition for free and equal participation and democracy. Charles Lindblom (1977: 132–3) lists nine fundamental rights as prerogatives of democracy. These are only civil and political rights, bearing a close resemblance to Marshall's description. Lindblom's list evidently leaves social rights to the 'output side' of political systems. A specific feature of Lindblom's list is the strong emphasis given to the right to form and join organizations. This corresponds to his view that democracy is the rule of the 'organized many' (Giddens 1985: 199). Starting-points in citizenship studies may be quite different. Marshall aims at a broad historical analysis while Held and Lindblom are making conceptual analyses of the preconditions for democracy.

These fragments of argumentation on citizens' rights refer to the complexity of issues at a more detailed level. The critiques presented here do not challenge the status of Marshall's studies as a point of comparative reference. However, the debates make it more difficult to achieve a unitary operational base for empirical studies. Of course, the research interest in the studies of Marshall, Turner, Heater and Mann focuses on broad macro-level analysis and 'theorized histories' (Castells 1983: 335), not so much on detailed empirical analyses of citizenship elements.

At least two kinds of problems emerge in relating broad classifications of citizens' rights to empirical analyses: (i) the categories (civil, political, social rights) are neither exactly stated nor easy to identify at a detailed level as the discussion about the place of 'economic rights' illustrates (Kartashkin 1982); and (ii) at an empirical level, the lists of citizens' rights are often broader and more detailed than Marshall's original descriptions indicate. This is partially due to a broadening and itemization of formal rights in the development of constitutional and legal systems. Issues like naturalization processes (the entry into citizenship), the rights of specific groups, e.g. children's rights, or the right to reproduction (Close 1995) have no clear position in Marshall's classification.

As stated above, citizenship as a status not only implies a set of rights, but also duties. In comparison with citizens' rights, the list of citizens' duties and responsibilities tends to be quite short. Evidently, the original idea was to create a balance between rights and duties. Citizens have duties in return for which they receive rights. In modern states, the duty to pay defined taxes seems to be the single duty shared by all citizens. Citizens apparently pay for their acquired rights through taxes. Increases in the levels of taxation in states is an indicator of the high tax burden required to satisfy the modern balance between duties and rights. There are some other general duties (e.g. military service, the duty to testify in judicial proceedings) but these are neither unitary nor of such general influence on all citizens as taxation is.

In fact, there is no declaration of human or citizens' duties and responsibilities. This raises questions about the effects of the marked shift of emphasis from duties to rights (Marshall 1964: 70). Is there an imbalance in the emphasis on human rights at the cost of human duties and responsibilities? Is the continued broadening of rights without the definition of corresponding duties and responsibilities based on an erroneous interpretation of the basic human condition? This problem relates to the relationship between common good and individual rights. The Aristotelian ideal of morally grounded citizenship is not well supported by the growth of individual rights. The modern state cannot ultimately bear the moral responsibility for the common good; the primary responsibility remains dependent on the morality of citizens (Rentto 1992).

Referring back to Figure 8.1, it is important to note that normative and institutional aspects of citizenship develop under conditions of multidimensional interaction with cultural and ideological factors and with practices of citizenship. Cultural and ideological patterns influence the direction and shape of citizenship reforms in the long run. Giddens (1982: 171–3) underlines the importance of political–ideological struggles in the development of citizenship. Turner (1990), Heater (1990) and Mann (1987) refer to national ideological traditions in analyzing the development of citizenship patterns. In the late twentieth century, different national traditions have become intermingled; cultural and ideological influences on national legislations have tended to become more internationally oriented.

Both formal and ideological issues of citizenship have often been bound up with the search for equality and justice. Of course, the ancient and medieval systems were very limited in the modern sense of these concepts. They were mostly orientated towards the creation of subgroups of equal citizens as privileged persons within collectivities. Historically, citizenship was a privileged status, reserved only for those who were assumed to be worthy of it on the basis of specific criteria (notably descent, civic merit and property; see Weber 1950).

It was only in the eighteenth century that universal equality emerged as a legitimate foundation for citizenship (Meehan 1994: 17). The progress towards equality in modern nation states is, however, far from the ideals of the American and French Revolutions.

Various perspectives can be employed in the empirical analysis of problems surrounding equality. With reference to Figure 8.1, it is possible to identify two alternative starting-points. On the one hand, the analysis of equality and citizenship can focus on normative preconditions underlying citizens' equal opportunities and their rights and duties. The study of formal rights and duties is important, as they translate idealized ideological objectives into rules of justice (Campbell 1986: 4). This, however, is no guarantee for the realization of citizenship. On the other hand, the analysis can focus on the realization of equality in societal practices and activities. This perspective deals with activities of governments (public policies), activities of citizens and their mutual encounter testing the degree of realization of formal principles. However, the practice of citizenship is not formed by public policies only. Rather, they act as relieving factors in unbroken inequalities of different societies and socio-economic structures. This view seems also to be Marshall's interpretation.

Studies analysing the inadequate and unequal realization of citizenship tend to use at least two different perspectives: (i) Identifying and analysing social groups for whom the realization of citizenship is deficient (e.g. women, children, aliens, poor, different minorities, prisoners, etc.). Such analyses often attempt to determine dynamic factors which account for 'citizenship deficits'. (ii) Identifying and analysing the development of specific dimensions of citizenship (e.g. specific rights and duties, critical cases, access to citizenship and so forth).

Equality and justice are essential perspectives in the analysis of citizenship and its constituent elements. Always hovering in the background is a certain antagonism between civil rights (liberty) and social rights (justice) (Close 1995: 159–61). This antagonism is partially relieved by public policies tending to increase equality within collectivities. John Rawls, in his *A Theory of Justice* (1973: 96), argues that the position of individuals concerning equality is dualistic. Individuals have both the position of equality through citizenship (formal rights and duties) and a position defined by their place in the distribution of income and wealth. According to Rawls, the tension between these two positions is resolved, at least partially, by adherence to the formal principles of liberty and justice. Rawls asserts that social and economic inequalities are acceptable if they are arranged in such a way that they improve the position of the least advantaged. This brings the role of public policies into the discussion. What is the relation of public policies to citizens' rights and duties?

In principle, it could be postulated that the task of public policies is to implement the principles of citizenship. In practice, however, the relation between public policies and citizenship is often quite loose (*Governance in Transition* OECD 1995: 73). In modern differentiated systems of nation states, the actors responsible for sectoral public policies often have quite different contextual powers and perspectives than the actors who formulate the principles of citizenship. This is connected with the broadened area of public policies. The highest state bodies have lost much of their coordinating capacity in sectorized and specialized institutional decision-making. Even 'Citizens' Charters' within different public services mostly use narrow perspectives correlated with institutionalized patterns of public activities. Citizens owing rights and duties tend to turn into clients of different specialized public services (Pollitt and Bouckaert 1995: 6). Client relationships between the individual and the collectivity are an essential part of modern citizenship (Habermas 1996: 31–2). They do not, however, cover the whole range of citizens' rights and duties. Rather, they present a specific mode of citizenship reflecting a fragmentation of 'principal citizenship' and a disintegration of relations between the principles of citizenship and public policies.

An attempt to bring formal citizenship closer to the context of societal practices has been made by Turner (1990). After criticizing the unitary concept of citizenship in the Marshallian tradition, he elaborated two principal dimensions in reference to the societal context of citizenship. These dimensions are relevant in developing empirical profiles of citizenship. The first is the active–passive dimension which depends on whether citizenship is developed from above or below. This implies an account of the degree of hierarchy and participation in the collectivity. The second dimension refers to the relationship between private and public arenas in the realization of citizenship. Some collectivities emphasize public arenas while others leave the realization of citizenship to the realm of private life and institutions (e.g. family, religious societies). Turner emphasizes the importance of different societal contexts in the analysis of the realization of citizenship.

An important perspective of citizenship emerges from the realities of citizens themselves. What possibilities do citizens have for the realization of their formal rights? How can and do citizens promote equal opportunities? Inequalities between different groups are revealed through the unequal resources and competencies of citizens. Furthermore, what is the place of citizenship in the experience and everyday life of citizens (Roche 1987)?

Figure 8.1 opens up a vast field for research on citizenship and its elements. Certain essential dimensions have been identified tentatively in preparation for proceeding towards empirical profiles. To sum up, these dimensions of profiles include:

- Normative and institutional aspects: formal rights of citizens, which can be divided into civil, political and welfare (economic, social, cultural) rights; formal duties of citizens.
- Cultural and ideological aspects: ideological patterns of citizenship; political struggles about the principles of citizenship.
- Practices of citizenship: realization of citizens' rights; realization of citizens' duties; public policies in relation to citizenship; active versus passive citizenship; private versus public citizenship.

- Contextual factors of citizenship dimensions which can be distinguished in external collectivities and interstate (inter-collectivity) agreements.

Thus, the development and articulation of citizenship depends upon several factors. Different restricting and enabling contextual factors modify the realization of citizenship. The identification of factors which prevent and promote the realization of ideal citizenship can be a meaningful challenge for empirical research.

An empirical illustration: elements of Finnish citizenship

The context and timetable of the development of welfare states vary from country to country. In the following, the framework of Figure 8.1 is applied to the example of Finland.

To start with normative and institutional aspects, we should note that in Finland, the completion of fundamental civil and political rights of citizens was achieved with independence and the Constitution of 1919. As of that moment, Finland has been a constitutional nation state with equality in formal civil and political rights.

This development did not take place in a vacuum. The contextual influence of international models is quite evident in the Finnish case. These models include both normative legal and ideological elements. One line of inter-national influence came from Sweden and from the period of Swedish rule (1155–1809), including the maintenance of the previous Swedish legislation during the period of autonomy under Russian rule (1809–1907). The Swedish Constitutions of the eighteenth century were one basis for the formulation of the Finnish Constitution of 1919. Another international influence came from continental Europe, particularly from Germany, in terms of professional legal thinking. The ideological background of the constitutional definition of rights has been characterized as belonging to the European liberalism of the late nineteenth century (Viljanen 1988: 46, 248). The background of civil rights lay mainly in the previous Swedish legislation, while the background for political rights came more from European liberalism and constitutionalism (Viljanen 1988: 250).

The development of the Finnish welfare state – another important part of the normative and institutional articulation of citizenship – followed, with a slight delay, the other northern European nation states. According to Kosonen (1987: 107–11), the development of the Finnish welfare state involved four main phases: the initial stage; a stabilization period; a period of expansion; and a period of re-evaluation. During the initial phase (*c.* 1890–1914) the emphasis was on minimum social security, not universal social rights. The stabilization period (1914–45) brought a gradual enlargement of selective social policy. Basic social, health and educational services became obligatory municipal tasks. The expansion period (1945–73) witnessed the most rapid growth in social rights and related public services. The focus of development, supported by economic growth, shifted from selective minimum security to responding to heterogeneous needs and the demands of different social groups. The re-evaluation period, beginning with economic uncertainties in the 1970s, has been characterized by criticism and re-orientation towards the rise of public services and consequent increased costs.

Elsewhere I have described the period 1945–65 as the institutionalization of the welfare state in Finland (Kiviniemi 1994). The 'early welfare state' was achieved during that period. This was demonstrated by the gradual growth of welfare services and benefits. The label 'early welfare state' is, however, an *a posteriori* construction. The Finnish reformers of the 1950s and early 1960s did not use the term 'welfare state'. The 1950s were dominated by the spirit-inspiring post-war societal reconstruction, and reforms were accepted as a part of this rebuilding. The acknowledged introduction of the welfare state by Pekka Kuusi came about in 1961.

The 'late welfare state' was achieved in Finland after 1966. The full transition to an institutional welfare state with broad social rights chiefly took place from 1966 to 1973. In the late 1980s and 1990s, a new trend in Finnish reforms became evident, officially characterized as an 'economic and political adaptation of the welfare state'. The recession of the early 1990s deepened and sharpened this trend. There have been continued pressures for reductions in public sector spending. The changes accomplished have not, however, made significant reductions in formal social rights. In this sense, the 'late welfare state' continues. Cut-backs have mainly affected the standards of service provision and benefits, generally maintaining the levels achieved in the mid-1980s. For instance, general access to social and health services has not weakened in the 1990s. Some particular groups of citizens (e.g. mental health patients, drug addicts) and specific services (particularly those for elderly people) have become less accessible, above all because of growing demand. Evidently the public policies in Finland have mostly been successful in maintaining the principal achievements of the 'late welfare state' (Laamanen *et al.* 1996: 327–9).

With respect to culture and ideology, developments in Finland demonstrate a movement from deep political tension in the early twentieth century to a culture of political consensus at the end of the century. Particularly the development of the 'late welfare state' since 1966 has involved the rise of a cross-party egalitarian welfare ideology, relatively stable economic growth, and consensual political leadership. This has been supported by the rise of central planning and a corporatist style of central decision making.

The 'late welfare state' has maintained a consistently high level of legitimacy among Finnish citizens (Pöntinen and Uusitalo 1986: 63; Forma 1996: 167). There is little empirical evidence of a 'crisis of legitimacy' in the welfare state in Finland. Citizens' attention seems to be focused on the practical effectiveness of public policies rather than on grand ideological issues. The political will of national élites to protect the main achievements of the 'late welfare state' was demonstrated in the constitutional reformulation of individual rights in 1995.

An important contextual detail of this reform is to be found in international declarations and conventions (*Perusoikeusuudistus* 1995).

The concrete practice of citizenship is relatively difficult to assess because of increasing differences in lifestyles and values. Under Turner's citizenship distinctions, Finland could be classed as a country of relatively active citizenship. The, internationally viewed, long tradition of citizens' associations in different fields as well as a relatively high voting rate are expressions of an active citizenship. Finnish people traditionally have faith in their ability to influence their own society (e.g. Hofstede 1980: 104). Recently, it has been suggested that public welfare policies have made people more passive than was previously the case. This is most likely the case only for subgroups of people. This issue is connected to the significant inequalities, which remain even after several decades of welfare policies, and their related risk of socio-economic marginalization.

The contextual influence of international models in the development of rights legislation has already been indicated above. Norms and institutions should also be mentioned as contextual influences. In the Finnish case, the contextual reference point for formal citizens' rights has gradually broadened from the traditional 'neighbourhood-orientated' pattern of northern Europe and Germany towards global citizenship models. In recent decades, the emergence of international formal human rights has tended to surpass traditional national ways of defining citizenship (Tiilikainen 1996).

Ideologies and cultures also serve to contextualize citizenship under-standings. Marshall (1964: 268) stated that welfare state policies are a mixture of liberal and socialist thoughts. In Finland, the most important ideologies have been the traditions of European liberalism and the Nordic welfare state. The former has been particularly influential in building the Finnish constitutional state and related legislation. In the latter category Swedish developments have been most closely followed. In Sweden, the welfare state has been characterized as a 'social democratic project' (e.g. Svensson 1994). In Finland, the welfare state was primarily built by a centre–left political coalition and was part of a gradual shift towards 'consensual politics'.

More recently, emerging notions of European citizenship have contextual-ized government approaches to citizenship, particularly from an institutional point of view. Changes in institutional patterns and governmental practices have been influenced by European level developments. The European context has also imported a new socio-cultural aspect to the citizenship debate: that of increased transnational mobility. The presence and activities of new immigrant citizens and resident non-citizens put the realization of citizenship principles to the test on a daily basis. This is, of course, illustrated in Figure 8.1 as contextualization due to the practices of non-citizens. So far, the effects of these tendencies in citizenship issues have been relatively marginal. They do, however, present factors which will probably exercise greater influence in the future. European citizenship may become further institutionalized in the next century, and the issue of a 'European social citizenship' is already being increasingly debated. Furthermore immigration statistics are expected to continue to show increases.

Figure 8.2 collects selected elements of Finnish citizenship from a historical perspective. The orientation of the Figure follows closely that of Figure 8.1. Its purpose is to condense complex phenomena into a limited picture. It does not aim to give a detailed profile of the Finnish citizenship. Rather, it is a preliminary outline for understanding and for further elaboration of empirical profiles.

Some general conclusions can be derived from the case of Finnish citizenship. First, the importance of contextual factors in the development and change of citizenship is quite evident. The institutional, ideological and practical elements of citizenship are not solely determined by the internal structures and processes of the collectivity. Neither does nationality determine the full range of characteristics of modern citizenship, although it is one influential factor (Meehan 1994: 9). The general trend has been towards increased internationalization of citizenship formation. This implies that the context in which citizenship develops, and is practised, has widened from the traditional regional context towards a more global arena.

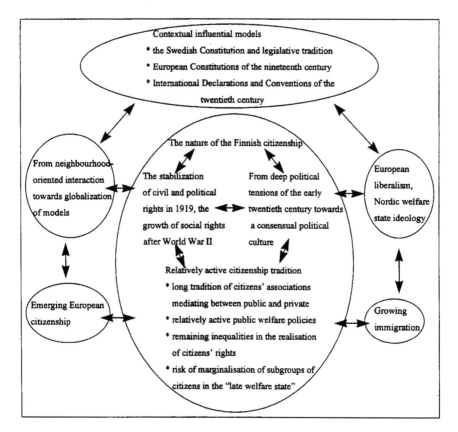

Figure 8.2 Selected elements of Finnish citizenship in historical perspective

Second, the development of Finnish citizenship broadly follows the Marshallian succession in the development of citizens' rights. Civil rights in Finland originate from the period of Swedish rule. The roots of political rights lie mostly in late nineteenth-century European liberalism. Welfare rights have gradually emerged during the twentieth century, and the stage of 'late welfare state' was achieved in the 1970s.

Third, the development of citizenship is not an evolutionary scheme. Rather, changes in citizenship can be traced to political struggles and political cooperation. The construction of the welfare state has been accompanied by the rise of a consensual political culture. It is a matter of interpretation whether the 'common game' of welfare state construction has gradually mitigated the deep political tensions of the early twentieth century. If this kind of interpretation is accepted, the integrating factor may be either the 'game itself' (societal construction) or the results of the 'game' (welfare policies) – or both.

Fourth, the developmental story of the modern welfare state is not yet completed. After the initial steps, covering some 50 years of expansion and subsequent re-evaluations, the ensemble of social rights has widened to include institutionalized patterns of welfare services and benefits. While these services and benefits have gained the status of social rights, the justification of this status has been much debated. From a long-term perspective, welfare states do not present fixed patterns of welfare provision. Rather, they are changing and adapting themselves according to contextual economic, political and cultural factors.

Fifth, a profile of citizenship does not have fixed dimensions. It is an instrument of analysis rather than an end in itself. Even if the main elements of citizenship are useful as a general conceptual framework, the dominant characteristics may be unique and vary according to the case studied. To estimate the usefulness of specific dimensions one would need to develop several illustrative cases.

Altogether, in the light of the single case used here, the natural research interest seems to be: what would other cases tell us? This should lead to comparative research interests.

Conclusion

During its history, the concept of citizenship has amassed much of the ideals involved in striving for democracy, justice and equality. Citizenship conceptions might be accused of being inclined to idealism. However, it is important to study those forms and contents of idealism as a source of institutionalized formal rights and duties. To develop a research agenda for the study of citizenship, it is important to integrate studies of ideas and formal systems with empirical analyses of the realization of citizenship under different circumstances. A long-term objective for citizenship research could be the improvement of knowledge of the profiles of citizenship which could be achieved by integrating empirical studies. This research could make use of contextual approaches and interpretations.

Figure 8.1 offers some principal elements and their mutual dynamics as a possible starting-point for empirical research. While modern citizenship is mostly anchored in nation states, it is important to recognize alternative levels of citizenship as a relationship between the individual and the collectivity based on the former's membership of the latter. The focus on nation states seems to be natural and to correspond to present realities. The global, continental and local levels may be regarded as contextual factors presenting alternative structural, cultural and practical models of citizenship.

The principal elements of citizenship may be conceptualized as institutional, cultural and practical. Equality and justice offer critical perspectives on these elements. Together, these elements and perspectives refer to a quite broad area of phenomena. Consequently, single research efforts are limited to more specific issues. However, in specified research settings a general conceptual orientation can function as a framework. Conceptual frameworks would add something to the comparability of empirical findings.

Empirical profiles of citizenship for different nation states would be useful for a better understanding of single-country studies. Even the most-referred British study by Marshall does not have, so far, any empirical equivalent in other countries. A useful line of proceeding would be comparative empirical studies on selected aspects of modern citizenship. While such studies are open to several alternative approaches, three principal alternatives can be suggested:

- A contextual–historical approach. A relatively concrete historical analysis of citizenship could move towards comparative aspects by introducing contextual factors such as normative models, ideological patterns and established practices of citizenship. The historical aspect involves the perspective on citizenship as developing in processes over time. This approach also involves interpretations at societal level which has been the telling message of Marshall.
- A formal–institutional approach. The study of formal institutionalized citizenship is needed as an 'anchor', implying connections among the principles, political doctrines and normative foundations of citizenship. Particularly, the inclusion of ideological aspects into formal–institutional studies would give a contextual element to these studies.
- Studies on the realization of citizenship in public policies. Empirical studies of citizenship could concern issues of particular institutionalized rights or duties and related public policies. The integration of studies on citizens' rights and studies on policy implementation might be fruitful in recognizing prevailing deficits in terms of justice and equality. An initial step towards selected empirical profiles would be the identification of the main features of a given sub-set of citizenship, e.g. educational rights and their realization in terms of educational policies. Empirical studies could also focus on situations of specified groups in terms of their formal rights/duties and the corresponding practices.

The result of such comparative studies would be the accumulation of knowledge of similarities and differences in citizenship profiles. While the general focus would be on comparing modern nation states, different types of comparative analyses have to be encouraged for progress of this research area. For understanding institutions of democracy, the study of citizenship is certainly as worthy as widely exercised election studies.

For Marshall, citizenship of a welfare state was the answer to the contradiction between capitalism and democracy (Turner 1993: 6). Probably, Marshall did not imply that modern citizenship would be a total solution for this contradiction but, rather, a way to achieve a tolerable coexistence. It is well worthwhile studying how Marshall's basic assumptions hold for 'late welfare states' of the 1990s.

Bibliography

Campbell, T. (1986) 'Introduction: realizing human rights', in T. Campbell (ed.) *Human Rights. From Rhetoric to Reality*, Oxford: Basil Blackwell.

Castells, M. (1983) *The City and the Grassroots*, London: Arnold.

Close, P. (1995) *Citizenship, Europe and Change*, Basingstoke: Macmillan.

Durkheim, E. (1992) *Professional Ethics and Civil Morals*, London: Routledge.

Forma, P. (1996) 'Kohdistuva, perusturva vai pohjoismainen? Hyvinvointivaltiomallien kannatus Suomessa', in O. Kangas (ed.) *Hyvinvointivaltiomallit, niiden toiminta ja kannatusperusta*. Helsinki: Ministry of Social and Health Affairs.

Giddens, A. (1982) *Profiles and Critiques in Social Theory*, London: Macmillan.

—— (1985) *The Nation-State and Violence*, Cambridge: Polity Press.

Habermas, J. (1996) 'Citizenship and national identity', in B. van Steenbergen (ed.) *The Condition of Citizenship*, London: Sage.

Heater, D. (1990) *Citizenship: The Civic Ideal in World History, Politics and Education*, Harlow: Longman.

Held, D. (1995) *Democracy and the Global Order*, Cambridge: Polity Press.

Hofstede, G. (1980) *Culture's Consequences*, London: Sage.

Kartashkin, V. (1982) 'Economic, social and cultural rights', in K. Vasak and P. Alston (eds) *International Dimensions of Human Rights*, Paris: UNESCO.

Kiviniemi, M. (1994) *Perspectives on Structure, Culture and Action. Studies in the Public Administration of the Welfare State*, Helsinki: Administrative Development Agency.

Kosonen, P. (1987) *Hyvinvointivaltion haasteet ja pohjoismaiset mallit*, Mänttä: Vastapaino.

Kuusi, P. (1961) *60-luvun sosiaalipolitiikka*, Porvoo: Werner Söderström.

Laamanen, R., Kalland, M. and Häppölä, A. (1996) *Palvelurakennemuutos ja sen onnistuneisuuden arviointi*, Helsinki: Ministry of Social and Health Affairs.

Lindblom, C. E. (1977) *Politics and Markets*, New York: Basic Books.

Mann, M. (1987) 'Ruling Class Strategies and Citizenship', *Sociology* 21, 3: 339–54.

Marshall, T. H. (1964) *Class, Citizenship and Social Development*, Garden City New York: Doubleday.

Meehan, E. (1994) *Citizenship and the European Community*, London: Sage.

OECD (1995) *Governance in Transition*, Paris: OECD.

Perusoikeusuudistus (1995), Helsinki: Ministry of Justice.

Pollitt, C. and Bouckaert, G. (1995) 'Defining quality', in C. Pollitt and G. Bouckaert (eds) *Quality Improvement in European Public Services*, London: Sage.

Pöntinen, S. and Uusitalo, H. (1986) *The Legitimacy of the Welfare State: Social Security Opinions in Finland 1975–1985*, Helsinki: Suomen Gallup.

Rawls, J. (1973) *A Theory of Justice*, Oxford: Oxford University Press.

Rentto, J.-P. (1992) 'Vapaus ja vastuu', in E. Kemppainen (ed.) *Yksilön vastuu ja sosiaaliset oikeudet*, Helsinki: National Board of Social and Health Affairs.

Riggs, F. W. (1980) 'The ecology and context of public administration: a comparative perspective', *Public Administration Review* 40, 2: 107–15.

Roche, M. (1987) 'Citizenship, social theory and social change', *Theory and Society* 16, 3: 363–99.

Svensson, T. (1994) 'Socialdemokratins dominans. En studie av den svenska socialdemokratins partistrategi'. Uppsala: *Acta Universitatis Upsaliensis* no. 120.

Tiilikainen, T. (1996) 'Rouva turvallissuuspolitiikka', interview by Katri Himma, *Suomen Kuvalehti* 80, 42: 71–3.

Turner, B. S. (1990) 'Outline of a theory of citizenship', *Sociology* 24, 2: 189–217.

——(1993) 'Contemporary problems in the theory of citizenship', in B. S. Turner (ed.) *Citizenship and Social Theory*, London: Sage.

Viljanen, V.-P. (1988) *Kansalaisten yleiset oikeudet*, Helsinki: Lakimiesliiton Kustannus.

Weber, M. (1950) *General Economic Theory*, Glencoe, IL: The Free Press.

9   Citizen (re)orientations in the welfare state

From public to private citizens?*

Lawrence Rose

Introduction

> ... rights of individual freedom and social security can just as well facilitate a privatist retreat from citizenship and a particular 'clientelization' of the citizen's role.
>
> (Habermas 1994: 31)

One of the critical issues raised in recent literature regarding citizenship in contemporary welfare states concerns the impact of welfare state policies on individual orientations to politics and the political sphere. This theme is perhaps most closely associated with the work of Habermas, but it is intertwined in the writings of others as well.[1] At issue is whether or not the welfare state, and in particular the proliferation of welfare state programmes based on principles of universal entitlements, may contribute to a shift in the manner in which individuals define their relationship to the public sphere. The underlying hypothesis is that such a shift has in fact occurred, or at least is likely to occur; the suggestion is that given a relatively encompassing set of social as well as civil and political rights, individuals will be inclined to turn away from the broader political arena and instead focus their attention more narrowly on securing the public goods and services to which they and their closest family members are entitled.

This suggestion is not without a logical theoretical base. Many welfare state policies introduce universal rights or entitlements, reducing or even totally removing more traditional tests of need as a qualifying condition. In many instances, moreover, entitlements are not connected to the individual's citizenship; individuals qualify for welfare state benefits merely by satisfying a set of stipulations in which citizenship is not a relevant factor. Of most critical importance, however, is that while entitlements grant collective rights of access, consumption of such benefits commonly occurs on an individual, often quite private basis. Consumption of public health services and care for the elderly offer two obvious examples of these conditions, but perhaps the most vivid illustration of collective rights and private consumption is found in connection with social security pensions, where it is up to the individual to decide how she or he will spend the benefits provided.

The crux of the argument, then, is that while the rights to many welfare state benefits are formally guaranteed through collective entitlements, arrangements involved in securing such benefits emphasize the individual's role as consumer more than his or her role as an active political citizen.[2] If this line of argument is valid, it suggests that the winning of more encompassing social rights may serve to weaken and undermine the use, if not the meaning, of political rights. Presumably this is not what T. H. Marshall had in mind when he set forth his treatise on the development of citizenship (Marshall 1950). The historical analysis presented by Marshall implies what has been interpreted as a linear and cumulative development of citizenship rights. From such a perspective, social rights are the result of and build upon previously won political rights; social rights should serve to reinforce the meaning of political rights, not weaken them.

Marshall's suggestion of such a linear development has of course been subject to criticism (cf. Giddens 1982 and Mann 1987 among others), and many authors prefer to interpret the interrelationship of civil, political and social rights as being more complementary and mutually supportive rather than sequential and cumulative. David Miller, for instance, has argued that 'the whole thrust of the citizenship idea is that different kinds of rights support each other. Protective and welfare rights provide a secure basis upon which the citizen can launch into his political role' (Miller 1989: 246). A similar perspective is argued by Twine (1994: 104). Such a line of thinking leads to an alternative hypothesis, one which runs contrary to that suggested by the concerns of Habermas and others – namely that the spread of social rights should *strengthen* the meaning and use of political rights rather than undermining and weakening them.

To date, relatively little systematic empirical evidence has been mustered to test the validity of either of these hypotheses. Some writers point to declining electoral participation, which has been observed in many countries, as evidence of a weakened meaning of political rights. Declining rates of party membership and difficulties reported by political parties in recruiting candidates to stand for election are also mentioned in this regard. Increased volatility in party choice has likewise been interpreted as a manifestation of strengthened consumer-based political orientations among voters. Yet at the same time there is substantial evidence suggesting a rise in alternative forms of political activity in many western societies, especially activities once labelled as 'irregular' or 'non-conventional' (cf. Bennett and Bennett 1986; Jennings *et al.* 1989; Parry *et al.* 1992; Pettersen and Rose 1996; Togeby 1993), as well as increased involvement in local community boards and user control organs which have proliferated in recent years (cf. Bogason 1996; Burns *et al.* 1994). Such activities, particularly those that have their basis in local organizations, may be interpreted as supporting the alternative hypothesis suggesting the complementary and mutually supportive interrelationship of social, political and civil rights.

These strands of evidence, while possibly relevant, have only an indirect bearing on the issue at hand. The present chapter offers evidence which relates more directly to the question of citizen orientations in contemporary welfare states. This evidence derives from a national survey conducted in Norway in 1996. Before this evidence is presented, however, a few words regarding the nature of the Norwegian welfare state are in order.

The Norwegian welfare state: provision and financing of services

To speak of the welfare state in Norway requires one to speak of the welfare municipality. Local authorities have long occupied a central position in the push for and implementation of basic social welfare programmes (cf. Grønlie 1991; Seip 1991). To be sure, stipulations regarding many fundamental welfare state programmes today are based on decisions reached at the national level. But the historical foundation for, and even more so the practical implementation of these programmes, has to a large degree been the domain of local government. Except for various standardized income maintenance programmes such as old age pensions, unemployment benefits and disability compensation, which national authorities administer, local governments currently have responsibility for providing all public goods and services of general significance. These include primary and secondary education, all primary medical care, care for the elderly, child day-care, social welfare benefits to the needy and a variety of leisure time and cultural services. For most citizens, in other words, the principal encounter with the welfare state and public service provision occurs in the context of local government. For purposes of considering the character of citizenship in contemporary welfare states, therefore, local government represents an important point of reference.

Of special relevance in this respect is the nature of public finance, especially as this relates to local government. Local governments in Norway obtain funding from three primary sources: (1) taxation on personal income and wealth; (2) intergovernmental transfers; and (3) user fees and charges. With the exception of user fees and charges, which traditionally have played a very modest role in most localities (cf. Rose 1996a: 172–8), local governments exercise no real discretion in determining the size of their revenue. Central government authorities determine a very limited range within which local authorities may set the local personal income tax levy, and local authorities have characteristically set their rates at the maximum level. Intergovernmental transfers are likewise decided by central authorities, and are in large measure based on a set of objective criteria. As a result of these conditions, revenues issues have not been a matter of particular political salience or debate on the local level. Local politics is decidedly more expenditure- than revenue-orientated.

Given these legal and financial arrangements, Norway offers an interesting case for testing a hypothesis positing a tendency for citizens in welfare states to turn away from the political arena and to focus their attention more on obtaining welfare benefits to which they and their family are entitled. The costs of such benefits, after all, are largely fixed, reflecting only to a small degree actual use, and there is little, if anything, to be gained by refraining from consumption. Hence, individuals could well be expected to stress their role as consumers more than their role as active political citizens and taxpayers. To what extent does empirical evidence support such a suggestion?

Citizen orientations: the predominance of consumerism

In a national survey conducted in early 1996 respondents were asked to indicate what importance they personally attached to different aspects of their relations to local government and politics. Three questions, each having a parallel structure, were used to register these orientations.[3] In each question respondents were first asked to indicate how important each of three different considerations was to them personally, with responses ranging from 'of little importance' to 'very important'. The considerations to be assessed in each question were designed to tap into three different facets of the individual's socio-political role orientations – a consumer role orientation, a (tax)payer role orientation and a citizen/voter role orientation, respectively.[4] Items designed to tap a consumer role orientation, for instance, emphasized aspects relating to public service provision and consumption, whereas items designed to tap a (tax)payer orientation emphasized the use of income tax revenues and the level of charges assessed for public services, while items designed to tap a citizen/ voter orientation emphasized political participation and a person's ability to influence local decisions. The three questions are reproduced in Table 9.1. The specific role orientation each item was intended to tap is noted by the terms enclosed in parentheses (these role designations were of course not included in the original questionnaire).

Once each of the three considerations within a given question had been assessed independently, respondents were then asked to indicate which one of the three they felt was most important, again for them personally. The intent, in short, was first to provide all respondents with an opportunity to express their views on the overall importance of each consideration, and then to require that they should assess all three considerations in relation to one another and select the one consideration which they saw as being of greatest relative importance to them personally.

As can be seen from Table 9.1, there is a general tendency for respondents to perceive all of the considerations to be quite important – not only the ability to participate in and influence public decision making, but also the nature of municipal services available to them and what these services are likely to cost. The average score was in every case above the midpoint of the importance scale, which ranged from 1 (of little importance) to 5 (very important). This result is not in itself surprising; all of the considerations were formulated in such a manner that, at least in the abstract, they are likely to be perceived as being quite import-ant by most people. Thus, in the absence of more explicit limiting conditions, all of the considerations could be expected to obtain a fairly high score.

What is more noteworthy is the *relative importance* attached to the respective considerations. This is evident both in the proportion of respondents who

Table 9.1 Residents' opinions regarding the importance of different aspects of their relations to local government*

When you think of your relations to the municipality where you reside, how important are the following three considerations for you personally?	*Percent 'very important'*	*Percent 'most important'*
A. To be able to influence decisions which are important for you. (Voter role)	32	18
B. That there are public services which are suited to the needs in your household. (Consumer role)	49	50
C. How much you have to pay in taxes, fees and user charges. (Taxpayer role)	41	32

From your point of view, how important are the following three considerations for you?	*Percent 'very important'*	*Percent 'most important'*
A. That your municipality holds user fees and taxes at the lowest possible level. (Taxpayer role)	34	22
B. That your municipality is sensitive to the opinions of a majority of the residents. (Voter role)	53	31
C. That your municipality offers good public services. (Consumer role)	57	47

How important is it for you personally that the municipality informs residents of the following three matters	*Percent 'very important'*	*Percent 'most important'*
A. What services the municipality has for its residents. (Consumer role)	61	37
B. How the municipality uses the residents' tax money. (Taxpayer role)	67	42
C. Which possibilities residents have to influence municipal decisions. (Voter role)	50	21

Minimum $N = 2,828$

* Percentage indicating specific aspects are 'very important' and 'most important' respectively. In each of the three questions presented here, respondents were asked initially to express their opinions concerning the importance of each aspect on a scale from 1 (of little importance) to 5 (very important). Then a follow-up question read as follows: 'If you had to choose, which of these three (A, B or C above) would you say is the *most important*'?

initially indicate each consideration is 'very important', and even more so by the proportion who, when forced to choose, select a specific consideration as being 'most important' to them personally. In two of the three questions, the consideration most frequently selected as very and most important is that designed to tap a consumer role orientation, whereas in the third instance the taxpayer item comes out on top while the consumer role item comes in second. Items designed to tap the political citizen/voter role orientation, on the other hand, obtain the lowest proportion as both 'very important' and 'most important' in two of the three questions, whereas in the remaining instance the citizen/voter item comes in second. Based on responses to these three questions, in sum, we observe a clear tendency for Norwegians to place greatest relative emphasis on their role as consumers of public goods and services. By comparison, much less importance is attached to their roles as taxpayers or politically active citizen voters, at least in terms of how they define their relationship to local government and politics.

One may wonder whether these findings are an artefact of the measurement techniques employed. It is quite possible, for example, that the items designed to tap consumer, taxpayer and political citizen orientations do not represent equally 'attractive' considerations; i.e. they may not have a logically or empirically comparable value, and may, for this reason, bias the outcome. Such a possibility cannot be dismissed out of hand. Other evidence from the same survey concerning citizen expectations relating to the objectives of local government and attitudes regarding municipal mergers, however, reinforce the impression gained from the results in Table 9.1.

Objectives of local government: efficiency over democracy

In Norway as elsewhere, arguments justifying local self-government have traditionally stressed three values – those of autonomy, democracy and efficiency respectively (cf. Jones and Stewart 1983; Sharpe 1970; Wolman 1995). Other values and considerations, such as equality in service provision and macro-economic control, have supplemented and tempered these values in the course of time, but the three traditional values continue to provide an important framework for discussions of local government (cf. Fevolden *et al.* 1992; Kjellberg 1988, 1995). In order to assess how the public perceives these values at present, therefore, respondents were asked to express their opinions regarding the importance of six different objectives of local government. These six objectives were designed to tap the traditional values of autonomy, democracy and efficiency respectively. Following a general evaluation of each objective individually, respondents were also asked to identify two of the six which they felt were most important to them personally.

Responses to these questions are displayed in Table 9.2, where the objectives are grouped according to the value they were designed to reflect. Once again the table contains information from both questions regarding the six objectives – i.e. both perceptions of the general importance of each objective as well as which two objectives were considered to be most or next most important. Looking first at the general evaluations (the left-hand column of numbers), we see that the objective considered 'very important' by the greatest proportion of respondents (73 per cent in all) is 'That residents are offered the best possible services for the taxes and fees they pay'. This objective involves a clear efficiency component, albeit not quite as explicitly phrased as the other item designed to tap the same value ('That municipal services are produced as cheaply as possible'). This latter objective was viewed as very important by 37 per cent of the respondents, thereby ranking third in terms of the proportion assessing alternative objectives as 'very important'. Ranking second, in between these

Table 9.2 Residents' viewpoints on the importance of different objectives of local government*

Objectives of local government	Percent 'very important'	Percent 'most important'	Percent 'next most important'
Autonomy			
That local evaluations count more than national standards.	24	3	10
That the municipality can make income and expenditure decisions without central government interference.	18	6	8
Democracy			
That there is good contact between residents and elected representatives.	49	28	22
That residents are involved in local political issues.	28	3	10
Efficiency			
That residents are offered the best possible services for the taxes and fees they pay.	73	51	28
That municipal services are produced as cheaply as possible.	37	10	23

Minimum N = 2,741

* Percentage indicating specific objectives are 'very important' (left column) and percent ranking specific objectives as 'most important' and 'next most important', respectively (centre and right columns). The introductory question read as follows: 'Municipalities can have different *objectives* which they attempt to achieve. Below we have listed several such objectives. How important do you feel each of these objectives is? Indicate your opinion on a scale from 1 (of little importance) to 5 (very important)'. Then a follow-up question read as follows: 'In your opinion, which of the objectives listed above (from A to F) are the *two most important*'? (Respondents had an opportunity to indicate the *most important* and the *next most important* separately.)

two efficiency objectives, is one reflecting a component of local democracy ('That there is good contact between residents and elected representatives'), which 49 per cent perceived to be very important. By comparison, an objective even more directly related to the participatory component of democratic self-government ('That residents are involved in local political issues') is viewed as very important by only 28 per cent of all respondents. Objectives receiving the most lukewarm endorsement, however, are those reflecting the value of local autonomy – i.e. 'That local evaluations count more than national standards' and 'That the municipality can make income and expenditure decisions without central government interference'. Only 24 and 18 per cent, respectively, perceived these as very important.

Responses to the initial question, in short, suggest that in evaluating alternative objectives of local government, Norwegians value efficiency and democracy more highly than autonomy, and efficiency of local government appears to be valued to a greater degree than democracy.[5] This tendency is even more evident in results from the follow-up question in which respondents were asked to identify the two objectives they personally considered to be the most important. These results are found in the columns centre and right hand in Table 9.2. Items relating to the value of efficiency once again end up in first and third place respectively, those relating to democracy occupy second and fourth place, while those relating to local autonomy attract the lowest level of endorsement.

Opposition to municipal mergers: services over democracy

This general pattern of findings is also evident in connection with a battery of questions concerning the issue of municipal mergers. The background for asking these questions is a debate concerning the restructuring of Norwegian local government, a debate which has occupied a prominent place on the political agenda for over 50 years (cf. Rose 1996a: 168–71). Central to the most recent round in this debate was a report submitted by a government commission appointed to look into the question anew. This report (NOU 1992: 15) contained a recommendation that municipalities should, as a rule of thumb, have a minimum of 5,000 inhabitants. This recommendation, were it to be adopted, would eliminate a little more than 55 per cent of all muni-cipalities existing in Norway today. Not surprisingly, the report raised a storm of protest, especially from the smaller municipalities. The recommendation was toned down in the white paper subsequently submitted for parliamentary consideration (St.meld. nr. 32 1994–95), but when Parliament finally dealt with this paper it went even further, formally rejecting the idea of compulsory mergers.

The important point here is that the topic of municipal amalgamation has been a major subject of debate in recent years, and there is therefore good reason to believe that most people have some familiarity with the issue. Opinions expressed on the matter, in other words, are not likely to be without some background and forethought. Under these circumstances, the results obtained from the national survey are quite noteworthy.

To begin with, a substantial majority – slightly over 80 per cent of those having an opinion on the issue – indicated they would consider a proposal to merge their own municipality with one or more neighbouring municipalities to be a bad proposal. Yet of greater note is what people indicated was of import-ance to them in evaluating such a proposal. Respondents were given a set of eleven different considerations, all of which have been raised in the public debate, and were asked to identify what they felt were the two most important considerations for them personally. Results from this question are presented in Table 9.3. For purposes of presentation, the eleven considerations are grouped in three general categories based on their content and then rank ordered according to the percentage of respondents evaluating each consideration to be either 'most' or 'second most' important.

The findings presented in Table 9.3 are consistent with the tendencies

Table 9.3 Residents' viewpoints regarding the most important considerations in relation to municipal amalgamation*

Relevant considerations	Percent 'most important'	Percent 'next most important'	Sum
Service-related conditions			
Effectiveness of municipal service delivery	29	12	41
The scope of municipal services	16	16	32
A just distribution of public services	16	16	31
Possibilities for adapting public services to the needs of residents	10	18	28
Social and political conditions			
Conflicts between different parts of the municipality	9	8	17
Contact between the residents and elected representatives	5	9	14
Conditions for local democracy	7	3	9
A sense of solidarity among municipal residents	3	7	9
Political involvement of residents	1	3	3
Municipal autonomy			
The need for financial transfers from central government	3	5	8
Municipal autonomy in relation to central government	2	5	7
N (= 100%)	(2,768)	(2,746)	

* Percentage indicating a consideration is 'most important' and 'next most important' respectively. The question read as follows: 'Which two considerations from the list above (from A to K) would you say are *the most important for you personally*, were an amalgamation to be suggested'?

observed previously. When forced to prioritize and make a choice among considerations reflecting different values and role orientations, the considerations ranking highest are those relating to the provision of public goods and services. Considerations of a social–political character, and especially those relating to democratic local self-government, are to a substantially lesser degree perceived to be among the two most important aspects. Particularly striking is the fact that 'political involvement of residents', a condition seen by many as critical for the maintenance of a vibrant local democracy, ends up with the lowest combined ranking of all possible considerations – only a little over 3 per cent. Two other considerations which also directly relate to the democratic character of local self-government – contact between residents and elected representatives, and general conditions for local democracy – obtain somewhat stronger support (a combined rating of 14 and 9 per cent respectively), but none the less rank no higher than sixth and seventh among all eleven considerations specified.

By comparison, two considerations pertaining to municipal autonomy again end up near the bottom of the list, being evaluated as most or second most important by only a small segment of the population. It would appear, in essence, that if Norwegians are inclined to take to the barricades to defend the present structure of local government, they will do so first and foremost based on considerations relating to service delivery, not out of concern for the maintenance or strengthening of local democracy and autonomy!

A preliminary summary

The results from all three batteries presented here converge in a mutually consistent pattern. Bluntly stated, it appears that local government is primarily valued as an instrument of efficient production of public goods and services, not as an arena for autonomous self-government and democratic citizen involvement. Residents, in turn, show a tendency to emphasize their role as consumers of public goods and services, not as taxpayers or active political citizens.

This conclusion is even more evident if responses to the three questions displayed in Table 9.1, regarding which of the three considerations within each question respondents perceived to be the most important to them personally, are combined. The results of such a procedure may be displayed with the aid of a triangle in which individuals who consistently select items reflecting one specific role orientation in all three questions are placed at one corner of the triangle (Figure 9.1). Those who choose one item from each of the three role orientations, by contrast, may be placed at the mid-point of the triangle, while six other points along the sides of the triangle represent alternative combinations of two choices of one role orientation and one of another.

The resulting distribution noted in Figure 9.1 reveals a clear tendency; there is considerable concentration of individuals around the consumer point of the triangle. In addition to the 17 per cent who make three choices reflecting a consumer role orientation (which is the largest single segment of the population), an additional 26 per cent emphasize a consumer role orientation in two

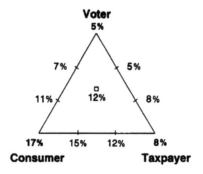

Figure 9.1 Salience of alternative citizen role orientations. Distribution of alternative response combinations reflecting what is most important to Norwegians in their relations to local government (shown as percentages)

of their three choices, while indicating either a taxpayer or citizen/voter role orientation in the third (15 and 11 per cent, respectively). In total these three combinations represent 43 per cent of all respondents, a proportion which constitutes a dominant plurality compared to other response combinations. By comparison, only 5 per cent make consistent choices emphasizing a citizen/ voter orientation, and not more than 17 per cent of the respondents made choices which place them in one of the three locations nearest the citizen/voter corner of the triangle.

Consumers, taxpayers and citizens/voters: who are they?

Just who are those individuals with more pronounced consumer, taxpayer and citizen/voter orientations respectively? Are they concentrated among specific segments of the population, or are they more evenly dispersed throughout the Norwegian population? Answers to these questions are not merely a matter of curiosity. To the extent that marked differences exist, they may well provide some insight into whether or not significant citizen reorientations are underway. From a practical political perspective, they may also serve to indicate a potential for socio-political conflict in which different groups may be pitted against one another based on their respective role orientations.

To answer these questions, three indices were constructed. Each index was based on the total number of consumer, taxpayer and citizen/voter items that respondents chose as being most important to them from among the three questions presented in Table 9.1. These indices were then regressed on selected population characteristics. The results of these regressions are presented in Table 9.4.

The findings reveal some interesting differences, the most prominent being those regarding individuals with high scores on the consumer and taxpayer indices. Those who score high on the consumer role orientation index, for example, are more typically younger, better educated women who work in the public sector, who sympathize with parties on the left, and to some degree the centre, of the political spectrum, and who live in households with relatively higher incomes. Those who score high on the taxpayer role orientation index, by comparison, are older, less well educated men who work in the private sector, who sympathize more with parties of the right, and, although not statistically significant, live in households with relatively lower income.

Those who score high on a citizen/voter role orientation are a much less distinct set of individuals, at least in terms of the characteristics considered here. In so far as these individuals in any way stand out from the population as a whole, they do so in terms of being somewhat younger persons living in smaller municipalities. They also sympathize more with parties of the right than they do parties of the left, although the tendency is weak.

Clearly there are factors other than those considered in Table 9.4 that may be associated with, and contribute to, individual role orientations, something confirmed by the low values of an adjusted R^2 for each regression. These findings

Table 9.4 Regression of indices regarding three citizen role orientations on selected population characteristics. Standardized regression coefficients. †

Population characteristics	Role orientation		
	Consumer	Taxpayer	Voter
Gender (women)	0.084***	−0.087***	−0.005
Age	−0.051*	0.100***	−0.051*
Education	0.166***	−0.200***	0.021
Income (household)	0.054*	−0.036	−0.026
Sector of employment	0.073**	−0.084***	0.005
Political sympathy‡			
Parties of the center	0.062*	−0.070*	0.002
Parties of the left	0.095***	−0.045	−0.067*
Size of municipality	0.038	0.011	−0.060*
Adjusted R^2	0.07	0.09	0.01

$N = 1,693$ Significance *** = 0.001   ** = 0.01   * = 0.05

† Indices are based on the total number of items reflecting a specific role orientation that were selected by a respondent as being most important to them personally (cf. Table 9.1). All of the indices have values ranging from 0 to 3.

‡ Political sympathy is operationalized by a set of dummy variables in which a variable representing two parties of the right – the Progress Party (Frp) and the Conservative Party (H) – serve as the reference point for the remaining two dummy variables, which are defined as follows: Parties of the centre = Christian People's Party (KrF), Centre Party (Sp), and the Liberal Party (V); Parties of the left = Red Electoral Alliance (RVA), Socialist Left Party (SV), and the Norwegian Labour Party (DNA).

must therefore be interpreted with caution. The profiles to emerge from these regressions, especially for those who are most consumer and taxpayer oriented, none the less open up some interesting interpretations. For one thing, they dovetail with work suggesting the emergence of a new public sector class in Norway, a class in which women predominate and that exhibits distinct value orientations and political behaviour (cf. Hoel and Knutsen 1989; Knutsen 1986; Lafferty 1988). The results also reveal a clear division between younger people who have a more pronounced consumer orientation on the one hand, and older individuals who display a greater propensity to emphasize a taxpayer orientation, on the other.

This latter difference may be no more than a life-cycle phenomenon, yet the fact that, especially older men with less education and somewhat lower household income, are over-represented among individuals stressing a taxpayer orientation suggests the possibility of a generational component. If there is indeed a generational effect involved, the implication is substantially different from that posited by Inglehart in his much debated work (Inglehart 1977, 1990). Rather than implying that those who have grown up under conditions of plenty turn their attention to the realization of 'post-materialist' values, while those who grew up under conditions of relative scarcity maintain 'materialist' interests, the findings suggest that the former have a more pronounced consumption or expenditure orientation, whereas the latter retain a (tax)payer or revenue orientation – a pattern which may apply to the public as well as private realm.

Discussion and conclusion

To recapitulate, many Norwegians appear to have a relatively weak orientation toward active political citizenship, and the role of local government as a democratic socio-political arena seems to have fallen into the shadow of local government as an instrument of public service production. The validity and generalizibility of these findings is of course open to discussion. The empirical approach is new and demands replication, both in Norway and in other settings. As stated here, moreover, the conclusion is a simplification: variations are to be observed, and additional nuances could be highlighted. It is important to stress, however, that further, more deeply probing analyses serve to confirm the major tendencies presented here. Those who emphasize their role as citizen/ voters, for instance, tend to a greater degree than others to place emphasis on democracy rather than efficiency or autonomy as an important objective of local government. Likewise, those who emphasize their own role as taxpayers tend more than others to see efficiency (and also autonomy, which can be seen as an important condition for the realization of efficient service production) as an important objective of local government.[6]

There is also a clear and logically consistent relationship between the individual's own set of role orientations and which considerations respondents perceive to be most important in assessing the issue of municipal amalgamation. Those who emphasize their own role as consumers are more concerned than others with the implications a merger could have on the scope of municipal services and whether or not services are well adapted to the needs of local residents, whereas these same persons are less concerned about the character of contact between residents and elected representatives. Those who emphasize their own role as voters and politically active citizens, by comparison, exhibit a nearly opposite pattern: they are most concerned about the implications of amalgamation for contact between citizens and elected representatives as well as the conditions for local democracy, while they are less concerned than others about the scope of municipal services.

There is good reason to believe, in short, that these findings are not merely a product of the measurement instruments employed, much less a reflection of random, poorly grounded and inconsistent attitudes as has sometimes been suggested is characteristic of responses to survey research.[7] On the contrary, the overall impression is that respondents have given expression to a set of reflected, internally consistent attitudes. That the findings appear to be robust and substantively valid does not, however, mean they offer unconditional support for a hypothesis suggesting shifting citizen orientations due to welfare state policies. Several caveats are in order. First, the findings relate to how Norwegians orient themselves in the context of local government. It was argued that this is the best context for investigating the possible impact of welfare state policies on citizen orientations since local government is the setting in which Norwegians and citizens in most other countries have their primary encounter with public authorities and the welfare state. Yet to say that a consumer orientation predominates over a citizen/voter or taxpayer orientation in the context of local government does not preclude the possibility that other orientations – e.g. that of a citizen/voter or taxpayer – may be more prevalent in other settings. Given the dominance of national authorities in making revenue decisions (decisions that affect local as well as national government), for example, it is possible that a taxpayer orientation might be more prominent in the context of national as opposed to local politics.

Likewise a citizen/voter orientation may have stronger salience in national as opposed to local politics. Indeed, given the absence of revenue issues of major significance at the local level in Norway, and the predominance of national issues in setting the framework for many of the activities for which local authorities are responsible, one might wonder what ground is left for local politicians to do battle over. That this is not merely a rhetorical question is underlined by extensive research results in which there is little evidence pointing to the importance of partisan political differences in decision making at the local level in Norway (Sørensen 1989).

A second ground for caution in interpreting the present findings is that they are of a static character. The fact that a consumer orientation and an emphasis on local government as an effective provider of public services predominate at present does not necessarily mean that this is more so today than previously. In a national survey conducted nearly 30 years earlier evidence was also found which suggested a marked tendency for individuals to emphasize considerations relating to effective service provision more than aspects of democratic self-government in justifying their preferences for strengthening local government (Kjellberg and Olsen 1968). These earlier findings underline the need to exercise caution in drawing conclusions about shifts in citizen orientations over time (cf. Hirschman 1982). However, recently published findings based on more systematic time series data do point to increased strength of 'materialist' cultural orientations among Norwegians in the last 10 years, and a comparable decline in more 'idealistic' cultural orientations (Hellevik 1996). A number of the value components comprising these cultural dimensions have a close bearing on the citizen role orientations discussed in the present chapter. A combination of findings suggests, therefore, that some reorientation of a short- if not long-term variety may indeed have occurred among the Norwegian population.

Even if Norwegians have become more consumer-orientated, both in politics and in more general cultural terms, such a shift cannot be unequivocally interpreted as a consequence of welfare state policies. Other developments may provide equally relevant explanations, or partial explanations, of such a shift in orientations. One development of particular relevance has been the manner in which public authorities in many countries, Norway among them, have shown increased fascination with models and metaphors drawn from the private sector. The work of Osbourne and Gaebler (1992) is one of the most widely known statements of this 'new public management' school of thought, the essence of which is greater use of market mechanisms in connection with public sector activities. The importance of these new public management practices is that they serve to highlight and emphasize the individual's role as a consumer of public goods and services, something which can only be expected to reinforce a 'privatization' in citizen orientations that may be spawned or nurtured by welfare state policies. If such a dynamic exists, it would seem that a shift in the relative focus of individuals from citizen/voters to consumers, from public to private citizens, is likely to be most pronounced in settings precisely such as those found in Scandinavia, where the welfare state has reached a fairly advanced stage of development, and where new public management practices have to a greater or less extent been implemented (cf. Klausen and Ståhlberg 1998). Evidence from Sweden (cf. Montin 1993; Montin and Elander 1995), moreover, suggests that this proposition applies every bit as much (and perhaps more so) in situations where welfare states have been forced to undertake cutbacks in the face of economic constraints as elsewhere (cf. Kuhnle 1988).

In concluding, it is appropriate to turn from the empirical to the normative realm. For it is important to make clear that a consumer orientation is not, in its own right, illegitimate. It is as much a component of contemporary citizenship as that of being a taxpayer or politically active voter, to mention the two other orientations considered here. The problem for democratic citizenship arises when one such role orientation becomes so dominant that it may overwhelm and weaken other role components – in particular should a consumer role orientation gain such prevalence that it overshadows the taxpayer/producer and citizen/voter role orientations. It is precisely in this regard that recent trends emphasizing consumer sovereignty and placing greater reliance on mechanisms of user control in the public sector are problematic. The reason is quite simple: user control is not necessarily synonymous with voter control. Indeed, user control and voter control may in fact be quite contradictory to one another. User control serves to shift the arena for decision making and, in the extreme case, even removes issues from the public domain, thereby under-cutting and depriving non-users of influence over decisions and activities which quite rightly belong in the public domain, where they are subject to influence by all citizens. Arrangements stressing user control, in essence, may give individuals even less reason to engage themselves as voters since the role as citizen/voter becomes less relevant and less necessary. Forms of citizen involve-ment which stress the individual's role as consumer and/or (tax)payer without at the same time underlining and encouraging the individual's role as voter and politically more broadly focused citizen, in short, imply a clear risk of eroding the broader meaning of citizenship, and may therefore rightly be met with some scepticism. Recent work summarizing Scandinavian experiences with new forms of local organization (Bogason 1996; Nyseth and Thorpe 1997) serves to underline this problematic side of increased consumer orientation in public service delivery. Other findings from the same research project as this chapter is based (e.g. Rose 1996b; Rose and Pettersen 1995, 1997), likewise suggest that this is a risk which must be taken seriously.

Notes

* This chapter draws upon data gathered in connection with a research project entitled 'Consumers, Taxpayers, Citizens – The Individual's Relations with Local Government'. The project was financed by the Norwegian Research Council (project nr. 103187/510) as part of a broader programme of research on local government. The programme was also supported by the Ministry of Local Government Affairs, the Norwegian Association of Local Authorities, and the Ministry of the Environment. Some of the analyses reported in this chapter have been carried out in collaboration with Audun Skare and reported elsewhere (Rose and Skare 1996a, 1996b). This support and collaboration is gratefully acknowledged. Responsibility for the viewpoints and interpretations contained in this chapter, however, rests with the author alone.

1 See, for example, Dahrendorf (1994) and Walzer (1989). In the Norwegian context this issue is evident in the work of Eriksen (1993), Eriksen and Weigård (1993) and Hansen (1995).

2 In this chapter the term consumer is used to cover all forms of usage of public goods and services, including those forms which might otherwise make the terms patient, client and/or customer equally appropriate.

3 These questions were interspersed in a postal questionnaire sent to individuals who had first been interviewed by telephone. 2,994 of the 3,833 persons interviewed by telephone completed and returned the postal questionnaire. Except for slight under-representation of individuals with less formal education, respondents are representative of the population between 18 and 80 years of age.

4 The notion of citizenship may well encompass other role components – a producer role for example (cf. Carens 1986). For the current research project, however, a decision was taken to limit attention to the three components suggested here.

5 It is important to stress that in the initial evaluation respondents were free to indicate that all of the objectives were equally important or, alternatively, equally unimportant should they have so desired.

6 All these differences are significant at the 0.05 level or better.

7 The debate following in the wake of Converse's classic article (1964) is well known in this regard. For a review of important developments relating to this debate since the 1970s, see Sniderman (1993) and Sniderman *et al.* (1991).

Bibliography

Bennett, S. E. and Bennett, L. L. M. (1986) 'Political participation', in A. Long (ed.) *Annual Review of Political Science*, vol. 1, Norwood, NJ: Ablex Publishing Corp.

Bogason, P. (ed.) (1996) *New Modes of Local Political Organizing*, New York: Nova Science Publishers.

Burns, D., Hambleton, R. and Hoggett, P. (1994) *The Politics of Decentralization*, London: Macmillan.

Carens, J. H. (1986) 'Rights and duties in an egalitarian society', *Political Theory* 14, 1: 31–49.

Converse, P. E. (1964) 'The nature of belief systems in mass publics', in D. E. Apter (ed.) *Ideology and Discontent*, New York: Free Press.

Dahrendorf, R. (1994) 'The changing quality of citizenship', in B. van Steenbergen (ed.) *The Condition of Citizenship*, London: Sage Publications.

Eriksen, E. O. (1993) *Den offentlige dimensjon*, Oslo: Tano forlag.

Eriksen, E. O. and Weigård, J. (1993) 'Fra statsborger til kunde: Kan relasjonen mellom innbyggerne og det offentlige reformuleres på grunnlag av nye roller?' *Norsk statsvitenskapelig tidsskrift* 9, 2: 111–31.

Fevolden, T., Hagen, T. P. and Sørensen, R. (1992) 'Mål med kommunal organisering', in T. Fevolden, T. P. Hagen and R. Sørensen, *Kommunal organisering*, Oslo: Tano forlag.

Giddens, A. (1982) 'Class division, class conflict and citizenship rights', in *Profiles and Critiques and Social Theory*, London: Macmillan.

Grønlie, T. (1991) 'Velferdskommunen', in A.-H. Nagel (ed.) *Velferdskommunen*, Bergen: Alma Mater Forlag A.S.

Habermas, J. (1994) 'Citizenship and national identity', in B. van Steenbergen (ed.) *The Condition of Citizenship*, London: Sage Publications.

Hansen, T. (1995) 'Lokalt demokrati ved et vendepunkt?' in T. Hansen and A. Offerdal (eds) *Borgere, tjenesteytere og beslutningstakere*, Oslo: Tano forlag.

Hellevik, O. (1996) *Nordmenn og det gode liv*, Oslo: Universitetsforlaget.

Hirschman, A.O. (1982) *Shifting Involvements*, Princeton: Princeton University Press.

Hoel, M. and Knutsen, O. (1989) 'Social class, gender and sector employment as political cleavages in Scandinavia', *Acta Sociologica* 32, 2: 182–201.

Inglehart, R. (1977) *The Silent Revolution*, Princeton: Princeton University Press.

Inglehart, R. (1990) *Cultural Shift in Advanced Industrial Society*, Princeton: Princeton University Press.

Jennings, M. K. *et al.* (1989) *Continuities in Political Action*, Berlin: Walter de Gruyter.

Jones, G. and Stewart, J. (1983) *The Case for Local Government*, London: George Allen & Unwin.

Kjellberg, F. (1988) 'Local government and the welfare state: reorganization in Scandinavia', in B. Dente and F. Kjellberg (eds) *The Dynamics of Institutional Change*, London: Sage Publications.

Kjellberg, F. (1995) 'The changing values of local government', *Annals of the American Academy of Social Sciences* 540: 40–50.

Kjellberg, F. and Olsen, J. P. (1968) 'Det kommunale selvstyre: En opinions-undersøkelse', *Tidsskrift for samfunnsforskning* 9, 1: 1–18.

Klausen, K.K. and Ståhlberg, K. (eds) (1998) *New Public Management i Norden*, Odense: Odense Universitetsforlag.

Knutsen, O. (1986) 'Sosiale klasser og politiske verdier i Norge: "Middelklassen" i den offentlig sektor som "den nye klasse"', *Tidsskrift for samfunnsforskning* 27, 4: 263–87.

Kuhnle, S. (1988) 'Political reconstruction of the European welfare states', in H. Cavanna (ed.) *Challenges to the Welfare State*, Cheltenham: Edward Elgar Publishing.

Lafferty, W.M. (1988) 'Offentlig-sektorklassen: I støpeskjeen mellom de private og kollektive verdier', in H. Bogen and O. Langeland (eds) *Offentlig eller privat?* FAFO rapport 078, Oslo: FAFO.

Mann, M. (1987) 'Ruling class strategies and citizenship', *Sociology* 21, 3: 339–54.

Marshall, T. H. (1950) *Citizenship and Social Class*, Cambridge: Cambridge University Press.

Miller, D. (1989) *Market, State, and Community*, Oxford: Clarendon Press.

Montin, S. (1993) *Swedish Local Government in Transition*, Örebro Studies No. 8, Örebro: University of Örebro.

Montin, S. and Elander, I. (1995) 'Citizenship, consumerism and local government in Sweden', *Scandinavian Political Studies* 18, 1: 25–51.

NOU (1992) *Kommune- og fylkesinndelingen i et Norge i forandring*, Oslo: Kommunal-og arbeidsdepartementet. Norges offentlige utredninger, NOU 1992: 15.

Nyseth, T. and Thorpe, L. (1997) 'Borgerstyre eller brukerstyre i lokalsamfunnet? Institusjonelle nydannelser i demokratiperspektiv', *Norsk statsvitenskapelige tidsskrift* 13, 4: 483–508.

Osbourne, D. and Gaebler, T. (1992) *Reinventing Government*, Reading, MA: Addison-Wesley.

Parry, G., Moyser, G. and Day, N. (1992) *Political Participation and Democracy in Britain*, Cambridge: Cambridge University Press.

Pettersen, P. A. and Rose, L. E. (1996) 'Political participation in local politics in Norway: some do, some don't; some will, some won't', *Political Behavior* 18, 1: 51–97.

Rose, L. (1996a) 'Norway', in E. Albæk *et al.* (eds) *Nordic Local Government*, Helsinki: The Association of Finnish Local Authorities.

Rose, L. (1996b) 'The notion of local citizenship: is it meaningful?' Paper prepared for the National Conference of Political Science. Bardøla Høyfjellshotell, Geilo, Norway, 8–9 January 1996. Oslo: Department of Political Science, University of Oslo.

Rose, L. E. and Pettersen, P. A. (1995) 'Borgerdyder og det lokale selvstyret: Politisk liv og lære blant folk flest', in T. Hansen and A. Offerdal (eds) *Borgere, tjenesteytere og beslutningstakere*, Oslo: Tano forlag.

Rose, L.E. and Pettersen, P.A. (1997) 'Civic virtues and political behavior: theory and practice in the Norwegian case'. Paper delivered at the Midwest Political Science Association annual meeting, Chicago, 10–12 April 1997. Oslo: Department of Political Science, University of Oslo.

Rose, L. and Skare, A. (1996a) *Lokalt folkestyre i klemme?* Forskningsnotat 01/96, Oslo: Institutt for statsvitenskap, Universitetet i Oslo.

Rose, L. and Skare, A. (1996b) 'Kommuneinstitusjonen mot sekelskiftet: Hvor bærer det hen?' Working paper. Oslo: Institutt for statsvitenskap, Universitetet i Oslo.

Seip, A.-L. (1991) 'Velferdskommunen og velferdstrekanten – et tilbakeblikk', in A.-H. Nagel (ed.) *Velferdskommunen*, Bergen: Alma Mater Forlag A.S.

Sharpe, L. J. (1970) 'Theories and values of local government', *Political Studies* 3, 2: 153–74.

Sniderman, P. M. (1993) 'The new look in public opinion research', in A. W. Finifter (ed.) *Political Science: The State of the Discipline, II*, Washington, DC: The American Political Science Association.

Sniderman, P. M., Brody, R. A. and Tetlock, P. E. (1991) *Reasoning and Choice*, Cambridge: Cambridge University Press.

St.meld. nr. 32 (1994–95) *Kommune- og fylkesinndeling*, Oslo: Kommunal- og arbeidsdepartementet.

Sørensen, R. (1989) 'Den kommunale demokrati: En fortsettelse av rikspolitikken med andre midler?' *Norsk statsvitenskapelig tidsskrift* 5, 3: 267–92.

Togeby, L. (1993) 'Grass roots participation in the Nordic countries', *European Journal of Political Research* 24, 2: 159–74.

Twine, F. (1994) *Citizenship and Social Rights*, London: Sage Publications.

Walzer, M. (1989) 'Citizenship', in T. Ball, J. Farr and R. L. Hansson (eds) *Political Innovation and Conceptual Change*, Cambridge: Cambridge University Press.

Wolman, H. (1995) 'Local government institutions and democratic governance', in D. Judge, G. Stoker and H. Wolman (eds) *Theories of Urban Politics*, London: Sage Publications.

10 Citizenship and the struggle against social exclusion in the context of welfare state reform

Rob Atkinson

Introduction

Over the last decade within western Europe a growing interest has been expressed in the idea of European citizenship within the context of the EC/EU. Such a view holds that as economic integration proceeds apace political and social integration should take on an increasingly prominent role and that economic, political and social rights ought to be formalised into and guaranteed by an EU 'Bill of Rights'. At the same time the European Commission and many Member States have expressed a concern that significant sectors of the population have been, and are being, marginalized within European society threatening the breakdown of social solidarity and cohesion. These concerns have focused on the concept of social exclusion and the need to integrate/insert excluded individuals and groups. Citizenship has taken on a central role in these debates as the socially excluded have increasingly been identified with those for whom citizenship rights have either not been actualized or denied. A cohesive, and competitive, Europe is seen by many as one in which citizenship rights are realised for everyone. This of course leads us back to the issue of an 'EU Bill of Rights'.

Simultaneously major concerns have been expressed regarding the future viability of the 'European Social Model' in the context of increasing globalization. The essence of these arguments is that Europe can no longer afford to maintain the present welfare state arrangements as they act as a restraint upon the global competitiveness of Europe's economy (European Commission 1993a; Flynn, 1996a,b). The outcome of this has been a growing consensus that the welfare state must be reformed and social expenditure reduced.

In this chapter I investigate the role of citizenship in combating social exclusion in circumstances where substantial pressures are being mobilized to develop a new model of welfare which is 'leaner, fitter and meaner'. The first section of the paper outlines the problems confronting welfare states within the EU, highlighting not only 'economic' issues but also those arising from the declining working population, the changing age structure and pressures for increased levels of service provision. The second section examines theories of citizenship and proposals for a European citizenship, and in the third section I investigate the concept of social exclusion and how this links into arguments over the nature of citizenship.

Problems of the welfare state in contemporary Europe

Since the 1970s all European models of welfare provision have come under considerable pressure as the 'Golden Age' of post-war capitalism gradually disintegrated, severely affecting many staple industries employing large numbers of workers and providing reasonably well-paid, secure jobs and corresponding benefits. As a result economic growth, full employment and high levels of labour market participation declined, intensifying and creating new demands at a time when the financing of the welfare state was increasingly problematic, creating a new 'fiscal crisis' (see Rhodes 1996, for an overview). Before going on to discuss the various models of welfare provision I will provide some indications of the common problems facing all welfare regimes.

The first and most obvious problem facing all European states is the high level of unemployment. In May 1995 there were almost 18 million people unemployed within the fifteen EU states, just under 11 per cent of the working population (Eurostat 1995a: 7). Of these 48 per cent were long-term unemployed in 1994 (i.e. for one year or more) and half of the long-term unemployed had been out of work for 2 years or more (ibid.: 27). In addition the employment rate (ratio of employment to population of working age) had fallen from its peak of 62 per cent in 1992 to 60 per cent in 1994 (Eurostat 1995a: 8, rates for the US and Japan were 70 per cent and 78 per cent, respectively).

Despite the recovery in economic output since mid-1993 in most EU states '. . . unemployment rates have either stabilised or fallen slightly in the first part of 1995' (Eurostat 1995a: 7), nor is there any expectation that conditions will improve quickly, leaving the possibility of 'jobless growth'. There are of course major variations in levels of unemployment between Member States as Table 10.1 shows.

The situation outlined above has played a major role in increasing the percentage of GDP spent on social protection, reaching an all time high of 26.6 per cent of GDP in the EU in 1993 (27.7 per cent if the former German Democratic Republic is included). As can be seen in Table 10.2 functions associated with unemployment grew rapidly between 1989–93, although as Table 10.3 shows the old age/survivors category still remains the largest element of social protection expenditure.

However, the problems are not simply those caused by unemployment. As Esping-Andersen (1996a) has noted, systems of social protection are facing significant pressures to increase expenditure because of a growing elderly population, whose pensions have to be financed by a declining working population, and by the escalating costs of health care.

These developments have combined with the effects of increasing global competition to create considerable pressure for a reduction in social protection

Table 10.1 Percentage of working population unemployed, EU 1994

	EU15	EU12	B	DK	D	GR	E	F	IRL	I	L	NL	A	P	FIN	S	UK
% Unemployed	11.2	11.4	9.6	8.0	8.7	8.9	24.3	12.7	15.6	11.3	3.5	7.2	3.7	6.7	18.5	8.0	9.7
6 months		32.1	24.8	46.0	36.2	27.2	26.8	41.4	23.1	20.5	45.3	22.5	34.2	42.8	na	61.2	36.6
6–11 months		19.7	17.0	21.9	19.5	22.4	20.5	21.4	17.8	18.0	25.1	28.1	7.0	13.9	na	21.3	18.0
12 months plus		48.1	58.3	32.1	44.3	50.5	52.7	37.5	59.1	61.5	29.6	49.4	58.8	43.4	na	17.5	45.4

Source: Eurostat 1995b, Table 1.

B, Belgium; DK, Denmark; D, Germany; GR, Greece; E, Spain; F, France; IRL, Ireland; I, Italy; L, Luxembourg; NL, The Netherlands; A, Austria; P, Portugal; FIN, Finland; S, Sweden; UK, United Kingdom. na, not available.

Table 10.2 Growth of social benefits per head in real terms, 1989–93.

	Old age/survivors (%)	Unemployment/ promotion of employment (%)
Belgium	12.7	14.1
Denmark	7.2	51.2
Germany	1.9	36.3
Greece	–3.8	82.7
Spain	21.5	64.4
France	10.1	45.5
Ireland	12.6	41.1
Italy	22.4	50.9
Luxembourg	23.8	62.9
The Netherlands	14.0	10.1
Portugal	46.4	277.8
UK	21.5	17.2
EU 12	13.1	45.1

Source: Eurostat, 1995c, Table 1.

Table 10.3 Percentage of total social benefit expenditure, by function in 1993

	Old age/survivors (%)	Unemployment/ promotion of employment (%)
Belgium	45.3	11.6
Denmark	34.0	18.9
Germany	41.1	7.6
Greece	66.2	3.4
Spain	40.4	21.1
France	43.6	8.3
Ireland	28.1	17.1
Italy	62.8	2.2
Luxembourg	46.8	1.0
The Netherlands	37.1	9.2
Portugal	40.6	6.5
UK	41.3	7.3
EU 12	44.7	8.4

Source: Eurostat, 1995c, Table 2.

expenditure, as noted in the European Commission's White Paper on *Growth, Competitiveness and Employment*:

> The macro economic framework in the Community is being affected by certain fundamental imbalances which have caused a vicious circle to be created. The current levels of public expenditure, particularly in the social field, have become unsustainable and have used up resources which could have been channelled into productive investment. They have pushed up

the taxation of labour and increased the cost of money. At the same time, the constant rise in labour costs – affecting both its wage and non-wage components and caused, at least in part, by excessively rigid regulation – has hindered job creation.

(European Commission 1993a: Chs.1.1)

Clearly there is a perceived need to reduce the costs of social protection and also to create a more 'flexible labour market'; flexible both in terms of wages and working practices. In addition there is a clear implication that not only are wages too high but also that employers are bearing too much of the cost of social protection. Regardless of how the social protection system is financed these pressures have seen a reduction in the employer's contribution; over the period 1980–91 employers' contributions to social protection within the EC fell from 45 per cent to 41 per cent with the shortfall being made up by a mixture of higher employee and/or government contributions (European Commission 1993b: 50; Eurostat 1995c).

From the above we can see that European welfare states face a common series of problems – a sense of crisis (see European Commission 1995b). However, the manner in which they have tackled these problems reflects the particular welfare state in each county. Now we must turn to the work of Esping-Andersen and others to begin to make sense of the issues. Each of the three models of welfare state has been placed under considerable pressure to adapt to the changing conditions outlined above. However, while Esping-Andersen's models are extremely valuable there is a danger that they could be interpreted in an over-rigid manner. He himself acknowledges that any particular welfare regime will be a composite of the three models with one dominant. Moreover, it is widely acknowledged that a 'southern European' variant of the conservative/Catholic model exists (see Ferrera 1996; Gough 1996; Mingione 1995) with its own highly particularistic and uneven systems of social insurance and social assistance, variable standards of health care and considerable levels of political clientelism.

The German variant of the conservative/Catholic model is heavily reliant on the social insurance principle which both reflects and maintains status differentials. The German response to the problems of rising and persistent unemployment, an ageing population and the attendant increase in health and pension costs has created its own contradictions. According to Esping-Andersen (1996b) the principal reaction has been to encourage early retirement within the core workforce, thereby maintaining productivity increases. However, this strategy has aggravated the problem of financing pensions and failed to create new jobs. The outcome has been increasing numbers of workers, and their families, unable to gain access to the privileged core workforce and the benefits which go with it. This has created an increasingly sharp divide between a shrinking group of 'insiders' and a growing group of 'outsiders' who are either unemployed or working in the informal sector, both of which create problems for the welfare state. However, it seems unlikely that any radical reforms will be forthcoming in the near future (see Taylor-Gooby 1996).

The southern European variant of the conservative/Catholic model has recently attracted attention (see Ferrera 1996; Gough 1996; Mingione 1995) for its lack of a coherent and integrated social protection system when compared to its northern European counterpart. In countries such as Italy, Spain, Portugal and Greece social insurance systems, albeit often of byzantine complexity, exist, with access determined by an individual's employment status and contributions to a particular insurance scheme. With regard to social assistance, however, there is no universal citizen-based system through which the state guarantees those outside insurance-based schemes a minimum income. In countries such as Italy social assistance is provided by a complex, and sometimes chaotic mixture, of local authorities, the church, voluntary associations and the family (see Ferrera 1996; Gough 1996). Access to assistance provided at the local level may also be heavily reliant upon political clientelism as a means of deciding who does, and does not, gain access to benefits (Ferrera, 1996). The combined outcome of these developments is a geographically uneven, complex and highly polarised system of social protection in which the family retains a crucial role in the provision of 'welfare'. However, in circumstances where the state and economy are weak, such as in southern Italy, the family lacks the resources to combat poverty, leading to what Mingione (1995: 26) has described as '. . . the pauperization of a large part of the population. . .'.

The Scandinavian model, particularly in Sweden, is widely acknowledged to have the most egalitarian and redistributive welfare state. Access to benefits and services is largely as of right, i.e. on the basis of citizenship entitlements. However, this model has come under increasing pressure since the late 1980s to at least contain, if not actually reduce, the costs of the welfare state (see Gould 1993; Stephens 1996). These pressures have emerged partly as a result of high levels of unemployment and the concomitant cost of maintaining generous benefit payments. Were unemployment merely a short-term problem this would be manageable, however, it is widely assumed within Sweden that unemployment is unlikely to fall below 5 per cent in the future (Stephens 1996). Such a situation breaks the crucial link between full employment, where everyone works and pays taxes, and the financing of the welfare state. As a result benefits are now to be tied more closely to contributions. Further problems are also likely to emerge from the ageing population and the pressure which this places on both pensions and health-care costs. Moreover, if pressure continues for the Swedish State to reduce expenditure it could resort to a form of privatization where services are 'contracted out'. The implications of this are quite serious, particularly for the very large numbers of women employed in the state sector.

In the UK, under the influence of neoliberal ideas (see Atkinson and Savage 1994), the liberal model has strongly reasserted itself since 1979. As a consequence the UK has taken the most 'radical' measures in western Europe to address the pressures of competition, continuous high levels of unemployment, the rising costs of welfare and an ageing population. In the period since the early 1980s benefits have generally been forced downwards and targeting greatly increased. The other side of this approach has been an increase in flexibility within the labour market. One of the outcomes has been an increase in inequality (Barclay 1995), with a growing number of people exiting from the state and purchasing services in the private sector leaving the economically weak dependent upon declining state services.

The preceding paragraphs broadly indicate how each particular welfare regime has adjusted to meet the challenges outlined earlier. However, the particular strategy adopted was strongly influenced by the prevailing consensus and the ability of the institutional matrix of each regime type to respond to new circumstances. It is hardly surprising that in the UK, where the economic problems have been sharpest and the post-war consensus has actually disintegrated, that change has been most radical. The other regimes have as yet managed to 'maintain their shape', perhaps becoming leaner, fitter and meaner in the process. However, whether they will be able to resist more fundamental reforms in the future remains a moot point.

The problems facing welfare states will also be exacerbated for those who have joined the European Monetary Union (EMU) as governments focus on controlling public expenditure and public deficits in line with the conditions laid out in the Stability Pact. Social expenditures are likely to be a prime target in this process suggesting that further rounds of cost-cutting and even privatization/contracting-out may occur over the next few years.

It seems increasingly unlikely that a 'European Welfare State', mirroring national welfare states, will emerge in the foreseeable future. Despite all the hopes expressed for the expansion of the 'social dimension' and the Social Protocol of the Maastricht Treaty conditions seem to have forced something of a retreat from what may never have been a realistic option (see Leibfried and Pierson 1992; Lange 1993; Leibfried 1993). As Majone (1993) has argued, such an outcome was always unlikely given the massive transfer of resources from Member States to the Commission entailed and the former's unwillingness to surrender control over social policy.

Contemporary debates over citizenship

As the preceding section indicates there is considerable pressure in western Europe to reform the welfare state and, less overtly, the corresponding conceptions of citizenship. I will outline the dominant approach to citizenship in the post-war era before going on to review more recent attempts to rethink citizenship in the context of economic, social and political restructuring.

The dominant concept of citizenship in post-war academic discourse has been that of Marshall (1965). His work remains the touchstone for much contemporary debate. Marshall viewed citizenship, notably the social element, as a way of ameliorating inequalities in society, in particular he regarded it as a way of moderating class inequalities in the UK. He considered it essential, if a more or less unified society was to be created, that every citizen should not only have legal and political rights but also social rights – that every one, regardless of who they were, should have the right to a guaranteed standard of living.

We ought to acknowledge that Marshall was writing during the 'golden years' of the post-war era when almost everyone assumed that there would be perpetual economic growth which would pay for the establishment and (constant) expansion of the welfare state. It is important to recognize as Bottomore (1992: 59) has argued, that of the two – economic growth and citizenship – priority was given to economic growth which became the precondition for the maintenance and expansion of social citizenship (and the welfare state more generally). Today these conditions no longer prevail and key elements of social citizenship are in doubt.

More recently there has been a 'backlash' against the citizenship rights approach by those who argue that it places too much emphasis on rights/ entitlements and largely ignores the issue of duty/responsibility. The argument relating to duty/responsibility has been most cogently developed by Mead (1986) who argues that the welfare state, and its attendant social rights, has created an underclass. Mead emphasizes the 'permissiveness' of the welfare state – rights allow people to claim benefits without requiring anything of them in return (i.e. no duties or responsibilities are placed upon claimants). Long-term claimants become detached from the world of work and society creating a situation in which 'deviant' cultural norms develop and an underclass thrives. What the preceding emphasizes is the extent to which there is no one single authoritative definition of citizenship, it is a contested concept and issue, part of a political/social struggle and capable of being utilized/mobilized by a variety of different, and competing, forces.

In the context of the EU, the push towards greater economic integration has increased the prominence given to issues of political and social integration. This, in turn, raises questions about the degree to which citizenship is tied to nation states and the extent to which the EU can develop a European notion of citizenship. Once again, the issue of inclusion and exclusion is posed. The Medium Term Social Action Programme (1995–97) notes that:

> Social progress and social solidarity must form an integral part of the European approach to competitiveness. . . . Further support for the future construction of Europe will be forthcoming only through action which is both credible and visible, in which all citizens of the Union feel involved. . . . Europe should aim to provide 'opportunities for all' to play an active part in society in the years ahead and to engage in building Europe together.
>
> (European Commission 1995a: Introduction)

As part of this strategy a Comité des Sages was set up to investigate how the 'social and political dimensions' of integration might be furthered as part of the strategy of 'competitiveness with a human face'. Such a strategy entails a restructured welfare state that will not only support competitiveness but also act as a force for social solidarity and cohesion (Comité des Sages 1996). In essence, whilst acknowledging the existence of different forms of citizenship within the Member States, the committee argued that the time had come to systematize the different forms of citizenship and develop an EU 'Bill of Rights' which would consolidate and develop key social and political rights thereby countering the excessive emphasis on the economic dimension of integration (Comité des Sages 1996). Such a strategy would also help counter the democratic and social deficit at the heart of the EU and address the fact that most rights guaranteed in the Treaties apply to individuals as workers and not as citizens. The key rights advocated are a mixture of civil, political and social rights including: equality before the law, anti-discrimination, freedom of movement, right of workers to organize in defence of their interests, right to work or minimum level of income, right to education, health and housing (for more detail see Comité de Sages 1996: 48–52). Thus the committee argued:

> Economic progress, which is really only a means to an end, has become an end in itself . . . the object of the Union is to enable every citizen to realise his/her potential in conjunction with his/her fellows, bearing in mind the necessary solidarity with future generations, and that legal rights and economic and social progress must be subordinate to that aim.
>
> (Comité des Sages 1996: 26)

The parallels with Marshall's theory of citizenship are striking, demonstrating the important influence which it still exerts as we approach the new millennium.

The committee strongly advocated that these issues be a central part of the 1997 Amsterdam Treaty negotiations. However, such issues were largely ignored and much greater emphasis placed upon defining who is not eligible for European citizenship (i.e. who is excluded) and maintaining 'Fortress Europe' (see Pugliese 1995; Robins and Aksoy 1995).

Social exclusion and citizenship

Anyone familiar with social exclusion will be aware that there is no generally agreed definition of the term – it is a contested concept. I will therefore focus on two broad attempts to construct concepts of social exclusion. The first concept derives from the 'French tradition', while the second has its origins in European programmes and institutions most notably the Poverty 3 Programme and the Observatory on National Policies to Combat Social Exclusion.

The French tradition

This tradition has not produced a clear and unified concept within French social and political discourse (see Yépez Del Castillo 1994; Silver 1994; Martin 1996). However, two factors do seem to unite contemporary accounts. First, there is a dissatisfaction with the (Anglo-Saxon) concept of poverty. Second, is the idea that there is a common moral and social order in society which transcends particular individual, class, ethnic and regional interests. It is held that the state (the embodiment of the Republic) has a duty to ensure all citizens are assimilated into this moral and social order. Of course this French 'tradition' reflects a particular development, under the influence of the French Republican ethos, of the continental approach to poverty which stresses social solidarity rather than competitive individualism.

The concept of poverty is essentially seen to lie within an Anglo-Saxon liberal individualist discourse which acknowledges that society is fragmented and that the various groups which make up society are in open competition with one another. Moreover, poverty is viewed as a static concept – an outcome rather than a dynamic process – mainly concerned with income distribution and defining what constitutes an adequate level of income.

The French tradition, whilst not unaware of the importance of income distribution, places much greater emphasis on the need to create social solidarity and to ensure that all citizens are integrated into and participate in a national social and moral order (the *conscience collective* in Durkheim's terms). The nation as a living, almost spiritual, organism lies at the heart of this conception. Thus social exclusion is primarily concerned with relational issues and the dynamic processes which lead to the breaking of social ties and the marginalization of groups in relation to the nation. Social exclusion is seen as a result of the profound social and economic transformations which the modern world is undergoing, via mass long-term unemployment and the creation of isolated and dangerous spaces which are socially and spatially segregated from the rest of society. These developments pose major challenges to the unity of the state/nation.

The most interesting and potentially useful notion of social exclusion to emerge from this tradition is to be found in the work of Paugam (1995, 1996). Paugam (1996) makes the important point that those categorized as poor are not defined by their own internal relationships but by the collective attitude which society adopts to them – what he terms the 'social orientation to poverty'. He constructs three ideal types of the social orientation to poverty: (1) integrated poverty; (2) marginal poverty; (3) disabling poverty. My main concern is with Paugam's notion of disabling poverty, which is more concerned with social exclusion than integrated and/or marginal poverty. In these societies we find growing numbers of people who are not only outside the labour market, but who experience inadequate housing, poor health and high levels of welfare dependency, i.e. cumulative disadvantage. Excluded groups are seen as posing a threat to social cohesion and social order as they become increasingly isolated from the rest of society. Such developments are most common in societies characterized by high unemployment and unstable labour markets, such as France and Britain.

Paugam's notion of social exclusion retains the concept of poverty but locates it within the wider universe of exclusion. The poor are not a homogeneous category, he argues, and poverty is a multidimensional phenomenon – a dynamic process. It is important to identify what he terms '. . . indicators of economic and social precariousness (precarious employment, marital instability, economic poverty, inadequate social and family life, inadequate support networks and low levels of participation in social activities) . . .' (Paugam 1995: 50). Precariousness in one area (e.g. in social life) is unlikely to lead to social exclusion; however, if it is reinforced by precariousness in other areas (e.g. unemployment) then a vicious downward spiral may be initiated producing exclusion.

The European Community/Union discourse

While the Anglo-Saxon definition of poverty tended to dominate in the European Community until the mid-1980s, during the second half of that decade social exclusion began to appear in Commission documents. This reflects a view that during the 1970s capitalism entered into a period of profound and long-lasting structural change which affected every sphere of society. Hence, a notion was needed which could encompass the full range of outcomes produced by structural change. Social exclusion was already well established within sections of the Commission and appeared to offer a more complex understanding of these changes. Thus the Commission argued:

> The concept of social exclusion is a dynamic one, referring both to processes and consequent situations . . . it . . . states out the multidimensional nature of the mechanisms whereby individuals and groups are excluded from taking part in social exchanges, from the component practices and rights of social integration and of identity . . . it even goes beyond participation in working life: it is felt and shown in the fields of housing, education, health and access to services. . . .
> (European Commission 1992: 8; see also Green Paper 1993: 20–1)

However, it should be noted this approach is largely descriptive, lacking any clear definition of exclusion or identification of causal processes, a fact acknowledged by the Commission but attributed to the complex reality the concept represented.

Citizenship and social exclusion

In the 1990s a new version of social exclusion, which combined elements of the French and Anglo-Saxon traditions, emerged. This view was most clearly articulated by the Observatory on National Policies to Combat Social Exclusion (established by the European Commission in 1990) and in the European Communities' Poverty 3 Programme (or to give it its full title, Community Programme concerning the Economic and Social Integration of the Economically and Socially Less Privileged Groups in Society). It sought to reconcile the French and Anglo-Saxon traditions through the use of the concept of citizenship rights. Robbins *et al.* (1994) explicitly adopt Marshall's theory of citizenship as a means to identify social exclusion. As Room (1995), a key figure in these developments, noted:

> ... the Observatory sought to investigate social exclusion in both relational and distributional terms. To evaluate, on the one hand, the extent to which some groups of the population are denied access to the principal social and occupational milieux and to the welfare institutions that embody modern notions of social citizenship; to examine on the other hand, the patterns of multidimensional disadvantage to which these groups are vulnerable, especially insofar as these persist over time.
>
> (Room 1995: 7)

Social exclusion can be conceived '... in terms of the denial – or non-realisation – of citizenship rights ...' (Berghman 1995: 19).

Building upon the work of Irish Poverty 3 researchers, Berghman drew attention not simply to citizenship rights but to the societal institutions in which those rights are embedded and actualized, namely

1 the democratic and legal system, which promotes civic integration;
2 the labour market which promotes economic integration;
3 the welfare system promoting what may be called social integration;
4 the family and community system which promotes interpersonal integration. (Commins quoted in Berghman 1996: 10)

Social exclusion occurs when one or more of the systems breaks down, thus allowing us to focus on a comprehensive, multidimensional and dynamic process. This approach directs attention not simply to a lack of income but also to a range of living conditions such as housing, health, education, community, etc., which are anchored in the societal institutions outlined earlier. If, for instance, the labour market begins to break down this may lead to impoverishment and then to poverty (a form of social exclusion). Social exclusion can thus result from breakdowns in any of the institutional systems. But it seems likely that we can only genuinely talk of social exclusion when, for individuals or groups, several of these systems breakdown either as part of a chain reaction or simultaneously.

Despite the potential such an analysis offers, a citizenship approach to exclusion also has its problems. First, as already noted, citizenship is a contested concept. Thus, the meaning of social rights (or entitlements) is open to interpretation. As noted earlier within Europe there are major differences over the development and meaning of citizenship and social rights. Garcia (1996: 10) argues

> ... social justice was a major consideration in the development of social rights in the British and Scandinavian cases, whereas in continental Europe, the French revolutionary tradition on the one hand, and Catholic traditions on the other, stressed social solidarity.

Nor, as Giddens (1985) has noted, should we expect citizenship and associated rights to remain static. For instance in the UK of the 1980s and 1990s social justice has come to play a secondary role with much greater emphasis placed on rights in relationship to the market (Robbins 1992).

Moreover, Duffy (1995: 46–7) points out that the materialization of (social) rights differs considerably between countries and hardly provides the basis for a consistent rights-based approach to measuring and combating social exclusion. Yépez Del Castillo (1994: 617) points to the distinction between formal and substantive rights, asking: '. . . what is the true significance of social rights if the citizen is not in a position to demand that they be upheld or applied?. . . what is the use of a social right . . . without the necessary material conditions for its application . . .'.

Given this we should not expect the notion of citizenship to resolve the problems surrounding social exclusion.

Problems with social exclusion, cohesion and integration

The counterparts to exclusion are cohesion and integration which are seen as central to the achievement of solidarity and citizenship. However, as already noted, the attempt to understand and combat social exclusion through the concept of citizenship is not without its difficulties. Indeed, there are deeper and more serious problems with the concept of exclusion, particularly as it operates within the discourse of the EC/EU. As Levitas (1996) has persuasively argued, the dominant meaning of social exclusion within the EC/EU has taken on a pseudo-Durkheimian conservatism, one subordinated to a neoliberal economic discourse which emphasizes the market, competitiveness and efficiency. Within this context paid work is seen as the primary mode of integration into society. As a result, issues of gender, race, class, low pay, the working poor, etc., are largely absent. Thus attention is largely focused upon those living on the margins of society who display socially unacceptable forms of behaviour, e.g. drug addicts, criminals, welfare dependents, the homeless, the mentally ill, etc., i.e., '. . . the poorest of the poor, a sub-set of poverty; . . .' (Abrahamson 1996: 5). Thus a simplistic and reductive model is created which '. . . fails to distinguish between different situations and ends up imposing too simple a picture of a dual, or two-speed society divided into those who are "in and those who are out"' (Strobel 1996: 174). Social exclusion is thus reduced to manageable proportions by defining it as a problem of marginalized individuals and their pathologies while more problematic and emotive terms such as poverty and inequality are avoided.

Terms such as social cohesion and integration are also problematic. Such concepts tend to be presented in neutral terms, but as we have already noted the dominant discourse of exclusion is located within a particular social and economic discourse (social conservatism and economic neoliberalism). With reference to cohesion Pahl (1991: 348) has argued with regard to Britain:

> Since the capacity of occupational associations [e.g. trade unions] to generate social cohesion is at best partial and at worst seen to be dangerous, the focus has shifted to 'the family' and the 'community' not so much as counters to state power but rather to aid the state as appropriate loci of social control and social responsibility.

With reference to integration, Potter (1996) has argued that such a notion presumes a social consensus into which individuals/groups can be inserted, but this is to disregard the very different, and potentially conflictual, interests of those concerned. Given these points, notions of cohesion and integration must be treated as social and political constructs and, therefore, as problematic.

To a large extent, discourses of social exclusion and citizenship have avoided even posing, let alone tackling, these issues and the danger is that they may become profoundly conservative concepts largely assimilated to market liberalism and social conservatism. Thus, any associated concept of citizenship is equally likely to be tainted unless it specifically functions as '. . . an articulating principle that affects the different subject positions of the social agent . . . while allowing for a plurality of specific allegiances and for the respect of individual liberty' (Mouffe 1992: 235).

Conclusion

The interest in social exclusion and citizenship within the EC/EU has developed during a period of profound economic, political and social change. Esping-Andersen (1996c) argues that the concepts of equality and citizenship, partially rooted in workers' movements, which underpinned the establishment of the welfare state have been undermined by the emergence of demands for equality and equal citizenship from groups outside the traditional working class, thus undermining the consensus which established the welfare state. In the economic climate of the 1990s the welfare state has found it extremely difficult to satisfy old demands let alone meet new demands thus further undermining its support. He argues that we need to:

> . . . rethink the idea of redistribution and rights: accepting inequalities for some, here and now, but guaranteeing at the same time that those who fare less well 'here and know' will not always do so; that underprivileged will not be a permanent fixture of anyone's life course.
>
> (Esping-Andersen 1996c: 264)

Such a view implies that today's sacrifices will, somehow, be compensated tomorrow, a view reminiscent of traditional reformism which can see no alternative to the prioritorization of liberal notions of economic growth. Ironically, such a model seems likely to merely widen social divisions and exacerbate social polarization and marginalization leading to further expansion and intensification of social exclusion. In the meantime, social exclusion may become so deeply entrenched that when the 'good times' do return it may prove so intractable as to become a permanent feature of society similar to the 'underclass' in the US.

Moreover, the EC/EU has always been primarily an economic institution and in the 1990s this aspect has reasserted itself through an emphasis on the need for competitiveness within an increasingly global economy, which in turn has created strong pressures for the reform of the 'European Social Model'. In this context the concern over citizenship and social exclusion has largely been a sideshow, perhaps designed to give the impression that European institutions do recognize the fears of citizens (see Eurobarometer 1990) and are reacting to these fears. I would suggest that there is an element of policy symbolism (see Edelman 1977) at work here, i.e. appearing to do something without actually doing very much. Certainly the pressures on national welfare states prevents them from doing any more than attempting to counter the worst excesses of social exclusion. At worst the socially excluded are seen as deviants (the 'undeserving poor'). The attempt to extend full citizenship rights to all, seeking to counter social exclusion and poverty and create cohesion/solidarity, would appear to be prohibitively expensive.

Nor does the prospect for the development of a 'European citizenship' appear bright. Citizenship in each Member State is embedded within particular historical, political and social conditions which make it difficult to imagine a coherent European concept emerging. Of course there may well be another reason for this attempt to develop a European citizenship. Since 1789 citizenship has often been associated with the process of nation building, and any attempt to create a federal Europe requires the construction of a common European identity and citizenship – a 'European nation'. However, as Anderson (1983) has argued, a nation '. . . is an imagined political community – and imagined as both inherently limited and sovereign' (1983: 15). This first and foremost involves defining who is to be included and who is to be excluded (the other), which involves the construction of a sense of European homogeneity and identity. However, as Robins and Aksoy (1995) argue 'Whatever coherence and identity is achieved, it is at the cost of a perpetual vigilance in maintaining the boundary between "natives" and "strangers"' (ibid.: 94). This also involves a spatial element which clearly defines the boundaries of Europe:

> This desire for clarity, this need to be sure about where Europe ends, is about the construction of a symbolic geography that will separate the insiders from the outsiders, those who belong to the community from the strangers that threaten its unity. Through the same process by which it is creating itself, this small white and western European community is also creating the aliens that will always seem to haunt its hopes and ideals.
> (ibid.: 95)

The most obvious expression of this is the 'Fortress Europe' stance. However, within the EU groups are also being defined as insiders and outsiders, the most obvious case being ethnic minorities. But more widely the socially excluded risk being defined as outsiders – non citizens – spatially and social segregated (ghettoized) from the rest of European society. They run the risk of being seen as a burden upon the welfare state and a drag upon the economy. An expansive, other regarding and open concept of European citizenship could have a vital role in countering such developments, but in a climate which prioritorizes economic growth and competitiveness there seems little chance of such a notion of citizenship developing.

Bibliography

Abrahamson, P. (1996) *Social Exclusion in Europe: Old Wine in New Bottles*, mimeo.

Anderson, B. (1983) *Imagined Communities*, London: Verso.

Atkinson, R. and Savage, S. (1994) 'The conservative approach to policy', in S. Savage, R. Atkinson, and L. Robins, (eds) *Public Policy in Britain*, London: Macmillan.

Barclay, P. (1995) *Inquiry into Income and Wealth*, York: Joseph Rowntree Foundation.

Berghman, J. (1995) 'Social exclusion in Europe: policy context and analytical framework' in G. Room (ed.) *Beyond The Threshold*, Bristol: Policy Press.

—— (1996) *Conceptualising Social Exclusion*, Paper presented at European Science Foundation Conference on 'Social Exclusion and Social Integration in Europe', Blarney, March.

Bottomore, T. (1992) 'Citizenship and social class forty years on', in Marshall, T. H. and Bottomore, T. (eds) *Citizenship and Social Class*, London: Pluto.

Comité des Sages (1996) *For a Europe of Civic and Social Rights*, Report by the Comité des Sages, European Commission Directorate-General for Employment, Industrial Relations and Social Affairs, Brussels.

Duffy, K. (1995) *Social Exclusion and Human Dignity in Europe: Background Report for the Proposed Initiative by the Council of Europe*, Brussels: Council of Europe.

Edelman, M. (1977) *Political Language. Words that Succeed, Policies that Fail*, New York: Academic Press.

Esping-Andersen, G. (1990) *The Three Worlds of Welfare Capitalism*, Cambridge: Polity.

—— (1996a) 'After the Golden Age? Welfare state dilemmas in a global economy', in G. Esping-Andersen (ed.) *Welfare States in Transition. National Adaptations in Global Economies*, London: Sage.

—— (1996b) 'Welfare states without work: the impasse of labour shedding and familialism in continental European social policy', in G. Esping-Andersen (ed.) *Welfare States in Transition. National Adaptations in Global Economies*, London: Sage.

—— (1996c) 'Positive-sum solutions in a world of trade-offs', in G. Esping-Andersen (ed.) *Welfare States in Transition. National Adaptations in Global Economies*, London: Sage.

Eurobarometer (1990) *The Perception of Poverty in Europe in 1989*, Brussels, Brussels: Commission of the European Communities.

European Commission (1992) *Towards a Europe of Solidarity: Intensifying the Fight Against Social Exclusion, Fostering Integration*, Brussels: Commission of the European Communities, COM(92) 542.

—— (1993a) *White Paper on Growth, Competitiveness and Employment*, COM(93) 700 final, Brussels: Commission of the European Communities.

—— (1993b) *Social Protection in Europe*, Luxembourg: Commission of the European

Communities, Directorate-General Employment, Industrial Relations and Social Affairs.

—— (1995a) *The Medium Term Social Action Programme*, Brussels: Directorate-General Employment, Industrial Relations and Social Affairs.

—— (1995b) *Social Protection in the Member States of the Union*, Luxembourg: European Commission, Directorate-General Employment, Industrial Relations and Social Affairs.

Eurostat (1995a) *Employment in Europe 1995*, Luxembourg: Eurostat.

—— (1995b) *Statistics in Focus. Population and Social Conditions. Labour Force Survey. Principal results*, No. 6, Luxembourg: Eurostat.

—— (1995c) *Statistics in Focus. Population and Social Conditions. Social Protection in the European Union*, No. 15, Luxembourg: Eurostat.

Ferrera, M. (1996) 'The "southern model" of welfare in social Europe', *Journal of European Social Policy* 6, 1: 17–37.

Flynn, P. (1996a) *European Social Policy: Perspectives and Challenges*, Wirschaftsrat, Brussels.

—— (1996b) *IEA Lecture*, Dublin.

Garcia, S. (1996) 'Cities and citizenship', *International Journal of Urban and Regional Research* 20: 7–21.

Giddens, A. (1985) *The Nation State and Violence*, Cambridge: Polity.

Gough, I. (1996) 'Social assistance in Southern Europe', *Southern European Society and Politics* 1, 1: 1–23.

Gould, A. (1993) 'The end of the middle way?', in C. Jones (ed.) *New Perspectives on the Welfare State in Europe*, London: Routledge.

Green Paper (1993) *Green Paper. European Social Policy. Options for the Union*, Luxembourg: European Commission.

Lange, P. (1993) 'Maastricht and the Social Protocol: why did they do it?', *Politics and Society* 21, 1: 5–36.

Leibfried, S. (1993) 'Towards a European welfare state?' in C. Jones (ed.) *New Perspectives on the Welfare State in Europe*, London: Routledge.

Leibfried, S. and Pierson, P. (1992) 'Prospects for social Europe', *Politics and Society* 20, 3: 333–66.

Levitas, R. (1996) 'The concept of social exclusion and the new Durkheimian hegemony', *Critical Social Policy* 16: 5–20.

Majone, G. (1993) 'The European Community between social policy and social regulation', *Journal of Common Market Studies* 31, 2: 153–70.

Marshall, T. H. (1965) *Class, Citizenship and Social Development*, New York: Anchor.

Martin, C. (1996) 'French review article: the debate in France over "Social Exclusion"', *Social Policy and Administration*, 30: 382–92.

Mead, L. (1986) *Beyond Entitlement: the Social Obligations of Citizenship*, New York: Free Press.

Mingione, E. (1995) 'New aspects of marginality in Europe', in C. Hadjimichalis, C. and D. Sadler (eds) *Europe at the Margins. New Mosaics of Inequality*, Chichester: John Wiley & Sons.

Mouffe, C. (1992) 'Democratic citizenship and the political community', in C. Mouffe, (ed.) *Dimensions of Radical Democracy*, London: Verso.

Pahl, R. (1991) 'The search for social cohesion: from Durkheim to the European Commission', *European Journal of Sociology* XXXII: 345–60.

Paugam, S. (1995) 'The spiral of precariousness: a multidimensional approach to the process of social disqualification in France' in G. Room (ed.) *Beyond the Threshold*, Bristol: Policy Press.

—— (1996) Elements of a comparative research perspective on poverty in European societies, Paper presented at European Science Foundation Conference on 'Social Exclusion and Poverty'.

Potter, P. (1996) Alternatives to the concept of 'Integration' in the struggle against exclusion, paper presented at the ENHR Conference, Denmark, August 26–31.

Pugliese, E. (1995) 'New international migrations and the "European Fortress"', in C. Hadjimichalis and D. Sadler (eds) *Europe at the Margins. New Mosaics of Inequality*, Chichester: John Wiley & Sons.

Rhodes, M. (1996) 'Globalization and West European welfare states: a critical review of recent debates', *Journal of European Social Policy* 6, 4: 305–27.

Robbins, D. (1992) *Social Exclusion 1990–1992: The United Kingdom*, EC Observatory on Policies to Combat Social Exclusion, Lille: European Economic Interest Group.

Robbins, D. *et al.* (1994) *Observatory on National Policies to Combat Social Exclusion. Third Annual Report*, Lille: A and R.

Robins, K. and Aksoy, A. (1995) 'Culture and marginality in the New Europe, in C. Hadjimichalis and D. Sadler (eds) *Europe at the Margins. New Mosaics of Inequality*, Chichester: John Wiley & Sons.

Room, G. (1995) 'Poverty and social exclusion: the new European agenda for policy and research', in G. Room (ed.) *Beyond the Threshold*, Bristol: Policy Press.

Silver, H. (1994) 'Social exclusion and social solidarity: Three paradigms', *International Labour Review* 133: 531–77.

Stephens, J. D. (1996) 'The Scandinavian welfare states: achievements, crisis, and prospects', in G. Esping-Andersen (ed.) *Welfare States in Transition. National Adaptations in Global Economies*, London: Sage.

Strobel, P. (1996) 'From poverty to exclusion: a wage earning society or a society of human rights?', *International Social Science Journal* 148: 173–89.

Taylor-Gooby, P. (1996) 'Eurosclerosis in European welfare states', *Policy and Politics* 24, 2: 109–23.

Yépez Del Castillo, I. (1994) 'A comparative approach to social exclusion', International Labour Review 133: 613–33.

11 European social rights towards national welfare states

Additional, substitute, illusory?

Anna-Karina Kolb

Introduction

The European Union (EU) has been developing a series of new social rights.[1] This development has been taking place during a period of considerable stress for national welfare states as they attempt to increase social cohesion. Against this backdrop, European-level social action may offer new perspectives and options for combating further social fragmentation.

The development of an EU social policy faces three main challenges. The first lies in the fact that the impressive variety of EU social action and objectives do not easily lead to a coherent policy. Second, institutional and national interests present in the EU pose a serious challenge to achieving consensus on the social policy front. A third challenge arises from the context within which these decisions are to be made, that of European integration, defined as a new political and institutional 'regime' with a multitiered decision-making system. With these three obstacles in mind, European citizens cannot be sure of the type of social rights they will have and this raises many fundamental questions. What kind of social rights have been developed so far in the special political and institutional 'regime' which is the European Union and how comparable are they to existing national rights? Do these rights offer a real new window of opportunity for social integration and participation by European citizens? And can a dynamic for the implementation of social rights already be detected in the chaotic setting of EU social policy?

This chapter will begin with the introduction of some characteristics of European integration that directly affect the implementation of social rights on a supranational level. This will be followed by a brief presentation of EU social rights according to Majone's typology of regulatory and redistributive policies (Majone 1996). The regulatory category covers social rights developed in accordance with the Common Market and the freedom of movement of workers, and the redistributive category describes those promoted through Structural Funds support. Finally, the paper will outline the main dynamics in European social rights and their meaning for a possible European social citizenship.

Social rights on a (supra)national level

Article 8 of the Maastricht Treaty introduced the notion of European citizenship, with the definition of certain political rights. This article serves as a legislative response to the growing concern of EU authorities about the democratic legitimacy of the European project. By institutionalizing the notion of a European citizenship, they aimed to create a symbolic, legitimating status, with the objective of narrowing the gap between the citizens of Europe and European integration (European Commission 1993a; Marias 1994; Wolton 1993).

A large part of the legitimacy of a citizen's status is linked to the (re)distributive action of the state, through social policy. Social security is considered a basic democratic right in welfare states. Social rights are intrinsically linked to civil and political rights as they serve to guarantee the minimum socio-economic conditions underpinning the concept of civil rights and provide significant legitimizing potential. Widely held social rights, such as at the level of the state, also reflect a national agreement on the redistribution of public wealth and therefore a unique conception of solidarity.

European social rights did not develop in the same way as national social rights, nor do they have the same meaning for citizens. The Treaty of Rome of 1957 did not make express reference to social legislation apart from that necessary for the implementation of the Common Market and the free movement of workers. Social issues became a more important theme during the mid-1980s. This is reflected in the Single European Act of 1985, particularly in Article 130 on economic and social cohesion, in the Charter of Fundamental Rights for Workers of 1989, and later in the Social Chapter of the Treaty of the European Union (TEU) of 1992. This development followed the accelerated implementation of the Common Market and aimed at mitigating some of the expected negative effects of deregulation.

The historical and institutional background of EU social rights is quite different from the state experience in many ways. First of all the EU is not a state with a redistributive social policy, backed by an adequate budget and administration. Member States have maintained their grip on the social policy area, and supranational activity is thus largely excluded. As control over social policy is perceived as a means of state legitimization this situation will not easily be altered (Pierson and Leibfried 1995).

As a result of the Common Market, the most extended EU social competencies relate to freedom of movement for workers. Member States have grudgingly accepted this supranational authority because of the fundamental objective of promoting labour mobility. For Pierson and Leibfried, the existing 'competitive state-building' between national and supranational action is nevertheless not a zero-sum game because the original type of social rights implemented by the Community creates opportunities for all actors to develop their own strategies. For example, states – which retain major social competencies – are to implement EU regulations in their own welfare state based on their own traditions, priorities and sets of actors. It is only logical that states will implement EU rules according to their interests. EU social policy is therefore not merely social regulation, but a process of adapting and interpreting policy measures by various national and institutional actors.

There is also little consensus among Member States about the character future EU social policy will have. Most notable is the long-standing disagreement between Britain and its European partners on the orientation of EU social action. That disagreement, in fact, tends to obscure the wide gulf that exists among Member States on many social topics, due to different national social histories, traditions and socio-economic levels. One well-known example of contested legislation was passed in 1996, and pertained to posted workers (European Council 1996a), which was accepted against Britain and Portugal's wishes (Europolitique 2121/2137). The intent of the directive is to prevent abuses in the posting of workers throughout Europe by setting minimum standards for their working conditions. The major obstacle was setting a threshold period for the application of national provisions relating to minimum pay and paid holidays. Some states considered the immediate application of national provisions as a protection against social dumping. Britain and Portugal – whose social standards are among the lowest ones – were opposed to this restrictive application which would considerably affect European competitiveness. The arguments about workers' social interests are intrinsically linked to the protection of national standards and fears of losing some competitive advantage. Controversy about the role of the EC as a 'social warrant' regime is therefore always mixed with attempts to protect national interests.

Dissension among Member States has also led to the complicated institutional framework created by the Maastricht Treaty for social policy. In the Social Protocol and Agreement of that treaty, Britain has allowed the Fourteen to carry on a wider and deeper social policy inside the EC, while it abstains from implementing certain social norms. The effects of such an institutional agreement have been somewhat negative. With the possibility of implementing two social policies – one with fifteen members and one with only fourteen – the uniformity of Community legislation on the entire European territory is at stake (Watson 1993; Séché 1993). For fear of damaging European legal homogeneity the Fourteen have been trying to include Britain in the decision making, lengthening the consultation and negotiation procedure, although the Protocol should have helped accelerate decision making in social matters. The result is that Member States have used the Social Protocol as little as possible because of its weak legislative basis and its complicated institutional framework. Differentiated social integration in the EC does not seem to be a practical way of implementing new social rights.

National disagreements cover some social action programmes. For example, Germany and Britain did not accept the budget of two social programmes – one in favour of the aged, the other against poverty and social exclusion – on the official grounds of the unclear legislative basis for majority voting (Europolitique 2161). The 1997 Treaty of Amsterdam should temporarily solve this problem as it includes the fight against exclusion in the objectives of EC social policy. But even deeper disagreement exists. On the one hand, Britain does not share the same vision of poverty and social assistance as the Commission and some other Member States. On the other hand, the German federal system gives significant autonomy to the *Länder* in social assistance and these latter do not want their role to be reduced by European social programmes. The achievement of new European social rights is resisted by many actors for strategic reasons that have nothing to do with the main objectives of EU social policy; whatever moral or ideological dimension social rights could have from a European citizenship perspective, they become bargaining chips in the political arena.

Finally, the construction of European social rights is influenced by the increasingly apparent limitations of the national welfare states, which cannot simply serve as a model of what should be created on a supranational level. The so-called crisis of the welfare state also affects the economic and socio-cultural basic values of the dominant paradigm of welfare states (Roche 1992). The persistence of, and at times increase in, poverty and social exclusion, as well as the burden of unemployment, serves as a reminder of the limits of welfare state action (Room 1990: 117–18). The Commission's position toward these limits is not very clear. In the copious EU literature on social problems the limits of the welfare state are recognized, but few alternatives are proposed. This clamouring for new solutions based on the notion of a 'European social model' (of which the abstract definition refers to general values such as democracy, free collective bargaining, market economy or solidarity) is no longer very helpful. Delors himself advocates adapting the liberal model, with only minor reservations (European Commission 1994: 207–08). More generally, Commission discourse offers an overall analysis of the difficulties of the welfare state without questioning the basic principles of liberal models in a concrete way. Most of the difficulties of welfare states remain to be solved at the national level, according to national needs and resources.

The ambiguity of European social models are revealed when social objectives are confronted with the possible deregulating effects of EU liberalization policies, and with the budgetary restrictions imposed on welfare states by European Monetary Union (EMU). One of the most recent examples is the resolution taken on the employment chapter of the Amsterdam Treaty during the extraordinary European Council on Employment in November 1997. This resolution includes specific quantitative objectives in terms of providing national education and training programmes for different types of unemployed workers: these expensive measures are difficult to reconcile with national efforts made in order to respect the restrictive Maastricht criteria for the EMU.

European social rights

We will divide European social rights into two analytical categories: social rights firmly anchored in EC legislation and jurisprudence and related to the creation of the Common Market, and the more diffuse rights promoted through different Structural Funds programmes. This schematic, dichotomous approach is adapted from Jallade's presentation of the welfare state as being split between two main objectives: the rights of workers on the one hand and reducing inequalities through programmes fighting social exclusion, unemployment and poverty on the other hand (Jallade 1992). It also corresponds to Majone's distinction between regulatory and redistributive policies in the European political system (Majone 1996). Regulative policies are motivated by an efficiency criterion and have only indirect redistributive consequences. 'Redistributive' here refers to political values used to justify the distribution of resources to some groups in society. Regulative policies are, therefore, typical of EC social action related to the functioning of the Common Market. More specifically, those social rights are aimed at implementing freedom of movement of workers and services and creating a labour market at the European level. EC redistributive policy tries to reduce inequalities between the different countries and regions and foment social cohesion in the EU. That distinction does not impede interconnections: labour legislation is reinforced by many structural programmes on unemployment, vocational training, etc.

Workers' social rights[2]

Workers' social rights cover four fields:

- Rights directly related to the implementation of the freedom of movement of workers. These cover co-ordination of national social security systems and the implementation of the principle of non-discrimination for professional mobility (Articles 48 to 57 TEU);
- Rights that guarantee health and safety in the workplace (Article 117, 118 TEU);
- Equality in working conditions between men and women (Article 119 TEU);
- Social dialogue (between social partners) (Article 118B TEU).

Compared to national social rights, the scope of European rights is quite limited. Many essential fields have been excluded from Community competency, for example wages, union rights, strike and lock-out situations; other areas require unanimity in decision making (e.g. social security), which is a major hindrance to progress in social legislation. Yet workers' rights are the only European social rights *per se*, as they legally entitle workers and their families to social benefits in a Member State other than their own.

As a result, EU social rights are tied to the implementation of the internal market and free movement of workers. For example, workers would not move if they could not receive social security benefits in other EC countries. This transfer is prescribed and guaranteed by Community legislation; it has also been interpreted and implemented under the jurisdiction of the European Court of Justice (ECJ). The present social security regime for migrant workers fulfils minimum conditions for working in another EU country, particularly in relation to pension provisions. This does not represent a harmonization of the different national social security systems, which still offer workers and their families distinctive rights.

Under judicial interpretation by the ECJ, the basic principle of non-discrimination (Article 48 TEU) between national and EU workers has progressively entitled the EU migrant worker and her/his family – regardless of the family members' nationality – the same provisions as a national worker (Verschueren 1996). Relatives of the holder of the original rights – the worker in this case – can profit from the complete social security system of that state, ranging from admission to regular education to reduced railway fares for large families, not because of special EC-level social rights, but because of the prohibition of discrimination between EU Member State nationals (Alexander 1993: 488). The worker's family is also entitled to most social security benefits even if they do not live in the same EU country. These obligations for national authorities put an end to the major historical characteristics of national social rights: territoriality and nationality (Leibfried and Pierson 1995). Moreover, the ECJ has developed an extended interpretation of fundamental concepts: 'family' includes three generations: grandparents, parents and dependent children and the notion of employment includes categories of workers not recognized as such in some national legislation. EU social rights are, in a way, an extension of national ones; new European standards prohibit discrimination based on nationality and prescribe the territorial unit as the EU rather than just the Member State. This represents a new dynamic in implementing social rights at the national level and also a new way for citizens to enjoy social rights.

The impact and use of this set of social rights for migrant workers is, nevertheless, tempered when looking at the reality of labour mobility in Europe. The most recent EU statistics (General Directorate X 1996) reveal that slightly more than 2.14 million EU-national workers are employed in another EU country, out of a total EU population of 371 million. In total, 5.59 million EU citizens (1.5 per cent) were living in another Member State in 1993. This includes 501,100 pensioners (one out of every ten EU residents living outside their Member State is over 65 years old) and about 140,000 students. These statistics illustrate that free movement of persons is largely used by pensioners and students, not workers. Thus, pensioners and students, while not the intended targets of EC social legislation, have become the main beneficiaries. The principle of free settlement, corollary to freedom of movement, has been extended to all citizens in the EU – as long as citizens can provide for their needs – in an attempt to give some 'flesh' to the rather bony new concept of citizenship (Marias 1994: 17). The poor or unemployed have little if any access at all to that basic EU right.

More generally, the fact that only a minority of EU workers are affected by migrant social rights has resulted in the irrelevance of those rights for most of the population. Rights concerning health and workplace safety as well as social dialogue are more pertinent and enjoy wider popular interest among workers.

The restricted labour mobility of blue-collar workers is not surprising as emigrating is still a serious decision, made more difficult by its cultural and familial aspects. That decision is perhaps easier for managerial staff and professionals whose resources and aptitudes facilitate cultural and professional adaptation. The free-moving *Europe des élites* is also a reality in that sense. The potential legitimating power of EU social legislation could, thus, be diminished by its restricted scope and the social discrimination that it reveals.

The EU has set minimum standards on rights that guarantee health and safety at the workplace – 'minimum' in the sense that each country is then free to strengthen the EU required level of safety and health. Here the dynamic of EU social rights is based on the scope of the definition of workers' health and safety, on which Member States disagree. So far the Commission has included working time and parental leave in that definition. Britain has strongly contested the inclusion of working time under workers' health regulations and was unsuccessful in its bid to overturn the regulation before the ECJ (Riley 1997). The flexible interpretation of the Commission was possible because of the very vague definition of health and safety in the Treaty; such flexibility is also foreseen in the new Article 118c of the Treaty of Amsterdam that vaguely refers to social action relating to 'labour law and working conditions' without further specifics. The lack of precision in the treaties is often due to disagreements on the objectives of the article; those disagreements reappear when making legislation. The extension of the notion of workers' health places them in the wider context of their needs and concerns and comes closer to the notion of a citizen. It also means that the European Commission starts playing the traditional state role of a regulative authority responsible for a certain socio-economic 'order'.

The third field of EU social legislation is gender equality in working conditions. The original article (Article 119 TEU) only focused on equal salaries for men and women in comparable jobs. It was introduced in the Treaty of Rome because of French fears that their new gender equality legislation would diminish their competitive strength in Europe. Granting women equal social rights was not the primary objective of negotiators but rather the indirect result of national protectionist reaction to market liberalization. Protection and benefits for female workers have been improved by extensive regulation and various specific promotion programmes. Some initial national regulation was developed due to a 'pro-European' social dynamic. This was the case in Italy, which stimulated the implementation of full legislation for migrant workers because of the great number of Italian migrants all over Europe in the 1960s.

The extensive interpretation of the ECJ served to transform a competition argument into a general principle, dealing with numerous aspects of gender inequality in the workplace (Dehousse 1995). One example of the powerful ECJ interpretation is the Barber case which includes contracted-out pensions within Article 119 TEU.[3] Implementing equality in that field involves such massive financial transfers that the court prescribed a limited application before 1990; that limitation created a dispute and a continuing debate as to the extent to which Article 119 TEU may be amended (Honeyball and Shaw 1991). And the Kalanke case in October 1995 – which prohibited affirmative action in public administration posts because it gave unconditional priority to women in a job – has initiated a large public discussion on the application and legitimacy of the ECJ interpretation of affirmative action and has led to legal changes in the treaties.[4] The Treaty of Amsterdam explicitly allows Member States to apply discriminatory affirmative policies in order to implement gender equality in employment.

Social dialogue is the fourth major labour legislation field. It requires that the Commission consult acknowledged European social partners before presenting proposals in the social policy field. Partners can decide to negotiate an agreement on the issue at hand or they can request that it be transmitted to the Council for adoption as a EU decision (Yonnet 1995: 35–8; European Commission 1996a). The Commission has been using this new procedure with positive consequences for social rights, as in the case of the Directive on Parental Leave (the right of men and women to take a career break in order to look after a child) (European Council 1996b) and that concerning the Framework Agreement on part-time work (European Council 1997). This opens the possibility for social partners to seriously participate in the EU legislative process and tends therefore to extend their influence on labour legislation. It can be considered as something quite positive for the legitimization of EU decision making and a way of granting new rights to civil actors. It nevertheless creates problems for national governments that could be bypassed by social partners. The Amsterdam Treaty, therefore, specifies that the agreements developed through collective bargaining imply no obligation for Member States to apply them or to adapt their national legislation. The other problem comes from the relative weakening of traditional social partners' representation in Western countries.

Rights promoted through the Structural Funds

The other set of social rights promoted by the EU are much vaguer and have no legal roots in EU legislation. These rights emanate from various social programmes of the European Structural Funds. There are three Structural Funds: the European Regional Development Fund, the European Agricultural Guidance and Guarantee Fund and the European Social Fund. They cover a full range of programmes tackling various social problems and the establishment of a series of forums and networks (European Commission 1993c; European Commission 1996c). These funds and programmes try to prevent the causes and consequences of unemployment, inequality, poverty and social exclusion; they aim also at maintaining and developing economic and social cohesion among the different counties and regions of the EU (Articles 2 and 130A TEU).

These funds can also be considered as the counterpart of the Common Market programme and its deregulating effects over regions and the most underprivileged segments of the population. According to economic theory, the Common Market should tend to equilibrium and an optimal distribution of resources over time; compensatory measures such as the Structural Funds should therefore be transitional in nature (Room 1990: 122). The social objectives of EU social programmes should however be interpreted through the specific conditions of the creation of the Structural Funds and their development. The funds were mostly negotiated by Member States in exchange for accepting further integration. The Regional Fund was created to satisfy countries like the UK which, unlike France, did not receive substantial amounts from the Common Agriculture Policy. The creation of some social cohesion funds was also a condition of the poorest countries for their approval of the 1992 Common Market programme and further enlargement. The Maastricht Treaty followed the same dynamic with the creation of the Cohesion Fund for the four less-developed countries (Ireland, Greece, Spain and Portugal). The reluctance of these southern countries to eastern enlargement is tied to the fear of losing part of these quite substantial revenues. The essential dynamic of these funds is primarily political and strategic, which explains why their development depends on the results of repeated negotiations. The negotiations leading to the structural budget distribution has been transformed into a struggle to retain or increase benefits for particular countries or regions. As a result, the direct role of national and regional interests in the distribution of Structural Funds could prevent a real 'Europeanization' of social policy (Anderson 1995: 158).

In the on-going debate over eastern enlargement, one of the most controversial points is the necessity to increase the EU budget if the new eastern Member States want to take part in structural programmes at the same level as the present members; any budget increase is opposed by the net contributing members. That diffuse part of European social citizenship now includes a bargaining stance, which was not the original intention of the Structural Funds. They were developed to implement the Common Market by mitigating negative externalities: the deeper the deregulation, the higher the redistribution price for those negatively affected by the deregulation. The funds were channelled to poorer countries to offset their structural problems. This system works as long as the richer countries are ready and able to make such side payments in order to ensure the gains from continued liberalization.

The existing legal instruments for social programmes consist mainly of the rules pertaining to the use of Structural Funds and the conditions for countries and regions to take part in the various programmes. There is also a list of various recommendations and joint opinions of the Commission and the Council about social protection, employment, social exclusion, and so forth. That legislation does not grant direct social rights to citizens; citizens can participate in programmes co-financed by the EU. The EU provides a complement to the action of Member States in that field. This is evident when looking at its competencies and its budget relative to national ones; subsidiarity is a central concept here. The Community structural budget is 26 billion European currency units (ECU), roughly 30 per cent of EU total public spending. The total EU budget represents slightly more than 1.2 per cent of the European gross domestic product (European Commission 1996b). That cannot be compared to amounts available for social policy in Member States and is not meant to substitute European social rights for national ones in the redistribution field. Yet, for the four poorest countries, net transfers represent an important part of their GDP.

Although millions of citizens take part in programmes partially financed by the EU, the redistributive character of those funds is minimal in comparison to national programmes. The funds are redistributed in some regions and economic areas, and there is absolutely no guarantee that they will have a redistributive effect towards the poorest EU citizens. Thus far, the observed effects of the Structural Funds do not allow for a conclusive evaluation of their redistributive effects and utility. The latest Commission report on economic and social cohesion reveals on the one hand a decrease in the richness differential between countries and an additional annual economic growth of 0.5 per cent, thanks to the structural help, for the four poorest countries (Greece, Ireland, Portugal and Spain) (Europolitique 2172/2173). On the other hand, it shows an increase in the gap between regions (The Netherlands excluded) and little real impact on employment which remains the main problem in Europe. According to the commissioner responsible for the Structural Funds, Mrs Wulf-Mathies, EU structural policy cannot effect miracles, especially those which the Member States cannot accomplish themselves with their greater resources (Europolitique 2173). If these programmes are aimed at restoring or strengthening some citizens' social rights, their mid- and long-term results remain obscure and so does their meaning for national social rights.

Due to the lack of resources and competencies, the role of the EU in promoting social rights is rather limited and at most may serve as a laboratory for ideas which are at the disposal of all Member States. The success of a programme such as 'Poverty 3' relies more upon the character of the projects than upon their number or size (European Commission 1995a). The objective is to identify and disseminate social policy best practices. The Commission's ambition is to serve as a catalyst for the exchange of ideas and experiences on a supranational level; the Community institutional framework and its philosophy of action should bring an added value to the programmes run in the different countries (European Commission 1995b: 10). The direct results for EU citizens of such a philosophy are difficult to judge, given the long-term objective. Moreover, EU action is intrinsically linked to state initiatives carried out by national partners.

As in many other spheres, Member States do not share the same vision of the EU's role in social policy. The notions of social cohesion and equality at the core of a redistributive social policy are linked to national cultural, ideological and political values. Dissension among national actors is more extreme than in the case of workers' social rights. The importance of historical traditions in handling social policy is at the heart of the problem. Those traditions are now questioned by the fact that all countries, rich and poor, have similar difficulties in tackling social problems and could be more interested in sharing their experience. The Commission has developed its own approach to social exclusion problems, under the French-orientated influence of its last president Delors, and has tested it in some programmes and institutions. Its latest reports show a kind of synthesizing and global approach that links together problems of social exclusion, citizenship and social rights. But the Commission discourse does not reflect a unified vision among Member States, as contested EU social programmes prove. Some European studies about poverty problems do, however, show the beginning of a convergence in the analysis of social exclusion, especially in what concerns the conception of responsibility. Increasingly, the basis for this responsibility is shifting from the individual to the collective or community (Room 1990: 72).

Perspectives of European social citizenship

There are no EU social rights in a traditional national sense. The new social rights emerge from the peculiar set of actors, principles and dynamics which characterize European integration and which have shaped a new kind of social citizenship. The liberal logic of the internal market with its four freedoms and its principle of non-discrimination has created a new space for the development of social rights, even if social rights were, from the very beginning, second rank objectives. That new space has very little in common with the historic conditions of the implementation of national social rights. The final product has much more to do with the development of favourable conditions for a European labour market than with the implementation of a social policy.

The implementation of the Common Market has created many social rights-orientated dynamics. First of all, the EC legislation and the extensive interpretation of the ECJ have challenged two of the basic notions of the national welfare state, territoriality and nationality (Leibfried and Pierson 1995). They have enlarged the circle of beneficiaries of national social security to all EU workers and their families, regardless of nationality. They have also extended the use of social rights to the whole European territory with the obligation of exporting some social benefits. By doing so, the Community logic has limited the use of state control instruments and traditions for granting social rights. Financially, the basic unit payer/beneficiary/resident becomes less significant and therefore maintaining budgetary and financial equilibrium could become increasingly difficult for national or regional communities. Administratively, the European standard of mutual recognition means that national social administrations must rely on the control methods of their European partners for many social benefits. Politically speaking, national social rights are democratically decided on the basis of a global project with reference to a peculiar concept of solidarity and social justice; ideally citizens enjoy a social system on which they have made common decisions. As a *Marktbürgerschaft* (market's citizenship) European citizenship allows the worker (but not yet all citizens) to demand national social rights and to take part in a welfare state, but without taking part in basic socio-political choices defining that welfare state.

The fact that some traditional state control instruments could be challenged by European social standards for migrant workers has not yet created stark conflicts among Member States. The absence of reaction could be due to the relatively infrequent use of freedom of movement by workers, which has not led to deep change in national social budgets and structures. Intra-community migrations remain a marginal phenomenon and have not had important consequences on the structure of welfare states. But how would national authorities react if those principles to implement freedom of movement in social security systems were applied to a larger number of migrant workers?

Furthermore, the expected competitive deregulation was quite often a source of European social legislation. This was at the request of Member States who wanted to protect their specific national regulation. That was the case of Italy promoting the implementation of the freedom of movement for workers because of its numerous emigrants all over Europe. Also, the principle of equal pay for men and women was introduced because of French fears of unfair competition towards its new anti-discrimination legislation. The fear of 'social dumping' is always a good reason for countries with high social standards to demand minimal social standards. Deregulation provokes reregulation, as a combined result of the implementation of the Common Market, competition between national standards, and social ambitions of some European institutions and actors.

In that respect, the reregulation of the European market includes freedom to choose one's service provider, another very important source of new social rights. Since the European citizen is also a consumer of social services, the liberalization of services directly touches many of his/her interests. For example countries with a private market-orientated health service must accept offers of non-national health insurance companies, according to the principle of non-discrimination. That increases the citizen's choice and possibilities for selectivity in one country and creates competition in some fields of national social services. Although the European citizen—consumer may not yet be entitled to look for and select social services all over Europe, some recent ECJ cases show that the problem is becoming increasingly relevant and will need to be addressed legislatively.[5]

The social rights promoted through Structural Fund programmes try to respond to an impressive range of objectives with restricted financial and administrative resources. The result of this inconsistency is uncertain and so far impossible to interpret. In the long term, EU action could help sustain national social rights by trying to find new solutions in collaboration with national partners and to favour their dissemination among Member States. Community action would take advantage of national diversity in social practice in order to compare and select efficient models. By comparing experiences, different models could be adapted based on national traditions.

The most important EU social dynamic is therefore regulatory and not redistributive in nature (Majone 1996: 1–95). The EU is not implementing a super-welfare state and will probably not do so in the future, due to budgetary and administrative factors. Under these conditions a regulatory social policy for workers and consumers seems the only large-scale possibility for producing social rights. The substantial ECJ jurisprudence on social policy co-ordination and working conditions proves the reality and the importance of EU social regulation as a fundamental part of the Common Market (Leibfried and Pierson 1995: 51).

EC social rights emanating from the regulatory dynamic are a new kind of right. They help citizens – especially workers – to use the opportunities and liberties of a larger regulated economic area. They do not directly strengthen their protection against socio-economic difficulties, but rather offer better conditions for various individual strategies that could improve their situation. They also build up the status of citizen as consumer. The European Union offers a list of new 'goods' to citizens, including political and social rights. The notion of consumer has the privilege of being universally understood and applicable, unlike the concepts of 'citizen' and 'welfare state'; it also covers more categories of people than the concept of 'worker' and therefore expands the beneficiaries of social rights. These advantages are interesting in the present situation of fifteen countries trying to integrate their economies but not knowing exactly what else to do, especially in the political field. As long as the political future of the EU remains so obscure and its meaning as a community so feeble, the status of consumer brings clarity and efficiency, strengthening the field of social rights.

The social rights inherent in workers' and/or consumers' rights also offer an efficient way to transcend culturally divergent positions. They obviously do not convey the same political and moral meaning as national social citizenship. But the European Union does not yet offer a meaningful citizenship. In spite of all the Commission's attempts to forge a complete and efficient set of political and socio-economic rights, current EU citizenship has little in common with the various national experiences and does not fill citizens with confidence. The use of the notion of 'European citizenship' with no clear and precise rights and responsibilities presents moreover the danger of playing with a symbolically powerful concept without any really solid background, and therefore risks jeopardizing its legitimating value. Such a danger is averted through the social rights developed via the implementation of the Common Market and offering real opportunities to citizens.

Notes

1 We will use the terminology 'European Union' and 'European Community' interchangeably in this article. All European social rights are developed in the context of the European Community.
2 The different treaties' modifications have tried to extend part of the social rights to other kinds of person (students, retired people, and so forth). But workers still enjoy the most extended European social legislation.
3 C-262/88 of May 17 1990.
4 C-450/93 of October 17 1995.
5 See the cases C-120/95 Decker/Caisse de maladie des employés privés and C-158/ 96 Kohll/Union des caisses de maladie.

Bibliography

Alexander, W. (1993) 'Non-EC Nationals and the ECJ', in H. Schermers *et al.* (eds) *Free Movement of Persons in Europe*, The Hague: TMC Asser Institute.

Anderson, J. J. (1995) 'Structural funds and the social dimension of EU policy: springboard or stumbling block?', in S. Leibfried and P. Pierson (eds) *European Social Policy, Between Fragmentation and Integration*, Washington: The Brookings Institution.

Caire, G. (1992) *L'Europe Sociale: Faits, Problèmes, Enjeux*, Paris: Masson.

Dehousse, F. (1995) *La Politique Sociale Européenne*, Courrier hebdomadaire, Bruxelles: CRISP.

European Commission (1992) *Vers une Europe des solidarités, intensifier la lutte contre l'exclusion sociale, promouvoir l'intégration*, COM (92) 542 final.

—— (1993a) *L'Europe des citoyens*, Bulletin des Communautés européennes, supplément 7/85, Luxembourg.

—— (1993b) *Politique sociale européenne, Options pour l'Union*, Livre vert, Luxembourg.

—— (1993c) *Options for the Union, Green Paper*, COM (93)551.

—— (1994) *Contributions à la préparation du Livre Blanc sur la politique sociale*, Europe sociale, 2/94, Luxembourg.

—— (1995a) *Rapport final sur la mise en oeuvre du programme communautaire pour l'intégration économique et sociale des groupes les moins favorisés 'PAUVRETE3'*, COM(95) 94 final.

—— (1995b) *Programme d'action sociale à moyen terme 1995-1997*, Europe Sociale, 1/95, Luxembourg.

—— (1996a) *Communication concerning the Development of the Social Dialogue at Community level*, COM (96) 448 final.

—— (1996b), *Vade-mecum budgétaire*, Luxembourg.

—— (1996c) *Politique sociale de la Communauté, Programmes, Réseaux et Observatoires*, mars 1996, Luxembourg.

European Council (1996a) 'European Parliament and Council Directive 96/71/EC on posted workers' of December 16 1996.

—— (1996b) 'Parental Leave Council Directive 96/34/EC' of June 3 1996.

—— (1997) 'Council Directive 94/45/EC concerning the Framework Agreement on part-time work concluded by UNICE, CEEP and the ETUC' of December 15 1998.

Europolitique, Bruxelles: Europe Information Service (EIS).

General Directorate X (1996) *Background Statistics, Citizens First*, compilation of statistics, autumn 1996.

Honeyball, S. and Shaw, J. (1991) 'Sex, law and the retiring law', *European Law Review* 16: 47–58.

Jallade, J.-P. (1992) 'Is the crisis behind us? issues facing social security systems in western Europe', in Z. Ferge and J. Kolberg (eds) *Social Policy in a Changing Europe*, Vienna: European Center for Social Welfare Policy and Research.

Leibfried, S. and Pierson, P. (1995) 'Semisovereign welfare states', in S. Leibfried and P. Pierson (eds) *European Social Policy, Between Fragmentation and Integration*, Washington: The Brookings Institution.

Majone, G. (1993) 'The European Community between social policy and social regulation', *Journal of Common Market Studies* 31, 2: 153–69.

—— (1996) *Regulating Europe*, London and New York: Routledge.

Marias, E. (ed.) (1994) *European Citizenship*, Maastricht: European Institute of Public Administration.

Marshall, T. H. (1992) *Citizenship and Social Class*, London: Pluto Press.

Pierson, P. and Leibfried, S. (1995) 'The making of social policy', in S. Leibfried and P. Pierson (eds) *European Social Policy, Between Fragmentation and Integration*, Washington: The Brookings Institution.

Rapport Veil (1997) *Rapport du Groupe de Haut Niveau sur la libre circulation des personnes*, présidé par Mme Veil, présenté à la Commission le 18 mars 1997.

Riley, A. (1997) 'A grave tactical error: the working time ruling', *European Current Law*, Monthly Digest, February 1997.

Rizzo, F. (1991) *La Jurisprudence Sociale de la Cour de Justice des Communautés Européennes*, Aix-en-Provence: Presses Universitaire.

Roche, M. (1992) *Rethinking Citizenship*, Cambridge: Polity Press.

Room, G. (1990) *New Poverty in the European Community*, Basingstoke: Macmillan Press Ltd.

Séché, J.-C. (1993) 'L'Europe sociale après Maastricht', *Cahiers de Droit Européen*, 509–36.

Verschueren, H. (1996) 'Libre circulation des personnes et protection minimale', *Revue du Marché Unique Européen* 2: 83–105.

Watson, Ph. (1993) 'Social policy after Maastricht', *Common Market Law Review* 30: 481–513.

Wolton, D. (1993) *La dernière utopie*, Paris: Flammarion.

Yonnet, J.-P. (1995) *Une redéfinition de la politique sociale européenne*, Courrier hebdomadaire, Bruxelles: CRISP.

Index

Note: 'n.' after a page reference indicates the number of a note on that page.

For Product Safety Concerns and Information please contact our EU
representative GPSR@taylorandfrancis.com
Taylor & Francis Verlag GmbH, Kaufingerstraße 24, 80331 München, Germany

www.ingramcontent.com/pod-product-compliance
Ingram Content Group UK Ltd.
Pitfield, Milton Keynes, MK11 3LW, UK
UKHW021057080625
459435UK00003B/31